LOW-INCOME STUDENTS AND THE PERPETUATION OF INEQUALITY

For Erica and José

Low-Income Students and the Perpetuation of Inequality
Higher Education in America

GARY A. BERG
California State University Channel Islands, USA

R Routledge
Taylor & Francis Group

LONDON AND NEW YORK

First published 2010 by Ashgate Publishing

Published 2016 by Routledge
2 Park Square, Milton Park, Abingdon, Oxon OX14 4RN
711 Third Avenue, New York, NY 10017, USA

Routledge is an imprint of the Taylor & Francis Group, an informa business

British Library Cataloguing in Publication Data
Berg, Gary A., 1955-
  Low-income students and the perpetuation of inequality :
  higher education in America.
  1. Low-income students--United States. 2. Discrimination
  in higher education--United States. 3. Educational
  mobility--United States. 4. Educational sociology--United States.
  I. Title
  378.1'9826942'0973-dc22

Library of Congress Cataloging-in-Publication Data
Berg, Gary A., 1955-
  Low-income students and the perpetuation of inequality : higher education in America /
  by Gary A. Berg.
       p. cm.
  Includes bibliographical references and index.
  ISBN 978-1-4094-0154-4 (hardback)
  1. People with social disabilities--Education (Higher)--United States. 2. Poor-
  -Education (Higher)--United States. 3. Education, Higher--United States--Costs.
  4. Universities and colleges--United States--Admission. I. Title.
  LC4823.B47 2009
  378.0087--dc22
                                                                        2009040125

ISBN 9781409401544 (hbk)

Contents

List of Figures

List of Tables

Foreword

Statistically, the least academically qualified students from wealthy families have as much chance of going to college as the highest performing kids from lower-class families.

This statement from Gary Berg's wide-ranging book defines a serious national problem. Although we take pride in our system of higher education as a chief source of opportunity for millions of students and see billions of dollars of private philanthropy each year flow into our colleges and universities, the reality is that the "system" hardly works for those who stand to benefit the most.

As a result, much in this book is not pleasant reading. Every college president, and perhaps almost every citizen, can tell wonderful stories of students lacking money, family experience in college, and academic preparation who became highly successful in spite of their disadvantages. I tell such stories all the time—and I hold as an article of faith the personal, social, and economic advantages of a college education. But the reality that all of us in the business must face is that for most such disadvantaged students, success is an exception. And Gary Berg's book helps us to understand why.

He sheds bright light, for instance, on the role of families, which often in the case of lower-class students is a source of pressure to stay home, bring in dollars, or, as I've sometimes heard, "help with the babies." He points out the difficulty we have in seeing the world as it seen by many of our students. As one of the students whom Berg has interviewed says, "They don't even know how it is to be like we are."

Low-Income Students and the Perpetuation of Inequality will open eyes and engage hearts. Berg's extensive interviews with students support and extend his reviews of sociological and educational literature. He tells several kinds of truth. Reading what he has learned, grimacing at times at our collective failings to serve poor and first-generation students, we can hope that while truth may not always conquer all, it can help widen the doors of opportunity in American colleges and universities.

William A. Bloodworth, Jr.
President
Augusta State University
Augusta, Georgia

Preface

This is a book of real life stories and I feel obliged as the narrator to tell mine. As I think is true of many, I haven't really thought about my own educational experience in relationship to class. However, when I view my college years in this way I see that they were clearly influenced by my family's social-economic position. Although both my parents attended college, they still had a marginal experience in education. Both left home as children. My father departed as a teenager, before finishing high school. After completing service during World War II, he took a comprehensive exam to get his high school diploma and entered art school. As I relate later in the book, my mother was raised on a 100-acre Minnesota farm and left home as a teen to work at the residence of a wealthy St. Paul family. Both of my parents worked heavily while attending college, and were to a large degree what we'd now call non-traditional students.

I grew up with the expectation of going to college, and the associated assumption that I'd do it completely on my own. I entered the University of Southern California (USC) as a freshman on a full scholarship and was instantly depressed. At the time, I thought of the discomfort in terms of my own immaturity, but there was at base a strong class chasm for me. While I felt proud of my full scholarship, I could see that it marked me with a social stigma. My suitemates in the campus residence hall were all from wealthy families, half from the East Coast. I felt distinctly out of place at formal functions, fraternity recruitment, and freshmen social events. I could add nothing to discussions about skiing and European travel—obvious marks of affluence. As a result of my unhappiness, I put in an application to the University of California, Berkeley and was accepted the following spring.

I hitchhiked to Berkeley (this was in the early 1970s) with an old suitcase in one hand and a portable Smith-Corona electric typewriter in the other, and took up residence in cooperative housing—the lowest rank of residence at the time, far less expensive than the dormitories. I felt more at home in this environment where students all had to work a certain number of hours per week to subsidize housing fees. Overall, I had much more in common with the students at the cooperative than I had at USC. Now lacking a scholarship, in my second year I was forced to take on a paying job 30 or more hours a week while attending school, eventually driving a truck three long days a week. I would attend class one day, and then drive across the state, leaving for work around 4:30 or 5:00 in the morning, and returning home often late in the evening. The next morning I was back in the classroom. It was as if I attended a completely different university than the other students: one day, a working-class trucker driving across northern California, and the next day, a budding but exhausted scholar.

I do not pretend that I was as disadvantaged as others who clearly faced many steeper obstacles than I have in my life. However, I did have an undergraduate college experience colored by my social position. When I graduated, I quickly found that my degree had less meaning in society than I expected it would. My work experience was more of a detriment than an asset because it labeled me as blue-collar. While other students went directly to work in corporations on a specific career track, I floundered. I did not have the connections they had through their college social network or their own family. I was in fact what will be discussed later in the book, a "marginal graduate." While I received an excellent education attending one of the premiere universities in the world, it did not advantage me as much as one might assume. Furthermore, after all these years, although both my wife and I have doctoral degrees from top institutions and years of professional experience now, I doubt that we are in a higher social-economic class than that of our parents. We might be more culturally aware and better read, and are higher education success stories of a kind, but our personal histories do not demonstrate social-economic mobility through education. Our experiences are not uncommon.

I am painfully aware of how dangerous it is to write about people of another class regardless of intentions. I found in writing this book that a defining characteristic of America, as opposed to other developed societies, is that a distressingly large percentage of the population experience poverty at some point in their lives. Although more people in America than in other modern countries have a first-hand feel for at least short-term poverty, living temporarily low on cash is not the same as suffering from a history of poverty and the related social problems that come with it. Even the simple act of identifying individuals and groups as "disadvantaged" or "poor" carries with it loaded connotations, unintended value judgments, the effects of which I saw while conducting the research and in reviewing quotations with interview subjects. It is with this knowledge of my own limitations and respect for those who are the primary focus that I offer this book to the reader.

I would like to thank the students and faculty of California State University Channel Islands (CSUCI) who generously participated in this study. I am especially thankful for the cooperation of the Osher Lifelong Learning Institute and its membership, and the Educational Opportunity Program for the opportunity to interview and observe its inspiring students. The inspiration for much of this book comes from my participation in the Summer College program at CSU Channel Islands and I am grateful for the open access granted to me by the Oxnard Union High School District and the Migrant Education Program, the faculty, staff and students. I also want to acknowledge the cooperation of Augusta State University and Montgomery Community College in contacting alumni students for participation in this study. The initial interest in this book project and support of Neil Jordan, the editor at Ashgate Publishing, is recognized and greatly appreciated, as well as Aimée Feenan, the Social Science editor. Finally, I want to once again thank my wife, Linda Venis, for her expert editing, counsel and support throughout the writing.

Introduction

A banker's family from the Twin Cities came by the Flohr farmhouse in rural Depression-era Minnesota. They were looking for someone to watch their children and clean up around the house. The wealthy family had originally asked a girl from down the road, but was turned away. Although only 14, the youngest Flohr girl wanted desperately to get out of the narrow farm life and agreed to take the maid position. Saving pennies, she paid her way through agricultural high school (public education only went through eighth grade at that time in Minnesota). After high school she worked in a munitions factory supporting the war effort. Encouraged by her older sister, she then went on to Hamline University to study nursing. Waiting on tables in the cafeteria three meals a day, she worked her way through college as well.

This is my mother's story. Like many of the children raised in the Depression Era, my mother is tough. This is a truth that only now in my fifties I am beginning to fully appreciate. My mother's struggle and eventual mobility through education is a Horatio Alger-type story, one deeply rooted in the American imagination. In fact an Alger novel and German Bible were the only books her family owned. Is her story still relevant today in America?

Importance

I had heard bits and pieces of my mother's story growing up, but never the details, and nothing about leaving home at 14 to work as a servant. The interview with my mother is one of the first I conducted when embarking on a search to understand the state of American social mobility through higher education. This journey has led me to talk with a wide range of people including university professors, administrators, students and alumni.

Why is this assessment of college's ability to move people up in society important now? In 2005 the *New York Times* ran a series of feature articles on the subject of class in America (Correspondents of the *New York Times*, 2005). Bill Keller explained why the *Times* picked the topic: "At a time when, by many measures, class seemed less and less a force in American life, it had become more so in some of the areas that matter most." Social mobility in America—long the central American value—appears to be an increasingly empty promise. Certainly there are still many cases of individuals moving ahead in society through education, but does higher education work in a general way to get people ahead in society? Or instead, have educators become gatekeepers to opportunity, sorting, selecting, and classifying students by convoluted measures of "merit"? If so, is this highly competitive system which leads to greater inequality what Americans want? We may be peering into a harsh future of increased separation between the haves and have-nots facilitated and justified by callous educational policies.

What do recent statistics say about social mobility and education? Overall, they show a marked difference in higher education access, retention, and impact of degree after graduation based on socio-economic status. Low-income students are less prepared, more likely to go to vocational school and community colleges, and often drop out of four-year institutions when they transfer. Once earning a degree, low-income students make less money. Overall while college attendance figures have risen, completion rates have been falling. In fact, completion rates fell by more than 25 percent between 1970 and 1999. This divergence is particularly large for students from low-income backgrounds, especially African-Americans. There is a mismatch between the high school push for "college for all" and the reality of stiff academic requirements in college that low-income students are often ill equipped to meet. Overall, what the numbers tell is a stark story of not only lessened access, but a much reduced impact for low-income students when they do manage to overcome poor preparation, lack of financial assistance and cultural capital, and earn a degree. To continue the often-used metaphor from the Civil Rights Era, even if they manage to get into the race and cross the finish line, students from low-income families generally receive a smaller trophy.

While the American population grows and the perceived value of a name-brand college education rises, parents scramble to get their children into the schools with the best reputations. As a result, there is much interest in admissions practices and policies, particularly at the highly sought-after elite universities. This concern in admissions practices and the struggle for acceptance at the top schools directly relates to the issue of social-economic class and mobility. If more people have college degrees, then those at the top in society increasingly value not just a college degree, but degrees from selective schools. From the university perspective, admissions decisions themselves become crucial in maintaining or improving reputations and seeking donors. For public institutions at the beck and call of the taxpayer, policies on who gets admitted come under greater scrutiny. All of these factors together have led directly to advocacy of a new meritocracy, or university admission based purely on academic measures. While such an admission practice might reduce the obvious forms of preference for the children of wealthy alumni, would it really improve the life chances of students from poor families?

The history of admissions practice in America is central to understanding the role of class in higher education. Ivy League schools have long practiced affirmative action, but primarily in favor of the rich and powerful. Jerome Karabel's book entitled *The Chosen: The Hidden History of Admission and Exclusion at Harvard, Yale, and Princeton*, shows how beginning in the 1920s, Harvard, Yale, and Princeton restricted admission because of fear of the rapidly increasing large enrollment of low-income Jewish students who were excelling academically (Karabel, 2005). The "big three" put a system of preferential treatment in place, the centerpiece of which was using the criteria of "character," "manliness," and "athleticism." The admission system became intentionally complex in order to hide an ethnic and class stratification process, and this was a conscious, documented effort of the elite colleges of that time. Through the 1950s, elite institutions such as Harvard University limited the number of "intellectuals," often Jews, to 10 percent of the student body. Legacies were given preference, with the criterion being whether or not the applicant could likely make it through four years satisfactorily. Eventually, the faculty began complaining of a need for higher academic quality students to help them with research, and the public objected to restrictions on Jewish applicants in particular. Aware that it is possible to tie their fortunes too closely to traditional elites, especially when in decline, the answer was to diversify the student body and strengthen its connections to rising social groups—the new professional class. Use of SAT and National Merit programs starting in the 1960s gave the outward appearance of openness, while still letting only a small percentage of extremely gifted low-income students into the Ivy League schools. However, the number of poor students admitted actually declined in Ivy League schools from 10 percent in 1954 to 5 percent in 1996. In sum, admissions to elite universities in America have never been truly open and are not so today.

The process whereby the elites moved from explicitly giving preference to the rich to more of a meritocratic admissions policy is fascinating sociology and reveals American philosophy towards the underprivileged. The role that education plays in assuring that everyone has a shot at moving up the social ladder is a deeply ingrained belief in America where economic inequality is tolerated because there is confidence in the possibility of mobility. What has come at the beginning of the twenty-first century a meritocratic revolution in American higher education is the logical conclusion of this deep-seated belief in letting the "best" succeed, while the rest fall into their natural place—what Thomas Jefferson termed the "natural aristocracy." This belief in a natural aristocracy is alive today in different forms and is the philosophy behind political changes in the past three decades that have led to increasingly unfavorable policies for students from poor families. College is a principle mechanism through which privilege is passed on from parents to children. Associated with the belief in a natural aristocracy is a stern approach which makes the poor primarily responsible for their own fate, and limits the perceived obligation of society. The American philosophy towards education then is two-part: first, that there are natural or innate differences in ability and that society should allow the best to rise to the top; and second, that those who are less able are largely responsible for their own fate.

Since the 1980s, American attitudes towards fairness in college admissions have taken a conservative political swing. This has led to questioning affirmative action policies that developed out of the 1960s Civil Rights Movement, and an emerging belief that an inability of individuals or particular groups to move up in society is not a problem to be addressed by public policy. In what may be a realization by the public of the economic disparity in those who attend college, a survey on the issue of class in America found that while 59 percent still favor affirmative action programs, 84 percent are inclined towards programs based on low-income status (*New York Times* Poll Class Project, 2005). Despite the widening gap between the upper and lower classes, some Americans persist in believing in their own social mobility. Sixty-six percent feel that they personally have either a much better or somewhat better standard of living than their parents. To an even larger extent, there is widespread belief in education as the engine for moving up, with 85 percent responding that a good education is essential or very important for "getting ahead in life." In this manner, Americans seem to lean towards income-based corrective public policy in recognition of a basic economic inequality, and are confident in their own mobility and the positive function of education in society.

Nevertheless, the long held confidence in education to correct inequality is eroding. According to a report by the National Center for Public Policy and Higher Education entitled *Public Attitudes on Higher Education: A Trend Analysis, 1993 to 2003*, the discontent is particularly noted in African-American parents of high school students (Immerwahr, 2004). Likewise, the percentage of parents of high school students who remain optimistic about educational opportunity has dropped 18 points with only 34 percent agreeing that the vast majority of qualified people have the chance to go to college. Furthermore, 58 percent thought that many people do not have a real chance to go to college. Overall, the report indicates a diminishing sense of opportunity for upper mobility through higher education.

How does America measure up today to the rhetoric of achieving the American Dream through education? The following are some of the realities about the poor and college explored in this book:

- Families are the Biggest Influence on Going to College
- Unfavorable Admission Policies Disadvantage Low-income Students
- Financial Aid Policies Work Against Low-income Students
- Funding for Higher Education Has Primarily Aided Students from the Middle and Upper Classes
- Private Universities Attract a Greater Percentage of Low-income Students than Public Universities
- Students from Poor Families Face Significant Psychological, Academic, and Financial Problems in College
- Degrees for Some Low-Income Students Have Marginal Economic Value
- Public Attitudes Have Turned Against the Poor and Influenced Educational Policy.

As one can see in the themes detailed above, the American public's attitude towards college is multifaceted and changing. While the myth of the power of education to move one up in society persists rhetorically, the public has an appreciation for the actual complexity of the impact of college on students from low-income families. I found that in writing this book while students talk of college as a route to a better life, many also speak about it as a place that is not appropriate for everyone. This attitude that assumes a natural inequality and individual responsibility is reflected in our more strident higher education policies today, many of which do not favor the poor.

Contribution and Purpose of the Book

While there are numerous books on inequality in primary and second education (e.g. Jonathan Kozol's *The Shame of the Nation: The Restoration of Apartheid Schooling in America*), there is little critical analysis in this regard to higher education. Much of the literature on higher education inequality has focused on admissions practices alone at universities as seen in *Privilege: Harvard and the Education of the Ruling Class* by Ross Gregory Douthat, and *The Chosen: The Hidden History of Admission and Exclusion at Harvard, Yale, and Princeton* by Jerome Karabel. However, these books do not concentrate specifically on the questions of social mobility and the experience of low-income students in college. This book is more broadly based on research collected from interviews, college classroom observations, and examination of national data on education and family income. In this way, the reader is provided with both a comprehensive review of the literature and statistics, but also vivid stories coming from interviews with low-income students. Although the intended audience for this book is primarily academic, the book is written in a way that is hopefully accessible to a more general public interested in the important topic.

Overall, the book argues that colleges in America largely fail students from low-income families, and in some ways perpetuate inequality. While the popular image of social mobility through education has a long and deep history in American and other societies worldwide, and many individuals from low-income backgrounds do in fact still benefit in extraordinary ways from going to college, those from underprivileged backgrounds as a group do not benefit as much as is commonly understood. Furthermore, there are indications that American society has begun to accept higher education's failure to make a difference in a general way for disadvantaged students.

Organization of the Book

The book begins in the first chapter by looking at the all-important manner in which low-income students as a whole are in various ways prepared to fail. The history of standardized testing emerging out of the eugenics movement is traced; the reliance on class-based forms of language proficiency and the limited availability of increasingly important Advanced Placement courses are discussed. The more subtle forms of insufficient psychological and social preparation for students from disadvantaged families is examined and illustrated by the perspective of two faculty members now instructing many low-income college students. This chapter argues that the American educational system has a long history of perpetuating inequality in explicit and subtle ways through the academic preparation of low-income students and standardized testing. According to the proponents of eugenics in an argument that has been made for two centuries, people are poor simply because they are intellectually less gifted and deserving. Surprisingly, there is a long history of support for the eugenics movement and the belief in racial genetic superiority in America which continues today. On the practical administrative level, the SAT as used first by the Ivy League colleges was motivated by a desire to restrict undesirable low-income students. This history of intelligence testing in America is the starting point for understanding how the educational system, at times intentionally, has perpetuated low rates of college attendance for children from poor families.

The second chapter argues that a long history of discrimination against low-income students in university admissions continues today in subtle forms. First, I present the statistics on admissions of low-income students and show that private universities, except for the elites, actually admit a larger percentage of low-income students than at the public universities which were founded to provide greater access. I then delve into the fascinating history and practice of admissions at elite American colleges. Although the public is not naïve about class privilege, I suspect most Americans would be surprised by the extent of the historical record of purposeful exclusion of ethnic minority and low-income students from these colleges. At public institutions, the changes in policy regarding affirmative action and recent efforts to use more just models for admissions are examined. The often underestimated impact of changes since the Reagan administration on financial aid distributions and the influence on low-income students are detailed. Although admissions policies on one level are simply bureaucratic ways of controlling enrollment at colleges, they reflect and perpetuate beliefs and values at specific institutions and throughout society. We shall see in this chapter that the ungenerous attitude towards the poor is evident in how low-income students are discouraged from attending college by various policies and practices. The chapter ends with a look at admissions practices from the point of view of a counselor who works in a special program for students from low-income families.

The next chapter argues that children from low-income families experience college in very challenging ways because of a variety of factors that lead to higher discontinuation rates. While participation in college for students from poor families greatly increased in number at the end of the twentieth century, the overall percentage did not increase significantly. Affluent students in the United States still outnumber poor students in high school graduation, college attendance, and college graduation rates. Additionally, low-income students disproportionately attend community colleges rather than going straight into four-year colleges. Students from low-income families discontinue their studies in much larger numbers both in high school and then later in college. This chapter identifies three main types of issues that confront these students: personal, family/cultural, and structural. The personal issues are those that often involve the individual human development and growth that is typical of college students, but perhaps more extreme in low-income students who carry the weight of additional stressors. Often the crux of the personal realm for these students has to do with self-image issues. I found conflict within the family to be a more important issue than anticipated. Finally, the larger socio-political structure has a direct impact on poor students through society's various systems, including higher education.

Chapter 4 argues that gender and race are interlocking categories of disadvantage with low-income students. I reflect on special challenges for women and ethnic minorities in college and how they have evolved over time. The chapter considers statistics showing that black and Latino students are far behind Asian and white populations in graduating from both high school and college today. Additionally, the impact on low-income students of the rollback of affirmative action policies is negative, and the outcomes of the new alternative method of comprehensive review in university admissions approach uncertain. The reality for many ethnic minority college students in America today is one of a web of disadvantage including limited progress in personal wealth, negative self-image, low academic expectations, and community segregation that perpetuate conditions. Additionally, the portraits of a current African-American student from South Central Los Angeles and a Black college professor educated at a Southern university are presented to deepen the discussion.

Chapter 5 examines how, in ways congruent with other low-income groups, educational institutions are inadequately serving the needs of immigrant populations. A case study of one group at a public university in Southern California illustrates this point in a program created in response to the dire statistics about large numbers of high school drop outs and miniscule attendance in college by the children of migratory farm workers. The local high school district requested the development of this unusual program which combines a university course in the afternoon, with a morning of intensive study and language skills. Most of the students are foreign-born, and approximately one-third of the students lack proper citizenship documentation. What is it like to be an immigrant today in America and go to college?

The sixth chapter argues that public attitudes and popular images as seen in popular newspapers and fictional accounts have perpetuated stereotypes of low-income students and assert an ideal social mobility function for higher education that now shows signs of fading. American beliefs about college have changed and are in the process of changing further. The book will show how the public is increasingly aware that the traditional image of college as an instrument of mobility in society simply does not fit the reality. Two major beliefs about the poor in American society are illustrated: first, that their position in society is a result of a combination of inadequate talent and flawed values. Second, that the individuals themselves have primary responsibility for changing their condition. I argue that popular college images as seen in newspapers and fictional accounts has perpetuated belief in the mobility of low-income students, but the representation has changed over time with a growing recognition of the hardened class lines drawn through the higher education system.

The seventh chapter presents evidence on the generally low rates of mobility in the United States and the weaker impact of a degree on low-income students. This includes the evaluation of the impact of a degree on college graduates from low-income families as a group in terms of subsequent wages and other indictors of social mobility finding that it is less significant than for those from more advantaged groups. Critics of higher education have for many generations in America doubted the value of a college degree. However, throughout the twentieth century as the doors of colleges were opened wider to the general population, there have been warnings of a watering down of the value of a college education.

The final chapter considers the implications of the argument. Findings include indications that the notion of meritocracy narrowly construed as test scores or grade point average without consideration of obstacles and the environmental context will not work for the poor. The larger socio-political context and function of higher education in society prevent a meritocratic admissions system from working. It is a simple truth that students from poor families do not go to college because they cannot afford to do so. Financial aid alone does not solve the problem for two reasons. First, even full scholarships do not replace foregone wages while attending college. In many cases, those families in extreme poverty depend on the wages of older children for survival. Second, for both practical and cultural reasons, college loans are not a practical option for low-income students. Students from low-income backgrounds often suffer from a lack of general experience and knowledge of the world. This lack directly impacts the students in the classroom because of a limited frame of reference and context for learning new things. The difficulty in adjustment for first-generation college students is first largely a cultural one. College has a culture with strong rules of behavior that is foreign to many students. For those who are not native English speakers, the pedagogical dependence in college on textbooks is an especially clear disadvantage.

In this final chapter I review the findings and suggest areas for further research while considering the things that might be done in higher education to better serve the needs of low-income students. I summarize how while there has been some increase in the number of students from poor families going to college, there has also been an increase in the failure of those same students to complete their degrees. Increasingly conservative views placing blame on the poor for their condition in America have become prominent at the end of the twentieth century and are behind public funding, financial aid and admission policy changes that do not favor low-income students. Reduced public funding for higher education over the past three decades, financial aid redirected to the middle-class since the Reagan administration, and the turning back of affirmative action policies all reflect the change in public attitudes towards the poor. Americans no longer hold a singularly idealistic vision of college. While students do talk of college as a route to better living and working conditions, many also speak about it as a place that is not appropriate for everyone and as four years spent with limited personal benefit. Furthermore, there is an understanding that students have very different college experiences, especially those from poor families. Finally, it is hoped by understanding our failings and confronting the truth about the successfulness of our college system for low-income students that we can do better in the future to provide real opportunity.

Sources and Method

The book is based on over 50 interviews and many days of classroom observations. I've drawn on data from the United States Census, the United States Department of Education, and numerous other publicly-available sources to provide a broad context for understanding the experience of low-income students in college. Additionally, I've delved deeply into the academic literature on the subject to interject the points of view of experts in the field.

The general methodology for this study consists of three parts: an in-depth review of the relevant research literature, an examination of national and international data, and the qualitative portion consisting of lengthy interviews and classroom observations. The strategy is to triangulate the views of experts, broad statistics, and the individual experiences of a limited set of interview subjects. Academics writing about research methods suggest that studies often benefit from a combined quantitative and qualitative approach because data sets can be compared for consistency. Additionally, interviews often conducted in qualitative studies allow some insight into the causal processes, while quantitative surveys provide indication of the prevalence of the phenomenon (Campbell and Stanley, 1966). The qualitative data are meant to give flesh and depth to the research literature and dry national statistics, and suggest patterns in line with the statistics and views of various experts in the field. According to Yin (1984), interviews should be used when "how" or "why" questions are posed, and when the focus is on contemporary phenomena within some real-life context. Determining patterns and linkages can be usefully done through using interview methods and consequently are appropriate in understanding the experience of low-income students in college. Furthermore, the interviews serve in a small way to check the validity of the quantitative data. Subjects are not chosen based on a statistical method from a population, but because their experiences could shed some light on a topic. Once the qualitative data are collected, the analytic process involves five basic modes per Marshall and Rossman (1989): data organization, categorization, uncovering themes and patterns, testing and searching for alternative explanations of the data, and finally, writing the analysis and integrating with the statistics and other material in the book. The qualitative data were coded, a process of grouping interview subject responses into categories that bring together the similar ideas, concepts, or themes discovered (Rubin and Rubin, 1995).

Quantitative Data

I've drawn on data sources from the United States Census, the Department of Education, and numerous other sources to provide the broader context for understanding the experience of the poor in college. As can be seen in the over three hundred citations in this book, I've delved deeply into the academic literature on the subject of low-income students in college and related relevant issues.

Qualitative Data

The qualitative data were collected over a year and a half period from two public universities: California State University Channel Islands (CSUCI) and Augusta State University (ASU). CSUCI, the 23rd California State University, opened its doors in 2002 and is located roughly 45 miles outside of Los Angeles at the base of the Santa Monica Mountains. Augusta State University can be traced to 1783 when the Academy of Richmond County was chartered. In 1958, the college became a member of the University System of Georgia and its name was changed to Augusta College. Still a two-year college, it wasn't until 1963 that four-year status was gained. CSUCI was chosen because of access by the author and the fact that it is part of the largest public university system in America concentrating on serving students from low-income families. Additionally, the university has two specific programs designed to focus on this population: Summer College and EOP. Augusta College was chosen because it offered a similar campus for study in a different region of the country.

The process of collecting qualitative data began with an extensive review of the research literature and national statistics. Common themes and issues where identified which informed the creation of a semi-structured interview instrument: students, administrator, faculty, and alumni (see survey instrument, Appendix B). Interviews were tape recorded and generally lasted about one hour in duration. I've changed the names of all of those interviewed for this book in respect of their privacy. The literature on research methods suggests testing survey instruments before using them to determine usefulness and reliability (Marshall and Rossman, 1989). As a result, the interview protocol was tested on a small sample first and minor adjustments were made to the interview questions.

Interview subjects for EOP were identified by the program director. Three EOP students and one program administrator were interviewed in-depth for this program. Twelve Summer College students were interviewed in-person and volunteered for the interviews with parental approval. Seven faculty and administrators were interviewed, all from CSUCI. The interviews with the alumni were conducted via email and included two groups: members of a CSUCI senior group, and alumni from Augusta State University. For the CSUCI group, an announcement for volunteers was made and direct contact was made. An email list of questions based on the survey instrument was sent out, and then with follow up questions posed by the author. In a few cases, in-person conversations followed for clarification. The August State University alumni were contacted through an email solicitation to alumni association members. The combined group of alumni resulted in 23 lengthy interviews. It should be noted that although the point of contact for the alumni was through two universities, this group included graduates from universities around the country. The demographics for the alumni group of students alone were as follows: 78 percent female, 22 percent male; 91 percent white; 78 percent first-generation college graduates.

Additionally, extensive classroom observations were made by the author using an original instrument to track verbal phrases, patterns and behavior linked to the issues identified in the literature review and in the interviews. Some of these direct observations are detailed in sections in the book. The observations took place over a one month period for Summer College, some of them timed randomly, others for key events such as scheduled student presentations and career discussions. The Summer College classroom had 34 enrolled students. The EOP observations occurred over a week during the beginning of a semester orientation and also involved some random attendance, as well as author identified key discussions on adjustment issues, etc. The EOP program observed had 29 students in attendance.

The chapter on the evolving public image of college in American society and the popular images of mobility was constructed using a method quite different from the rest of the book, a fusion of a research literature review and film and literary criticism. The chapter began with extensive searches of library databases for newspaper articles from major American newspapers going back as far as the eighteenth century. Keywords were drawn broadly from issues and themes developed out of the research literature review. A similar search was done of fiction and film directories looking for instances of college portrayal. I should note here that in additional to my doctoral degree in higher education, I have two graduate degrees in film and television and am accustomed to looking at the sociological implications of media. Initially, secondary sources on the subject of the college novel and film were consulted, but eventually the author was led directly to primary materials. In particular, research at the Academy of Motion Picture Arts and Sciences Margaret Herrick Library in Los Angeles was especially fruitful in this regard.

In regard to the limitations of the data presented in this book, I would urge the reader to consider the whole picture presented. The national statistics indicate various aspects of the complex experience of low-income students in college, the research literature gives one the points of view of many scholars coming from different directions, and the interviews and observations very specific experiences of a limited group of individuals.

A note up front on definitions and use of terms such as "poor" and "low-income" should be made here. Experts in the field tend to be very uncomfortable with the use of "class" and other imprecise terminology for socio-economic groups because they describe more than just wealth. Typical ways that class is defined by scholars are through father's education, father's occupation, respondent's education, status of first job, status of job later in life, and personal wealth (Blau, 1967). Others might point to associated signs of class such as social activities, social groups, and location of residence. The definition of poverty is similarly confused with no general agreement by experts on a definition (Iceland, 2006). Those working with poverty figures tend to either use specific or absolute economic figures, such as a government poverty level, or a relative definition which can vary by time and place. The definition I use in this book defines poverty as a relative or comparative disadvantage. John Iceland in *Poverty in America: A Handbook* gives an apt description of the utility of using a relative definition of poverty:

> Implicit is the assumption that people are social beings who operate within relationships. Those whose resources are significantly below the resources of others, even if they are physically able to survive, may not be able to participate adequately in social organizations and relationships, and are thus incapable of fully participating in society. Adam Smith argued that to be poor was to lack what was needed to be a 'creditable' member of society. (Iceland, 2006, p. 25)

Of course, one could take a relative definition to an absurd level so that someone within a very privileged group might be viewed as impoverished. However, within reason it is this relative definition of poverty as not being able to participate adequately in social organizations, specifically higher education, that I employ this is book. Generally, I use low-income and poor interchangeably and employ a relative definition focused on the idea of being less advantaged. When looking at statistical data often the definition is stated specifically and does vary to some degree from one source to another.

A second important notation I need to make up front is to explain how I treat the relationship of class to race and gender in this book. I don't believe that one can very effectively separate race and gender from class—they are connected. Esther Ngang-ling Chow expresses the linkage well:

> Race, class, and gender are conceptualized as 'interlocking categories,' as 'intersecting systems,' as 'interdependent dimensions' of inequality, and as 'intersecting systems,' as 'interdependent dimensions' of inequality, and as 'multiple bases' for oppression rather than separate types of identity as they normally are treated. This conceptualization requires us to focus our analysis on their interactive, reciprocal, and cumulative effects. (Chow, 1996, p. xxi)

Additionally, as in Chow's book, a major theme in mine is that private and public spheres of experience for the disadvantaged are linked. In this way, class, race, and gender are interconnected and the impact of historical and continuing inequality is pervasive. While poor white, ethnic minority, and female students certainly have different experiences in college, they have commonalities by virtue of their overall relative historical disadvantage in society.

What I'm impressed with in my interviews with students are the compelling stories of inspired dreams and bitter struggles to move up in society through education despite a larger social context that often works against them. I remember in particular a student facing severe challenges at home who, despite her own problems, looked at another student coming to the United States from Mexico with compassion, understanding and appreciation: "For other students it is really hard. I see some of them in my classes and they don't speak English very well. I think about, 'How would my life be different if I was one of them?' I think it would be really, really hard. And I think I would give up." These students remind us of the human side of low-income students in college. Finally, I asked all of those I interviewed if they thought higher education in America was working. My 88-year-old mother's response: "Definitely." A 20-year-old student's response: "Kind of."

Chapter 1
Prepared for Failure

This chapter argues that the American educational system has a long history of perpetuating inequality in explicit and subtle ways through the academic preparation of low-income students and standardized testing. According to the proponents of eugenics, in an argument that has been made for two centuries, people are poor simply because they are intellectually less gifted and deserving. Surprisingly, there is a long history of support for the eugenics movement and the belief in racial genetic superiority in America which continues today in books like *The Bell Curve* and, more subtly perhaps, in our enacted public policies that affect the disadvantaged. What few recognize is that the SAT test was originally designed by someone who believed, at least in the early part of his life, in the inferiority of low-income and racial minority groups. In *A Study of American Intelligence* the Princeton psychologist Carl Brigham claimed the inferiority of minority groups through the use of a test given to military personnel (Brigham, 1923). On the practical administrative level, the SAT as used first by the Ivy League colleges was motivated by a desire to restrict undesirable low-income students. This history of intelligence testing in America is the starting point for understanding how the educational system, at times intentionally, has perpetuated low rates of college attendance for children from poor families.

Additionally, the reliance on class-based forms of language proficiency and the limited availability of increasingly important Advanced Placement courses is also reviewed in this chapter. The more subtle forms of insufficient psychological and social preparation, a legacy of disadvantaged families, add an even more intricate obstacle for students. Finally, the chapter ends with the perspective of two faculty members experienced in teaching low-income students which reveal the forms insufficient preparation take, including the important general lack of worldliness. Taken together I present a case for understanding the philosophical and cultural attitudes behind educational policies impacting children from low-income families, and the specific mechanisms that work to perpetuate inequality.

The Intelligence of Low-Income Students is Questioned

Eugenics

There is a long history of looking at the genetic basis for intelligence and the consistent attempt to link disappointing performance of the poor in school to low intelligence. The notion of biological determinism holds that social and economic differences between groups are inherited, and position in society is a reflection of biology (Gould, 1981). Classical accounts of social mobility point out the natural tendency in human behavior to create leaders and followers: "Any organized social group whatever, once it is organized, is inevitably stratified to some degree" (Sorokin, 1959, p. 15). This analysis also leads to the notion that societies often become more, rather than less, economically unequal as they advance. Overall, economists looking at social mobility throughout the history of civilizations typically use terms such as "trend-less" and "fluctuating" to depict a lack of clear patterns. An early twentieth century sociologist saw social institutions as functioning to place individuals within the social hierarchy: "These institutions, such as the family, army, church, school, political, professional and occupational organizations are not only a channel of social circulation but are at the same time, the 'sieves' which test and sift, select and distribute the individuals within different social strata or positions" (Sorokin, 1959, p. 183).

In this context, schools are social elevators going to different floors based on the political structure. Their primary function in modern society is as a testing, selecting, and distributing agency. Scholars have typically found genetics and environment as the two main determiners of class position in society, with a heated argument over which is more important. Statistically, the members of the upper classes score higher on intelligence tests, are physically taller and heavier, healthier, and live longer. On the environment side, classes seem to perpetuate their positions by maintaining their physical separateness and creating consistently positive or negative surroundings. Social mobility then occurs through luck or accident, changes in the environment, or differences of children from their genetic parents.

Francis Galton, a leader in the eugenics movement and half-cousin of Charles Darwin, in his seminal book, *Hereditary Genius*, looked at generations of various professions in nineteenth century England from judges, politicians, poets, painters, religious persons, Cambridge students, oarsmen, and wrestlers. His conclusion was that intelligence and talent are indisputably passed along genetically: "I feel convinced that no man can achieve a very high reputation without being gifted with very high abilities" (Galton, 1998, p. 49). E.G. Conklin, another leader in the development of thinking about human intelligence, in *The Direction of Human Evolution* argues that the dream of perfect equality is impossible because of natural differences: "This ideal of absolute equality has never been, and can never be, fully realized in human society—physically, intellectually, and morally— and there is no possible way in which such natural inequalities can be wholly eradicated" (Conklin, 1921, p. 100-101). Conklin points out that the essence of our natural society developed through a process of evolution leading to difference and inequality. Through his analysis, he sees that low intelligence is passed generally from parent to child, and that formal education can do little to increase basic genetic intelligence. Given this evolutionary fact about intelligence, Conklin argues that a democratic society needs to instead look at behavior of individuals in seeking out merit, but that finally differences in intelligence will tend to win out in society.

A more recent proponent of the link between genetics and intelligence, Arthur Jensen became a controversial leading figure in the intelligence debate from his academic home at the University of California, Berkeley. In his 1972 book, *Genetics and Education*, Jensen claimed that he found the bias against a genetic link or pattern to intelligence was so strong in America because of a social philosophy insistent upon notions of intellectual equality (Jensen, 1972). Jensen argued that the scientific facts showed a natural inequality of intelligence. Studies which looked at children from the same family raised in different households established that intelligence was constant regardless of their environment. However, unlike IQ, scholastic achievement does vary, according to Jensen: "The fact that scholastic achievement is considerably less heritable than intelligence also means that many other traits, habits, attitudes, and values enter into a child's performance in school besides just his intelligence, and these non-cognitive factors are largely environmentally determined, mainly through influences within the child's family" (Jensen, 1972, p. 135). In this way intelligence, but not academic performance, is inherited. This distinction made by Jensen is extremely important in looking at the use of standardized tests for university admissions purposes. For instance, we shall see in the discussion of standardized tests later in this chapter how the University of California made this same distinction in pointing out that the SAT I, like IQ tests, failed to predict subsequent academic performance in college. Nevertheless, Jensen claims that there is a resulting direct relationship between intelligence and social class: "It is well known that children's IQs, by school age, are correlated with the socioeconomic status of their parents. This is a world-wide phenomenon and has an extensive research literature going back 70 years" (Jensen, 1972, p. 153). Additionally, Jensen found that intelligence measurements also correlated with occupational status: "In a society that values and rewards individual talent and merit, genetic factors inevitably take on considerable importance" (Jensen, 1972, p. 156). Most disturbing, Jensen finally argued that there are clear racial differences in mental ability.

One of the most controversial eugenics proponents in the United States was the Nobel Prize-winning physicist William Shockley. Shockley warned of "dysgenics" or the negative evolution of the human race through the reproduction of the "genetically disadvantaged" (Shockley, 1992). Although a politically self-described liberal on social policies, he argued for a hard scientific look at the negative effects of the excessive propagation of the less intelligent. But probably the most notorious book in recent memory on the racial basis of intelligence is Herrnstein and Murray's book *The Bell Curve* (Herrnstein and Murray, 1996). The authors claim intelligence is at a minimum 60 percent inherited and only 40 percent or less a result of the environment. They see differences in genes as the most important factor in predicting success in school and in life, resulting in class position. As a consequence, they doubt the "messiah" role for education, specifically that extra education for low IQ students helps significantly. According to these scholars, over time as society becomes increasingly meritocratic, those with higher IQ rates will reside in the upper-classes: "The twenty-first [century] will open on a world in which cognitive ability is the decisive dividing force" (Herrnstein and Murray, 1996, p. 25).

In addition to the eugenics movement's focus on intelligence, some have concentrated on the moral and ethical lapses of the poor. An example of the rhetoric of this position comes from Theodore Dalrymple, a well-known British psychiatrist, who treats the poor in slum hospitals and prisons in England, and argues that poverty is caused by a dysfunctional set of values which are reinforced by society (Dalrymple, 2001). He claims that low-income families fail to take responsibility for their actions. For instance, "the knife went in" is how one murderer describes his violent act. They see life, he claims, as a series of disconnected events with no thread or pattern of meaning. So in this way, Dalrymple claims that not only are the poor less intelligent, but they are also immoral.

Perhaps the best and most cohesive argument made in rebuttal to *The Bell Curve* was done by a group of faculty members in the Sociology Department at the University of California, Berkeley and published in book form in 1996 as *Cracking The Bell Curve Myth* (Fischer, Hout, Jankowski, Lucas, Swidler and Voss, 1996). The authors argue that "g," or general intelligence, is simply a reflection of disadvantage: "Around the world, members of disadvantaged groups usually score lower than members of advantaged groups, whatever their racial identities" (Fischer et al., 1996, p. 19). The authors point to the data showing how extremely unequal American society has become: "Groups score unequally on tests because they are unequal in society" (Fischer et al. 1996, p. 172). The poor tend to concentrate into isolated areas and schools which emphasizes their disadvantage. Why do Asians do so well? The authors submit that there is an important difference in voluntary versus involuntary immigration. Asians who have immigrated most recently to America come from middle-class backgrounds. Additionally, Asian culture emphasizes hard work. Finally, the Berkeley sociologists claim in their book, "A racial or ethnic group's position in society determines its measured intelligence rather than vice versa" (Fischer et al., 1996, p. 173).

In sum, eugenics is not an isolated set of ideas linked to Nazi Germany, but a set of assumptions that leads to an unwillingness to take aggressive corrective action to help the poor, or worst, to further institutionally disadvantage them. This public attitude took extreme forms in the 1927 Supreme Court ruling allowing compulsory sterilization for the unfit. At elite colleges, Yale and other Ivy League schools took part in a rather bizarre eugenic scheme to take nude photographs of students in an attempt to try and document physical superiority (Oren, 1985). This practice continued into the 1960s and was an effort by these elite institutions to try to demonstrate supremacy of its students through scientific measurement. While these are extreme examples of the eugenic disposition in higher education, many of the changes in public policy at the end of the twentieth century come from a belief that there are innate intellectual differences that follow particular patterns, and that therefore improvements in favor of students from poor backgrounds will have limited impact at best.

Standardized Testing

In America, the eugenics movement can be traced to various key thinkers including Carl Brigham, who was a professor of psychology at Princeton University. In 1923 he published his important book based on Army IQ tests, *A Study of American Intelligence* (Brigham, 1923). Brigham had played a role in administering the army tests that came out of World War I, and his book drew on that experience. He found through his study of military personnel data to support a race hypothesis of superiority of "Nordic type" versus the "Alpine type." Influenced by eugenics theory, Brigham outlined in clear terms the distinctions among the races:

> The Nordic is constitutionally introvert, the Mediterranean constitutionally extrovert; the instinct of self-assertion is strong in the Nordic; the Alpine is introvert but not so strongly introvert as the Nordic; The Alpine has a high degree of sociability, is perhaps relatively weak in curiosity, and strong in the instinct of submission. (Brigham, 1923, p. 186)

His book argued the test scores were clear indicators of innate intelligence, and that the results proved the superior intelligence of what he called the Nordic Race. Brigham claimed that beliefs that Jews were intelligent were incorrect and that Negroes are intellectually inferior as well. Not only did Brigham make generalizations by race, but also by class: "Children from the professional, semi-professional and higher business classes have, on the whole, an hereditary endowment superior to that of children form the semi-skilled and unskilled laboring classes" (Brigham, 1923, p. 188). It is important to note here that eugenicists from the start made claims that were class based, in some cases more than race based. Most importantly, Brigham commented that recent history in America showed a dangerous pattern of "inferior peoples" immigrating to the United States: "According to all evidence available, then, American intelligence is declining, and will proceed with an accelerating rate as the racial admixture becomes more and more extensive" (Brigham, 1923, p. 210). Later in life Brigham was said to have renounced his earlier views. Nevertheless, *A Study of American Intelligence* was used by the eugenicist Harry Laughlin in the 1924 congressional debates on immigration, and played a key role in the creation of restrictive immigration legislation which tragically impacted the flow of Jewish refugees to the United States fleeing the Holocaust. Brigham's perhaps most significant legacy is the creation of the Scholastic Aptitude Test (SAT). Few realize that the SAT, the predominant measure used in college admissions, was designed by someone who believed, at least in the early part of his life, in the racial inferiority of ethnic minority and low-income groups.

The use and history of standardized testing in the United States is fascinating sociology and falls within the nature-versus-nurture debate because the initial intent of tests like the SAT was to appear to remove privilege from the evaluation of ability to perform well in college. Such standardized tests became a way for colleges to validate and defend admissions choices. Like affirmative action policies, the SAT was a quick fix for one of the obvious shortcomings of meritocracy. Nevertheless, from the start, the SAT test has proven to be culturally biased. For instance, in 1951 the Educational Testing Service (ETS) found an extremely low number of Southerners scoring well on the test (Lemann, 2000). In 1980, Ralph Nader's organization printed a damaging report on ETS called *The Reign of ETS: The Corporation that Makes up Minds* (Naim, 1980). In this analysis, Nader's group essentially claims consumer fraud by ETS in that the testing group makes assertions regarding the analysis of student ability without proper statistical support with devastating effects:

> Imagine a process of evaluation where the educational and career opportunities of millions of people are significantly determined by multiple-choice examinations, which do not even purport to test their judgment, wisdom, experience, creativity, idealism, determination or stamina. (Naim, 1980, p. xiv)

Nader's report challenges the very notion of the possibility of an instrument foretelling success in college. Citing various studies, the Nader study concludes that the SAT test predicts an applicant's success in college only 8 to 15 percent better than a random roll of dice. Furthermore, the SAT consistently produces results of lower test scores for low-income and minority students. According to the Nader report, "ETS does not tell them that the assessment of their 'aptitude' is more a reflection of socio-economic status than their actual potential for future accomplishment" (Naim, 1980, p. 210). Furthermore, the report claims that the test destroys student self-confidence and is counter-productive to learning.

As early as 1960, the University of California found that the SAT was not a good predictor of performance in college. By the turn of the twenty-first century, the bias of the SAT, especially in the dreaded verbal analogies, was so clear that the University of California threatened to discontinue its use. According to a report issued by a special state-wide committee looking into the effectiveness of the SAT, the ability of the test to identify those who would perform well in college was not demonstrated: "The advantage that the SAT I is often assumed to possess—that it is effective at identifying students with strong potential who have not yet been able to demonstrate that potential—is largely a phantom, at least at the University of California" (Board of Admissions and Relations with Schools BOARS, n.d.). Indeed, the University of California found that student high school grade point average and SAT II scores were much more useful in predicting college academic success. Furthermore, the SAT II was less affected by socio-economic background, according to the study. ETS managed to reach a compromise with its largest client in revising the SAT, and the University of California in return decided to stress the SAT II tests which are based on content knowledge that students should have learned in high school (Sacks, 2007). The University of California on-going assessment of the SAT indicates a renewed awareness, or suspicion, of the use of standardized tests in college admissions altogether.

When the University of California decided that the SAT I was not a good predictor of college grades, the Ivy League schools were silent on the matter. Elite universities have for years weighed the verbal portion of the test more heavily giving students with a privileged secondary school experience a distinct advantage. Additionally, one clear statistical problem that Harvard and Yale face with the SAT is that since their grades are inflated, with an average grade point average of A- it was difficult to show how different SAT scores lead to varying success in college. This problem in evaluating critically their own students is seen in the fact that Yale University in 1992 graduated 58 percent of its class with honors (they subsequently enforced a limit of 30 percent) (Soares, 2007).

Finally, performing well on standardized tests as a goal for low-income students does not lead to equality—a study in the 1970s found that there existed nearly as much economic inequality among those who score highly on standardized tests as in the general American population (Jencks, Smith, Acland, Bane, Cohen, Gintis, Heyns, Michelson, 1972). So even if the standardized tests were fair, the larger admissions and social context overrides outstanding individual performance. Furthermore, standardized tests do not predict subsequent career success because they measure values linked to school, not jobs. Given the brief history of standardized tests related here, it is surprising that they have lasted so long in American higher education. One can see that these tests were originally designed as a way of rationalizing a belief in the intellectual superiority of middle and upper-class kids who are subsequently admitted in greater numbers to better colleges. Nevertheless, although it has taken too long, it seems that there is growing consensus against the plainly biased standardized tests.

Role of Basic Language, Math and Study Skills

Students from low-income families often lack basic language and math skills as they enter college. The sociologist Emile Durkheim in his book *The Evolution of Education Thought* (1977) traces the history and importance of language skills in higher education arguing that often observers are puzzled by the importance of "grammar" in the curriculum of early universities. He describes the original notion of grammar as being more of a focus on the study of logic and thinking rather than on arbitrary language conventions, as we understand it today: "Grammar was, as it were, the womb of logic" (Durkheim, 1977, p. 63). In modern times the link between sentence construction and thinking itself has been largely overlooked. But as any good English teacher knows, there is a direct connection between writing well and thinking. Durkheim aptly described it: "Thus with words, with language, we are dealing in some direct way with thought; and consequently the study of language is, if one knows how to set about it, to study thought itself" (Durkheim, 1977, p. 57). What this important nineteenth century thinker understood is well known by low-income students in college, suffering as they often do from inadequate language skills which impair clear thinking and expression.

In Miles Corwin's book *And Still We Rise*, the journalist spent a year in a high school classroom in South Central Los Angles observing the struggles of students and their energetic teacher in an Advanced Placement English course (Corwin 2001). The book dramatizes the challenge for teachers to make a traditional academic English literature curriculum relevant and understandable to students who not only come from a very different culture, but lack an understanding of Durkheim's classical grammar, the basis for Western European logic. Furthermore, with family problems, gangs, part-time jobs, and identity formation issues these students are hardly free of the "force of circumstance" Durkheim noted as typical for those pursuing liberal studies. In the experiences represented in this book of the group of talented students from a very poor area in Los Angeles we see the gap between the language skill expectations and traditions of higher education.

Similarly, many of those I talked with described students who are struggling because of very little adequate academic preparation in Math and English. These students are in college because somehow they were recruited or encouraged to attend, but they come with deficiencies in reading comprehension and study skills. Clearly academic preparation in English as well as in the sciences is a key for low-income college students trying to succeed. Particularly at the more selective institutions, high school preparation for low-income college students often falls short in writing. The form these deficiencies in preparation take are various but telling. In the following conversation with a student I am struck by both the obvious desire of low-income parents to support education, as well as the lack of knowledge or randomness of the preparation.

> AUTHOR: Growing up did you have a lot of books, magazines, or newspapers around home?
> STUDENT: I had books. Books that you'd read in elementary like *Charlie and the Chocolate Factory*. Magazines.
> AUTHOR: Do your parents read much?
> STUDENT: They don't do any of that.
> AUTHOR: Do they read in Spanish?
> STUDENT: Not really.
> AUTHOR: So why were the books and magazines around?
> STUDENT: I'd go to the store and see books and magazines that I wanted and would tell them to buy them for me. And they would buy them for me.
> AUTHOR: So it was really you?
> STUDENT: Yes. I had little coloring books with stories. I'd paint the pictures.

Part of the academic preparation is simply for students to be around intellectually and culturally enriching media, from books to magazines and newspapers. In this way, middle-class students and those from low-income students who do well in college often talk about going to the library on a regular basis.

Part of the general worldliness that faculty members mention in my interviews with them (as at the end of this chapter) has to do with active discussions in the household. For middle-class children, often these conversations take place informally at the dinner table, or in the car on the way to school or soccer practice. Low-income students report that they do not have these types of conversations. We will see later how experts note that one typical difference between middle-class and low-income home life is that low-income children often do not engage in serious conversation with adults. One person I interviewed described a process whereby the older children were engaged more in such conversation: "It was expected that the older children would participate more, and that at a certain point you were older and were considered more well informed."

In the little known but important series of lectures referenced earlier, Durkheim pointed to the clearly class-based history of education where a chief characteristic is that students be unemployed: "Aimed at the sons of a privileged aristocracy for whom the difficulties of serious living did not exist" (Durkheim, 1977, p. 210). In bold fashion, as seen from our politically-correct contemporary vantage point, the French sociologist argued that the humanist education was developed for and through this privileged leisure class and consequently has an inherent impracticality and class basis to it even today. What he calls the "force of circumstance" did not inform the traditional curricula of the university because the primary audience was for those removed from concerns of daily survival. In this way, historically the lack of language skills has been a distinct sign of low-income status in higher education. The force of economic necessity for the working-class and lack of resources to invest in culturally rich resources add up to a formidable obstacle to success in college for students from poor families.

Advanced Placement Courses

One way students seek competitive advantage in college admissions and better preparation for college is through high school Advanced Placement (AP) tests. There is good news and bad news in terms of Advanced Placement courses for low-income and ethnic minority students. In the College Board's *Advanced Placement Report to the Nation 2006*, signs of leveling of the playing field are reported claiming "a wider segment than ever of the US is achieving success" because 14 percent as opposed to 10 percent the previous year had scored a three, or a passing grade on an AP test (College Board, 2006). However, on a less happy note, the report admits that racial minority groups are still significantly under participating in Advance Placement courses.

In a book by Samuel Lucas entitled *Tracking Inequality: Stratification and Mobility in American High Schools*, the author argues that when tracking of students in K-12 was rolled back in the late 1960s and 1970s, schools turned to directing students by courses (Lucas, 1999). In what he terms the "Unremarked Revolution," American schools began to hide a tracking system in the guise of college preparatory and honors courses that formed natural sequences. These replaced the previously explicit tracks that had been clearly shown to disadvantage low-income and ethnic minority students. Because admission to advanced courses is dependent on previous coursework, an informal tracking system was maintained. Lucas presents data in his book indicating a clear link of social class to enrollment in advanced high school courses.

Advancement Placement courses were originally designed to help provide a base level of preparation for students preparing for college and to help universities better evaluate in-coming students. Previously, colleges had a great deal of trouble comparing the rigor of advanced courses at the high school level from one community to the next. However, the ability to support and schedule Advance Placement courses quickly became a resource issue that emphasized the inequality of schools. In this way, the class divide has become exaggerated by the growing popular use and importance of Advance Placement courses especially for top-tier university admissions. This importance occurs in three linked ways: first, through raising the level of academic preparation; second, through elevating a student's grade point average (since A grades are generally recorded as 5 points rather than 4); and finally in reducing the number of courses a student needs to take in college to earn a degree.

The low-income students I interviewed talked about taking fewer Advanced Placement courses than one finds in typical college-bound students. Additionally, they tend to avoid the more difficult hard science and math AP courses that are especially beneficial in competitive admissions decisions. I found students from Spanish-speaking families often enrolled in AP Spanish because of the built-in advantage they had as native speakers. Conversely, AP English Literature was rarely mentioned as a course that first-generation college students had taken in high school.

Knowledge and access to Advanced Placement courses is an increasingly important part of the adequate preparation for college. Low-income students talk about their family and friends lacking a basic knowledge of how to prepare for college through taking Advanced Placement Courses and standardized tests such as the SAT with test prep courses. While middle-class parents typically have their children repeatedly take the pre-SAT tests and enroll their children in preparatory courses after school and during the summer, low-income families lack both an understanding of the importance of these activities and the means to participate fully.

Psycho-Social Preparation

The psychological and social preparation of low-income students for college is informed by the lack of family knowledge of university life and in how parents, teachers, and counselors emotionally support college-going students. Experts in the field point to the way that the lack of cultural capital, or the things that are not taught in school, give middle- and upper-class children advantages in college, while in low-income families, the opposite pattern occurs (McDonough, 1997). As a result, poor students apply to lower-level colleges and send out fewer applications than middle- and upper-class students. The choice about colleges is made sense of within the context of friends, family, and general class outlook, so that their alternatives in life and for college are self-limited. Students from poor families expect less and have lower aspirations in relationship to college.

In terms of understanding the college experience, many of those I spoke with indicated that a central component of the lack of preparation comes from parents who themselves have not had a college experience. Students throughout my interviews and discussions remarked on the specific forms this lack of knowledge of college takes, and how it impacts them practically and psychologically. Some experts in the field argue that those who don't go to college typically have parents who expressed minimal educational ambition for them, and that those parental expectations are clearly linked to family income. Attitudes about education and career objectives of these students from alternate family backgrounds differ so greatly that they become self-fulfilling prophecies. Often upper-income students have more access to information about college earlier in the process, as well as more satisfying discussions with counselors and teachers about education after high school. The role of teachers and school counselors in emotionally and practically supporting low-income students is often mentioned: "If I didn't have that I wouldn't have known which schools to apply to, I wouldn't have known much about college at all."

The emotional and psychological support of parents is perhaps the most important factor. Although parents may not themselves understand college, they can still support their child's effort: "He don't know how, but if I tell him how he'll help." Sometimes this support takes the form of stories related to children about how parents have struggled and children need to pursue education to be different than their parents. For others it is easy to find encouragement to do something different than taking the path that has led to such a hard life of struggle and need. In these cases, it takes little direct encouragement of the students other than to point out the reality of their situation. Low-income students with supportive parents talk with some irritation about having their homework checked, grades looked over, and punishment for poor performance. Additionally, supportive parents of first-generation college students often pursue school resources even though they don't always understand the process: "They are always going to meetings."

The negative side of this parental support and encouragement is that low-income college students often feel a great deal of pressure to succeed. When I ask one low-income student how her parents would feel if she hadn't gone to college she tells me, "My parents would be disappointed, but they'd also try to understand." Furthermore, this same student talked of family members who are envious of her for having the college privilege. I repeatedly heard stories about relatives telling promising young female students that there was no point in going to college; that they'd just end up failing and going to work, or become pregnant.

Students also experience family pressure to work instead of going to college: "She didn't go, why should you go?" And then if it isn't stressful enough having one's life chances depend on success in college, their parents' and future generations' well-being is often tied up with the educational fate of a single low-income student: "It's going to be for your benefit, and your children's benefit." In this way, low-income students talk about succeeding not just for themselves, but for their family members and generations to come.

Students from poor families often speak of divergent parental attitudes towards brothers and sisters. Besides the obvious gender attitudes, parents express preferences towards one child over another, or question suitability for college by individual siblings. Students told me about how their parents expected a brother or sister to go to a private university or the University of California rather than attend a community college or California State University. Conversely, the expectations are lower for some: "They want me to go to an okay college. But they expect my sister to go to a good college. And the other night my sister was stressing out about college, because what if she doesn't make it? And she doesn't want to disappoint anyone." Lacking family support, others talk about the importance of friends in encouraging students to attend college. In this way, if a high school has a college prep aim, and the students are working towards and talking about college, then it is more likely a first-generation college student will follow suit.

Low-income students speak directly about how lack of comfort and self-confidence becomes a practical handicap in the classroom. Poorly supported students express shyness about approaching faculty with questions both in and out of the classroom. "I'm kind of embarrassed by what I might say," is a typical comment. This shyness for many is a legacy and symptom of a lower position in society. So we see that the emotional context for attending college is structured by family, friends, teachers and school counselors. Those who end up in college often point to attitudes such as this expressed by one person I interviewed: "You can be whatever you want to be. You can do whatever you want to do. I heard that throughout my whole life."

Importance of Environment for Low-Income Students

A great deal of attention has been given to looking at how the environment, broadly defined, impacts the life chances of individual students. Historically, experts have considered the broad socio-political and religious context. More recently, there has been an increased understanding of the complexity of an individual's environment and a special focus on the impact of the immediate family and cultural background of students. Figure 1.1 represents how the two lines of the nature versus nurture argument progress. Notice in particular how environment opposes talent, and the different approaches of conformity or self-direction oppose random biological characteristics that might influence intelligence.

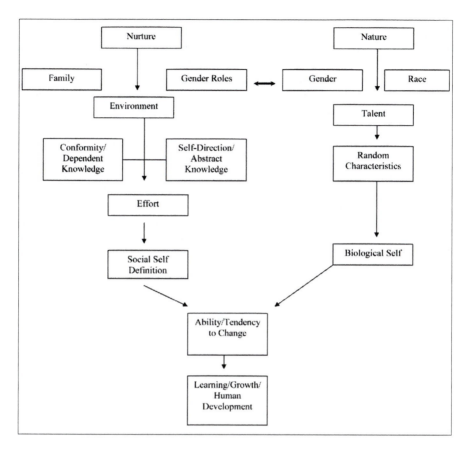

Figure 1.1 Nurture versus nature
Source: Author.

Some thinkers have long emphasized the importance of the environment in encouraging movement among the classes. The traditional formulation of class comes from the nineteenth century economists Karl Marx and Max Weber. For Marx, class relationships were embedded in the production process itself; ownership and control of production was at the root. For Weber, class situations reflected different life chances in the market. In *The Protestant Ethic and the Spirit of Capitalism*, Weber describes the notion of the calling to fulfill a duty to worldly affairs, a pseudo-religious obligation that characterizes the modern worker: "The earning of money within the modern economic order is, so long as it is done legally, the result and the expression of virtue and proficiency in a calling" (Weber, 1930, p. 19). One can see in this protestant ethic described by Weber a link to the American perception that the poor have primary responsibility for their own condition. However, by the end of the twentieth century the general perception by contemporary scholars was that these nineteenth century economists and their approaches did not lend themselves to the complexity of contemporary class relations (Crompton, 1998). In other words, the affects of the environment on individuals is multifaceted and may vary greatly for individuals.

What are the specific ways today in which the environment or the "nurture" part of the nature versus nurture equation contributes to class position? Scholars have looked at family influences on educational attainment and success and noted that the educational reforms of the 1960s focusing on race-based childhood education largely failed because parental inequality was not addressed (Jencks, Smith, Acland, Bane, Cohen, Gintis, Heyns, Michelson, 1972). According to these experts, the primary assumption of the reforms in the 1960s, that changing education could lead to breaking the cycle of poverty, has proven incorrect. Instead, some researchers have found that "inequality is recreated anew in each generation, even among people who start life in essentially identical circumstances" (Jencks et al., 1972, p. 8). Economic status and mobility depends on job competence and luck, and to a lesser degree, on schooling and scores on standardized tests. Thus some scholars have concluded that in order to have a real impact on the inequality in educational attainment, attitudes and values will need to be altered. Because not all students are driven to pursue mobility and wealth, educational attainment is partly a matter of values, and there may be collective standards by income group and ethnicity. These scholars then point to another one of the main public myths about the poor which is that their condition is partly a result of individual values. In this way, the importance of environment is discounted by pointing to the responsibility of individuals for their own fate.

Since personal values and attitudes are formed to a large extent by the immediate family, experts have looked closely at the home life impact on students and the notion of "cultural capital" (Bourdieu, 1993). Annette Lareau, in her book *Unequal Childhoods*, found distinct differences between how lower- and middle-class children are raised that directly impacts school performance (Laureau, 2003). She makes the distinction between "concerted cultivation" practiced by middle- and upper-class parents, versus "natural growth" approaches to child-rearing used by low-income parents. Middle-class parents tend to talk more directly to their children as adults, while low-income students are generally not engaged actively by adults and have more unsupervised or undirected free time. In this way, middle-class children gain more confidence and understand that they are entitled to adult attention. The greater amount of adult conversation in middle-class families tends to lead to greater vocabularies in children, a familiarity with abstract concepts, and a better understanding of rules of interacting with social institutions and adults. "Thus, one of the benefits of middle-class status appears to be the transmission of exceptional verbal skills that enable children to make special requests of adults in positions of power" (Lareau, 2003, p. 111). Lareau argues that middle-class children have many more organized activities, from soccer to after school tutoring, that teach them how to perform and interact in ways that are advantages both in school and in later professional life. Furthermore, low-income parents are often distant and distrustful of schools. Most importantly, Lareau claims that some of the common characteristics of low-income parenting, such as close family ties and less stress on the children, are positive in and of themselves, but that society clearly rewards the attributes that are imbued in middle- and upper-class children: "There are signs that middle-class children benefit, in ways that are invisible to them and to their parents, from the degree of similarity between the cultural repertoires in the home and those standards adopted by institutions" (Lareau, 2003, p. 237).

Similarly, Melvin L. Kohn claims that middle-class parents are more likely to emphasize children's self-direction, while working-class parents tend to promote conformity to external standards (Kohn, 1989). Self-direction requires opportunities and experiences that are available to those in higher social positions and occupations. What parents emphasize is transmitted in ways that influence child development:

> Middle-class mothers give higher priority to values that reflect internal dynamics—the child's own and his empathic concern for other people's. Specifically, they are said to be significantly more likely than are working-class mothers to value happiness (in particular, for sons), consideration, self-control, and curiosity. (Kohn, 1989, p. 21)

Kohn argues that working-class parents are considerably less likely than middle-class parents to expect or want their children to go to college. Class differences in values and orientation perpetuate class inequality: "Whether consciously or not, parents tend to impart to their children lessons derived from the conditions of life of their own social class—and thus help prepare their children for a similar class position" (Kohn, 1989, p. 200). The theorized overall conformist orientation of low-income parents is a poor fit for children needing to learn to deal with the problems of a higher-class professional life.

Norton Grubb and Marvin Lazerson point out that in the face of inattentive parents, teachers become substitute parents sponsored by the government (Grubb and Lazerson, 1982). These scholars trace the problem to a nineteenth century notion of the family which focused on individual family responsibility for children, rather than a larger village or social ownership of that responsibility. Poetically, they state that: "Children have been the 'bearers of the American Dream,' and children's institutions have usually borne the responsibility for fulfilling this version of the American dream" (Grubb and Lazerson 1982, p. 67). The authors identify the mixed goals of public education in America to essentially use a public institution to further individual or private goals of moving up in the world. This paradoxical tension between the public goal to educate all children, and the private goal of educating only one's children, leads to the unequal educational results: "As long as parents use public institutions for private ends, the public responsibilities of the schools will remain embattled and compromised, and the promise of public education will remain distorted by the demands of individualistic ends" (Grubb and Lazerson 1982, p. 132). Like Lareau, Grubb and Lazerson claim that middle-class parenting focuses more on developing independence and self-reliance in children whereas working-class parents tend to stress obedience and conformity. This difference in parenting is directly linked to a socialization process for different economic tracks: "Children of different class backgrounds are prepared for institutions outside the family in different ways" (Grubb and Lazerson 1982, p. 76). Furthermore, Grubb and Lazerson point to poor planning skills in the low-income students. Chronic unemployment and poverty condition the poor to understanding that their future is uncontrollable, making planning pointless.

Scholars have also written about how families pass along different attitudes and ways of thinking. Basil Bernstein, in *Class, Codes and Control*, cites three primary differences: understanding relationships between means and ends, behavioral discipline, and an ability to change behavior in pursuit of distant goals (Bernstein, 1972). Bernstein found that the differences in language that classes use carry some of these key differences: "It is reasonable to argue that the genes of social class may well be carried less through a genetic code but far more through a communication code that social class itself promotes" (Bernstein, 1971, p. 143). He found that the low-income subjects spent less time pausing and used a shorter length words than those from the upper classes. Most importantly in terms of education, Bernstein identified a tendency of low-income students to have trouble with abstractions, and suggests that its members have been socialized to look primarily at context-dependent knowledge.

Some scholars have focused on practical ways that the educational and cultural environment provided by privileged families leads directly to positive educational outcomes. For instance, the summer educational and cultural experiences typical of affluent families have been found to influence school performance in a large way (Heyns, 1978). The impact of having college educated parents is perhaps greatest during the summer when the gap between advantaged and disadvantaged students roughly doubles. Consistent use of the library, along with summer educational programs, helps wealthier children not only to maintain but increase their knowledge during the summer. In this way, the gap between poor and rich, black and white, widens during summer. In some ways the school acts as a surrogate parent during the school year. Because of the uneven resources for children during the summer, some argue for compulsory schooling during the summer for poor children.

William Julius Wilson (1987) looks at the challenges in terms of overall urban decay with the fleeing of middle-class ethnic minority groups to the suburbs, leaving behind a particularly disadvantaged segment. At the same time, this group was especially hard hit by economic downturns and changes in the industrial system found in cities. Wilson argues on a policy level that affirmative action and other such policies tend to mostly advantage the middle-class from ethnic groups, and not the ones who are especially challenged in urban poor areas.

In reviewing the disturbing history of eugenics in America, the belief is repeatedly expressed that the poor are responsible for their own unhappy fates, both by genetic inheritance and flawed values and attitudes. In Figure 1.2 the relationship between environmental factors and genetics are sketched out in the form that the influences take in a eugenic model. We see in this conception that intelligence is of primary importance in both the creation of inequality and social problems. Parents are only important, one presumes, in as much as they deliver or pass along the good or bad genes.

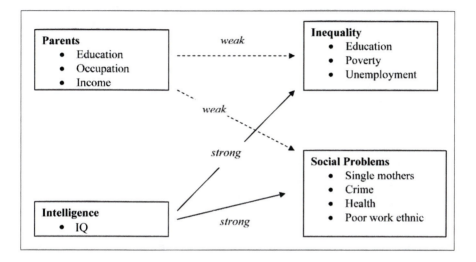

Figure 1.2 Eugenic model of educational performance
Source: Based on Fischer, Hout, Jankowski, Lucas, Swidler, and Voss, 1996.

Interestingly, the role of the parents as seen throughout this book is minimized in this model.

Although scholars disagree on the extent of the influence of environment on student success in college, it clearly has an impact. From subtle forms of family interactions and college expectations, to practical and direct advantages of summer programs and organized activities, experts have increasingly identified limitations for low-income students in their environment which work to perpetuate disadvantage.

Sidebar Portrait: Rick

Rick is a young and energetic Associate Professor of History. He looks like the former college wrestler that he is, and welcomes me to his office with a strong handshake. Rick describes growing up in Oxnard, California in a working class family. Although his mother was educated to the sixth grade, and his father to community college, he was encouraged from an early age to attend college. Nevertheless,

Rick clarifies that the support was not much beyond general encouragement and financial help because his parents did not have college experience themselves: "I don't think my parents had the background, in terms of what was needed to be successful, or even to get ready for college or the university." In discussing his own college experience, he tells me of the attitude in his own family, and that he has seen in other first-generation college student families, where it is assumed that by simply attending high school one is prepared for college: "Not knowing that there are differences in the courses you take, in terms of competencies, visiting colleges, and the background work that parents with a college education may be aware of." Rick describes the general impression of college in his community: "For my parents and the parents of many of my friends who grew up in my neighborhood, college was very mysterious." In contrast, he tells me that the world of work was typically much better understood and promoted to children in his community.

As with many first-generation college families, there is a general encouragement to go to college but with little supplied in the way of rationale: "They never said why." By the end of high school Rick's parents laid out the career options for him in plain terms: "My mother told me in no uncertain terms I was either going to go to school or I was going to get a job. There was no grey area." When he chose college they had enough means to fully support him financially at first at a local community college, and then California State Fresno in the San Joaquin Valley. He chose this university because of its wrestling program and a desire not to financially burden the family with more expensive University of California campus or private college options.

In college, Rick speaks about the athletics program as smoothing many of the typical adjustment problems from academic advising, to practical registration and housing needs. Additionally, the athletics program provided a ready-made community of young people with similar interests and often backgrounds. "I didn't go through EOP at community college, or the college level. But the sports program, more so at the community college, was my EOP."

When returning home, he noticed a "gap" between family and friends. Rick's parents did not ask about college; they just expected that he would finish and do well. This tension between parents and first-generation college students parallels what I saw in the children of migrant workers and the EOP students. While on the face of things the general encouragement and financial support seem like real advantages for Rick, he nevertheless still felt hindered because of poor academic preparation: "I knew that my preparation should have taken place a long time ago."

A history professor saw promise in the young wrestler and suggested he go to graduate school. Again, even though they did not fully understand the importance of graduate school, his parents supported Rick in this effort. He was again challenged in graduate school and always felt behind the other students. After graduate school he came home and worked at the United Parcel Service for a year before finding a teaching position at a community college. While teaching at community college he went back to school and earned a doctoral degree. He then was appointed to the position at the regional comprehensive university where he now teaches.

Rick understands the very real obstacles faced by low-income college students but is also critical of the attitudes he finds in some students. He points to a sense of entitlement some students display and a surprising lack of understanding of the personal importance of earning a college degree. Additionally, students who transfer from a community college typically experience transition problems with academic expectations and understanding differences in university culture. Rick sees the lack of academic preparation he experienced himself in his students: "They have deficiencies in skills, as I had back then, in terms of reading and comprehension, skills related to studying." Furthermore, he notes economic pulls on the students to work long hours outside of the classroom. Scheduling classes with work and family responsibilities while paying for expensive textbooks and fees is a typical burden.

Rick views the successful students as performing well because of natural talent: "Some just have gifts. They're talented so maybe they don't have to spend as much time trying to get through the material." This special group of students has not avoided the pressures and obstacles the other low-income students face rather, "they are successful despite their circumstances." Looking back over his teaching career, Rick sees the best students from low-income backgrounds as having both natural talent and desire to do well. He adds that they specifically tend to have good listening skills and high degrees of literacy.

When I ask Rick about the notion of merit-based admissions practices, he describes such a focus as masking a public lack of support of low-income and ethnic minority groups. The problem, he argues, is the impossibility of separating out merit from the larger social context. In his own case, his family was very aware of the status issues linked to education. Rick's father insisted that he not take wood shop or auto mechanics in order to avoid the tracking into vocational occupations. He is suspicious of the under representation of ethnic groups in particular high status professions: "I think everybody should have the opportunity to consider going to college, I don't think that question should be answered for them."

As an educator, Rick views public higher education as only partially working to improve the life chances of low-income children. He sees better efforts in recruitment and retention of students as key. Rick points to the fairly recently implemented policy at the California State University to remove students who cannot meet basic levels of writing and math competency: "If we're doing that, are we really supporting students?" He sees college as only minimally serving to move low-income students up in society. Rick reflects on his own experience of often hearing that he is a "credit to your community," while knowing that he is one of a very few Latinos from a working-class background to earn a doctoral degree. Meanwhile, in his old neighborhood half the students drop out of high school before graduating. Rick reflects on hearing his middle school teacher encouraging students to go to their graduation ceremony because they were unlikely to make it through high school. He subsequently saw friends slowly, one-by-one, dropout of school.

Rick describes earning a college degree as a "tremendous asset in mobility, if you can survive it." He feels that he is privileged in many ways, and wants to pass along what he has learned about the college culture to his children. In his community he sees those from his generation lacking college degrees struggling economically with health and addiction problems. Nevertheless, he admits that a college education does not necessary bring financial security and wealth: "It's not only economic." Rick points to the larger world view and perspective that is gained through a college education. He reflects on his own background and tells me that many uneducated people don't even understand that they are disadvantaged. "I never saw myself as disadvantaged, I had everything. I had two good parents, I never had a day of not having something to eat. I never went without new clothes. I had everything. But looking back now I understand that I was disadvantaged in other respects." Rick sees the whole notion of "disadvantaged" as being complex especially when it comes to education.

Finally, Rick points to the family as a key to education and social mobility. While he doesn't want to suggest that everything is the parent's fault, he does see the clear connection between the parents and the life chances of students and likelihood of earning a degree. A home life that is supportive and stable is more likely to encourage children to move up in the world through a college education. Nevertheless, it is the larger structures that form the background to the family and home life. Rick sees that in regards to affirmative action debates that the conversation usually turns to individual flaws rather than larger social structures, institutions and economic, because the discussion is "too complicated, too difficult."

Sidebar Portrait: George

George is a professor who was himself a first-generation college student. His father and mother are foreign born; neither has education beyond high school and did not discuss college with him. Even when George was identified as gifted as a child, his parents never pressured him to go to college: "I think there was the hope, but not the expectation." When he did enter a local private college, his parents were encouraging and supported his effort. Although he had been admitted to Stanford University on a full scholarship, his parents did not want him to leave home at 17. George recalls that his first college was "perfectly good," but that he felt out of place. A commuter at a primarily residential private Catholic college, he was left out of many of the traditional student experiences and did not fit into the campus social groups. Furthermore, he worked part time as a life guard and as an emergency room technician while attending school, which also pulled him away from the regular student life experience.

In search of a more suitable college and wanting to leave his Southern California nest, George transferred in his sophomore year to a public university in Texas. He describes a powerful culture shock living in Texas this first year, even greater than what he experienced in subsequent international travel. Nevertheless, he managed to fit in better in Texas than at his previous institution, partly because he formed an identity tied to California, which was a novelty at the new university. George describes his motivation for going to college as loosely linked to getting a job and that led him to be a business major. In college he became interested in other subjects, such as languages and sciences, and ended up spending a year studying abroad in Paris. However, even with this impressive undergraduate experience, he didn't go directly to graduate school. Instead George worked for a few years, went to a public university for a master's degree, and then on to a private research university for a doctoral degree.

Coming from what he describes as a "very tight knit traditional Hispanic family where really the only reason for leaving the house is because you got married," George said that his parents were not happy with him departing to attend in Texas. Over time, their nervousness passed and he was conferred adult status. He doesn't feel that he had to make sacrifices to fit into the atmosphere at college: "I didn't feel that going to college compromised my cultural self in any sense."

Nevertheless, George does feel that his choice to go to college meant a sacrifice in his relationship to his family: "a little something was given up in some sense." Although they don't completely understand his chosen academic profession, they do show him a great deal of respect: "My sister, my parents, my grandfather, my aunts and uncles take to heart whatever I say to them because somehow it comes from the voice of authority." He doesn't feel that he's lost familial affection, but that there is a barrier now from a lack of understanding. When I ask if his family understands what he does as a professor, he tells me that they are still trying to figure out why anyone would need to go to school for 26 years. While like many immigrant families there is a general belief in the value of an American education, George's father imparted a working class attitude about careers: "What you need to do in life is figure out how to work, how to make a decent living, without killing yourself." In this context, college is perhaps a way to find employment beyond manual labor.

As with many families, expectations regarding careers and education varied greatly for George's sister. "I think that there is the perception that because she is a girl she is inherently less able," George tells me, admitting that he doesn't have direct evidence of this—just a sense of the cultural attitude he felt growing up. Regarding college, "the expectation was that my sister would 'try' to go to college, but I don't think that they would have ever pressured her." He describes traditional family roles with the male as the "bread winner" and the woman as a housewife. Although his mother did work, she was never considered the main source of family support. Nevertheless, his sister did end getting a degree in business and is now a successful business person. George describes this occurrence as a "threat" for his parents because her path did not align with their image and expectations of her.

As a faculty member, George has worked with low-income and first-generation students at different universities. He claims some are very talented, while others "probably shouldn't be in college, and are wasting their time." On a psychological level, George sees low-income students struggling with issues of identity formation. Coming into the university with different primary languages, cultural backgrounds, and work and family expectations, all increase the pressure on their identities at a time when young people are going through very large developmental changes.

George characterizes the primary problem that many low-income students suffer from as a lack of broad cultural knowledge. He gives the example of trying to make the courses he teaches interactive and real-world based by bringing in newspapers articles and discussing how current events relate to the principles they are studying. However, many of the students have never read a newspaper: "They have no understanding of how to read the language that is presented there." He sees this as not just a second language issue, but a problem of students coming from families where proper and more formal forms of English are not spoken or read. Additionally, the mathematics and graphical representations he uses are difficult for many students to understand because of poor academic preparation. More broadly he sees the problem for many low-income students being based on simple lack of worldliness: "Just exposure even to the topic." George claims that it is not because they are incapable of understanding the material, or in some cases not even that they are poorly prepared academically, it is simply because they have no broader frame of reference of the world: "So that everything is hitting them as completely new." While he believes that everyone has some way of relating to a topic, the illustrations that he uses and are often used in higher education too often don't work for first-generation college students with a very limited range of experience. As a result, he has to change his examples and go out of his way to reach this group of students: "I use myself and my family a lot because that is something that they can relate to." While uncomfortable with the broad definitions of class and race, he tends to see this kind of lack of worldliness in first-generation students as primarily class based: "It's not their culture that makes the difference, it's their class."

How are public universities doing in addressing the needs of first-generation college students? George expresses mixed feelings of, on the one hand, realizing that there is an inherent inequality of opportunity, but on the other hand believes that individuals play a key role in forming their own life chances. He feels that public universities have a lot of resources available for low-income students that too often go untapped because of a lack of strong motivation to succeed. In addition to a university needing to try to accommodate low-income students, he sees a responsibility for the students in adapting themselves to the college culture. From his own experience, George sees that for young people deciding to go to college is a commitment that reduces and limits options to some degree. At a young age, many want more options and freedom to act and don't want to be stuck in a college career track.

When I ask about the social mobility impact of college, George has perhaps a balanced response in thinking that college for most results in maintaining the status quo: "I think for the average college student, college helps them maintain the social status they were brought up in." Nevertheless, he has no doubt that for low-income students college is an opportunity for mobility, one often times not pursued. He points out as an example that many low-income students go into lower paying "helping professions" such as teaching, medicine and social services. As noted earlier with the children of migrant workers, George observes that "they see this as a way to not justify, but legitimate leaving that community." He then notes a conscious decision by some students to choose professions out of college that give them less economic mobility than they might achieve in other arenas.

In regard to merit-based admission policies, George emphasizes such an approach can only be fair if there is a way to compare effectively people from different backgrounds:

> To me if you are going to have a meritocracy then you need to make sure those students coming from elementary, middle and high school are being supported to the extent that when they get to higher education that everybody is competing on a relatively level playing field.

When I ask him if that is the reality in America today, he quickly responds, "No." He sees the "diversity" that is valued in American institutions as one of the things preventing meritocracy from working. George points to other more homogenous societies around the world where the notion of merit-based educational systems is perhaps more workable as a concept. A beneficiary of affirmative action academic aid himself, he does see a need to work against inequality, but thinks the focus should be on class rather than just race. He finds the role of measured talent in admissions as a "terrifying" subject. He tells me he can't imagine a fair measure of real talent. Rather he sees the social responsibility in providing opportunity rather than in evaluating talent, balanced with individual student responsibility to take advantage of those opportunities. Finally, he believes talent will become apparent regardless of the system. He sees talent as one factor, but not the only one. "I can draw you a graph," he tells me as we wrap up the interview.

In interviews with Rick and George we see faculty members who understand the experience of low-income students from multiple perspectives. The limitations of their own parents, their own education experience, and the lack of skills and plain worldliness they note in their students are revealing and important issues.

Conclusion

In this chapter, the history of standardized testing emerging out of the eugenics movement was detailed, as well as the deficient psychological and social preparation of low-income students. Additionally, I examined the way that language skills have historically been central to a college education, and that associated math and study skill proficiency are all class-linked. Advanced Placement courses, initially designed to bring a uniform standard to advanced high school courses, have become resources aligned very closely to wealthy school districts and privileged students. The lack of psychological preparation for college is in many ways the most difficult obstacle to overcome for students from low-income families. Poor self-images reinforced by school performance and confidence-deflating grades, parental education limitations, and low expectations handicap low-income students. Students are encouraged by the rhetoric of our culture to pursue their educational dreams, while at the same time often carrying psychological self-images that are self-defeating. In this way, students from poor families too often are not just inadequately prepared for college, but set up for a failure in a way that is cruelly justified and document by our educational system.

Are low-income students solely responsible for their own fate? "The axiom of modern thought is that people are unequal, and the ensuing moral injunctions that they should be accorded a station in life related to their capacities. By dint of a long struggle, society has at last been prevailed upon to conform: the mentally superior have been raised to the top and the mentally inferior lowered to the bottom" (Young, 1994, p. 106).

In his well-known satirical book *The Rise of the Meritocracy*, Michael Young states plainly where we have arrived in modern thinking about education and the poor: rather than a class system based explicitly on blood lines, it is proposed that class position be assigned by mental ability. American beliefs about the responsibility of the poor for their own condition are alarmingly parallel to those expressed by the vocal eugenics proponents. The extensive influence of the eugenics movement in America continues today, at least in the spirit of our public disregard for the disadvantaged which is played out in our educational policies.

Critics of *The Bell Curve* point to the reliance of the eugenics position on the belief in a single sure-fire test an intelligence which is inherited and does not change: "If any of these premises are false, their entire argument collapses" (Gould, 1995, p. 12). One team of critics characterized the *The Bell Curve* as "a chilly synthesis of the work of disreputable race theorists and eccentric eugenicist" (Rosen and Lane 1995, p. 58). Others doubted Murray and Herrnstein's forecast that a caste of those with high intelligence will inevitably rule the world. Instead, Hacker describes *The Bell Curve* vision as a "testocracy," or a society led by those who succeed only at performing well on tests (Hacker, 1995). Finally, is America already by dint of genetic inevitability a meritocracy as Young claims? According to *Who's Running America?*, an exhaustive study by Florida State University professor Thomas Dye, 54 of the top corporate leaders and 42 percent of the leading governmental leaders hold degrees from 12 heavily endowed and prestigious private universities" (Dye, 2002, p. 12). The elite universities in America are housing and perpetuating the ruling class in America. This fact is indisputable. However, what we can argue about is the cause, genetic and/or environmental, and the fairness to concentrate power and opportunity in the few. Regardless, the image of a country controlled by an elite group of genetically superior families groomed and perpetuated in a select group of elite universities does not fit the image Americans like to have about college in the United States. In the next chapter I look specifically at the reality of how university admissions practices perpetuate inequality.

Chapter 2

Admissions Policies Favor the Advantaged

This chapter argues that a long history of discrimination against low-income students in university admissions continues today in subtle forms. First, I present the statistics on admissions of low-income students and show that private universities, except for the elites, actually admit a larger percentage of low-income students than at the public universities which were founded to provide greater access. I then delve into the fascinating history and practice of admissions at elite American colleges. Although the public is not naïve about class privilege, I suspect most Americans would be surprised by the extent of the historical record of purposeful exclusion of ethnic minority and low-income students from these colleges. At public institutions, the changes in policy regarding affirmative action and recent efforts to use more just models for admissions are examined. The often underestimated impact of changes since the Reagan administration on financial aid distributions and the influence on low-income students are detailed. Although admissions policies on one level are simply bureaucratic ways of controlling enrollment at colleges, they reflect and perpetuate beliefs and values at specific institutions and throughout society. We shall see in this chapter that the ungenerous attitude towards the poor is evident in how low-income students are discouraged from attending college by various policies and practices. The chapter ends with a look at admissions practices from the point of view of a counselor who works in a special program for students from low-income families.

Admission Differs for Lower-Income Students

If in fact there is a great deal of mobility through education in America then we should see more students from poor families applying and accepted to college in greater numbers. While the figures on applications to college are not concrete evidence of subsequent attendance and graduation, they do indicate which colleges are most attractive to low-income students. In this way, application patterns might be affected by the perceived value of particular colleges, personal and social fit, as well as the likelihood of acceptance. In this section we look at mobility trends in application and acceptance to different university types.

Public four-year universities, regardless of their selectivity, are relatively uniform in serving students from low-income backgrounds. The following figure (2.1) shows that the difference in the percentage of low-income student applicants (family income of less than $30,000 in 2004-2005) between low- and highly-selective public universities is not great (only a little more than 6 percent).

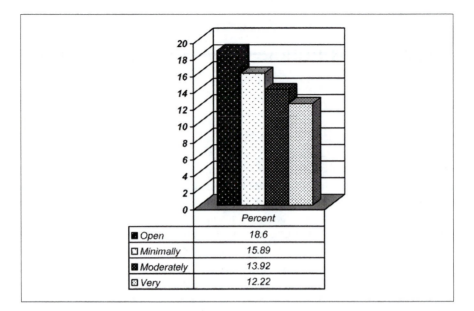

**Figure 2.1 Percentage of student applicants 4-yr public university by
selectivity and family income less than $30k in 2004-2005**
Source: Based on data from Economic Diversity of Colleges (in full in Appendix C).

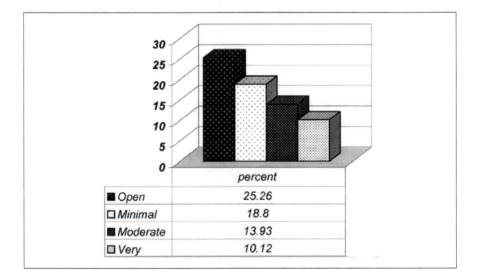

**Figure 2.2 Percentage of student applicants 4-yr private university by
family income less than $30k in 2004-2005**
Source: Based on data from Economic Diversity of Colleges (in full in Appendix C).

Contrary to common perceptions, private universities, except for the most selective colleges, have a larger percentage of lower-income applicants than public institutions. This fact is an indicator of how private or independent universities in some ways are filling gaps in providing access to lower-income students that the public universities fail to meet. In Figure 2.2 we see that the open admission and minimally selective privates surpass the public four-year institutions by a few percentage points (7 and 3 respectively) in drawing more applicants with family incomes of less than $30,000 per year.

How do the top privates fair in attracting low-income students? Not well. The following table (2.1) shows three of the top privates in America and how they rate on percent of applicants from poor families as indicated by graduates with debt and percent of enrolled Pell grant recipients in 2004-05.

Table 2.1 Student economic indicators comparison of top privates in 2004-2005

Institution name	Dependents: Percent of applicants below $30,000 (2004-05)	Percent of graduates with debt (2004-05)	Pell grants: Percent of 12-month enrollments (2004-05)
Harvard	5	49	6
Princeton	5	26	8
Yale	6	40	9

Source: Economic Diversity of Colleges.

In fairness to these institutions, note that the percent of those enrolled from low-income groups appears slightly higher than the percentage of applicants (although this may be attributed to different measures of poverty). Furthermore, the graduation-with-debt data are only a rough indication at best of economic class. Nevertheless, one international comparison shows that Oxford University has four times the number of students from low-income families as Harvard (Soares, 2007).

One way of analyzing class beyond race is to look at parallel student groups. When doing so, it appears that similarly academically prepared students out of high school enroll in college at very different rates depending on their parents' income and education (Ellwood and Kane, 2000). Additionally, the role of family background seems to have increased in importance a college education's payoff has improved. In an article on the link between family background and college going tendencies, Ellwood and Kane conclude: "College enrollment rates have risen at the top income quartile not only because family income itself has become a more important predictor of who goes to college, but because differences in average parental education for those in the top and bottom income quartiles have widened as well" (Ellwood and Kane 2000, p. 283). We can see the importance of parental background in the statistic of only 40 percent from the low-income students attending any kind of college within two years of high school graduation as opposed to 90 percent in the top quartile (Ellwood and Kane 2000, p. 286). In this same study, when taking achievement, demographics, tuition and parental education out of the equation, the gap is narrowed, indicating a lessened influence of family income alone in predicting the educational attainment of an individual. Ellwood and Kane summarized their findings in the following way:

> The source of the advantage clearly goes beyond income. Parents with more education must convey different expectations and information on the benefits to college. Overcoming this information and expectation gap may be the most important but difficult part of creating more similar enrollment patterns for similarly prepared children from disadvantaged families. (Ellwood and Kane 2000, p. 313)

We saw in the first chapter that more students of all types are better preparing themselves to compete for admission to universities by taking advanced placement courses, but ethnic minority students still lag behind in this area. In this chapter, in line with their institutional directives, we find that selective public four-year institutions such as the University of California and University of Michigan serve low-income students to a greater degree than elite privates such as Harvard, Princeton, and Yale. However, it is surprising to find data showing that private universities generally receive a slightly higher percentage of applications from lower-income students than public universities.

Getting in is More Difficult

Students from poor families have always had a more difficult time getting into college, especially at the elite universities. As college has become more broadly available in American society, it has increased pressure on the upper-classes to separate their children from the masses by getting them into selective universities. From the university perspective, as competition becomes more heated, admissions decisions themselves become crucial in maintaining or improving reputations and seeking donors. For public institutions at the beck and call of the taxpayer, policies on who is admitted come under greater scrutiny.

There is a long history of debate about college admission policies in America. James Conant, President of Harvard University and a leader in the development of standardized college admissions testing, wrote a series of influential articles for *The Atlantic Monthly* in the 1940s. In an article entitled *Education for a Classless Society*, Conant pointed to a need for Americans to be more realistic about their expectations for mobility through higher education: "Widespread enthusiasm for intellectual freedom can be rekindled only when a sufficient number of men and women readjust their expectations" (Conant 1949, p. 595). On the brink of a world war that was to bring great political upheaval internationally, Conant pointed out the discomfort Americans had with discussions of class and the need to understand its function in higher education:

> For a century and a half Americans have been saying with pride, 'This is a free country. There are no classes in the United States.' Note these words carefully, for the denial for classes in America is the denial of hereditary classes, not the denial of temporary groupings based on economic differences. (Conant, 1940, p. 596)

He argued that the function of education in America was to assess and develop talent, and then guide ambitions for college and careers accordingly regardless of social class. In reaction to the heavy weight of class privilege at institutions such as Harvard, he was arguing for a move towards meritocracy, or admissions based purely on academic merit. In a later 1943 article in the *Monthly*, the Harvard president continued his line of reasoning, contending that World War II occasioned an examination in America of class mobility (Conant, 1943, p. 44). The offer of education to returning soldiers was a key for him: "The demobilization of our armed forces is a God-given moment for reintroducing the American concept of a fluid society." If it is handled properly, it was an opportunity to redirect society, but if done wrong it could lead to unrest: "Sow the seeds of a civil war within a decade" (Conant 1943, p. 44). Post World War II college admissions practices were a conscious strategy for maintaining the social order he spoke of in this article.

The history of admissions practice in America has never been as open at the elite universities as advertised, where they have consistently favored the wealthy. One can trace the first significant restrictions on admissions to the 1920s when Harvard, Yale and Princeton began restricting the admission of Jewish students. In the 1920s, Jews began to take up a substantially increasing part of the student body at Ivy League schools, and dominated in winning scholarship awards. For instance, the percentage of Jews at Harvard had risen to 21.5 percent, and 7.5 percent at Yale, up from just two percent at the turn of the century (Oren, 1985). A major public relations fall-out at Harvard occurred after an explicit quota system was implemented by President Lowell. As a result, the elite institutions were forced to become more subtle in their restrictions of these undesirable low-income students, primarily using the loaded and highly subject criteria of: "character" (Karabel, 2005). Specific methods included requiring more detailed family history data to help identify ethnicity and implementing personal interviews. Low-income Jews were discouraged by simply giving out less financial aid to them. Throughout the Ivy League schools it became common to talk about character, personality, and promise in admissions decisions rather than simple academic qualifications. This strategy was successful at Yale in leveling off the tide of diversity increase, as can be seen in the fact that by 1930 only 8.2 percent of the freshman class was Jewish.

When the SAT was introduced in 1926, admissions deans at Ivy League schools hoped that it would be a test WASPs would do well on, and conversely Jews would struggle with. However, this was not the case, and led to the practice of weighing verbal scores on the SAT over the math section beginning in the 1930s. In this way, those students from prestigious college prep schools emphasizing language skills were given preferential treatment. Furthermore, Yale reportedly would not consider applicants from certain geographical areas, especially so called "Brooklyn boys." When applicant pools increased dramatically in 1950s, the emphasis shifted further to "leadership" and "character" rather than academics, or personal not academic promise (Soares, 2007). The admission system became murky in order to hide racial and class barriers: "This extraordinary emphasis on highly subjective qualities—pursued right down to the assignment of a single number reflecting the institution's summary assessment of the candidate as a human being—was central to the admissions process of the Big Three" (Soares, 2007, p. 485). Throughout the 1950s, elite institutions such as Harvard limited the number of "intellectuals" to ten percent of the student body. Legacies were given preference as long as the applicant was likely to make it through four years, regardless of high school grades.

While discrimination in admissions remained, the mechanisms continued to evolve throughout the twentieth century. As late as 1961, Yale's student body was only 12 percent Jewish, while Harvard's was 21 percent and Columbia's 45 percent (Oren, 1985). In his book on Jews at Yale, Dan Oren claims that finally the most pervasive form of discrimination was class-based, simply an attitude at Yale of "profound lack of interest in the lower class groups" (Oren, 1985, p. 292). For those Jews and others from "uninteresting classes" admitted to Yale and other Ivy League schools, the result was that they were shunned from the important campus clubs and societies. Oren further points out that the very words "college" and "club" have a common root meaning and that to join an elite college was to join an elite club. Those low-income students who attended college simply for the education were misunderstanding the nature of these privileged institutions. Finally, faculty and public pressure mounted and the use of SAT and National Merit programs gave the appearance of openness. Interesting, many have noted how in the late 1980s Asian Americans became the "new Jews" facing similar negative admission quotas of a sort. In fact, Asian Americans admitted at Ivy League schools scored an average of 112 points higher on the SAT than white students, pointing to the suspicion that the bar was intentionally held higher for some less desirable groups. Rather than becoming more open to low-income students, the percent of students from poor families admitted declined in Ivy League schools from 10 percent in 1954 to 5 percent in 1996. However, during the twentieth century they increasingly admitted students from the rising new professional class in addition to the older privileged legacies. "A strategy followed most dramatically by Yale in the late 1960s when, in the context of the emergence of postindustrial society and the increasing prominence of science and technology, it shifted its policy toward the brilliant children of the 'new class' of credentialed professionals while eliminating the last vestiges of anti-Semitism" (Soares, 2007, p. 545).

The controversial early action admissions policy at elite universities also gives preference to wealthy families who could afford to commit to attending expensive institutions without knowing about financial aid awards (Soares, 2007). Although Harvard's recent decision to move away from early admission is certainly notable, in 2002, 70 percent of the top-ranked private institutions offered early admissions and it remains a widespread practice (Avery, Fairbanks and Zeckhauser, 2003). This tactic was first used in 1954 with the so-called A-B-C system where feeder college preparatory school applicants were given a preliminary analysis for admissions at Harvard, Yale and Princeton and graded A through C, with A meaning almost sure admission. In 1973 the big three moved to "early evaluation" wherein students who sent early applications received evaluations by January with assessments of likely, possible, or unlikely. Early admissions clearly advantage privileged students and are a mechanism for elite institutions to limit the number of students from the low-incomes. Advantaged students are much more likely to know and exploit early admissions practices. Although elite colleges tend to deny publicly the advantage of applying early claiming that more qualified applicants tend to dominate this group, those needing to weigh financial aid packages cannot apply early, and according to one study, those who apply early receive what amounts to the equivalent of a 100 point greater SAT-1 score in the overall evaluation process (Avery, Fairbanks and Zeckhauser, 2003).

One sees that over a period of time at elite universities, personal qualities became 30 to 50 percent of the admissions scoring for potential students. Face-to-face interviews developed into another way to avoid admittance based strictly on academic qualifications, and ensure a student body with a sufficiently high enough percentage of privileged students. Furthermore, experts have remarked on how ironic it is that colleges that distance themselves from the NCAA provide the greatest boost to athletes in the admissions process. For instance, male athletes are just three percent of the students at the University of Michigan, but comprise 22 percent of the male student body at Princeton (Soares, 2007). Contrary to popular belief, even the special admissions for athletes tend to benefit white and wealthy students more that ethnic minority and low-income students. "Offsetting minority participation in basketball, football, and track, prestigious colleges give an admissions edge to athletes in spots played mainly by upper-income whites; for instance, crew, squash, horseback riding, skiing, sailing, fencing, golf" (Golden, 2006, pp. 5-6). In fact, a study of 19 Ivy League universities and liberal arts colleges found that only "6 percent of recruited athletes came from the poorest one-fourth of American families, as opposed to 12 percent of non athletes" (Middelbury College, 2002, p. 12). In this way, the "need blind" admissions put in place at some Ivy League schools did not change the basic admissions mix because of other controls, such as early admissions and exceptions for athletes.

So called "context" is the university's consideration of the qualifications of other students where admissions decisions have been made in favor of less qualified students for various reasons, such as legacy connections at private institutions. Often to admit one well-connected student with a less than stellar academic record, the college will also admit other, better qualified applicants from the same school. "This cover-up strategy—admitting a sub par candidate for institutional reasons and then defusing potential criticism from parents, teachers, or guidance counselors by taking every other higher-ranking applicant from the same school—is well known in admissions circles" (Golden, 2006, p. 12). In this way the higher education system is making opportunity at elite universities more unusual.

Golden's book, *The Price of Admission: How America's Ruling Class Buys its Way into Elite Colleges and Who Gets Left Outside the Gates*, presents unsettling information on admissions practices today at elite universities, much of which goes against commonly held perceptions. To begin with, Caucasian and wealthy students benefit from preferential admissions far more than ethnic minority students aided by affirmative action kinds of programs. In fact, "At least one-third of the students at elite universities, and at least half at liberal arts colleges, are flagged for preferential treatment in the admissions process" (Golden, 2006, p. 6). These special admit students are known as "hooked" or "unhooked" based on their family's clout with the university. Interestingly, "hooked" isn't only about being an alumnus, but one with money. Golden argues that the importance of family money is clear when one looks at the statistics on admissions of children of alums who apply for financial aid.

In this way, Golden (2006) claims that families are essentially buying their way into college at the rate of $50,000 at an exclusive college, and as much as millions at the most elite universities. Additionally, celebrity status is given preference at many elite universities according to Golden, especially at schools such as Brown where there is a long record of such special admits. Other private universities like Notre Dame rely greatly on legacies where 21 to 24 percent of each freshman class comes from children of graduates. Furthermore, despite claims that affirmative action admits lower the quality of the student body, a recent study found that minority students are far less likely to run into academic trouble in college than wealthy legacies (Massey and Mooney, 2007). Those private colleges who are most committed to giving preferences to children of alumni have the highest dropout rates from such legacy students. The reality is that there isn't much of an incentive for elite universities to change their ways. As Latty L. Goodwin points out in her book following a group of disadvantaged students at an elite college, "There is an elephant in the room that needs to be acknowledged at this point. And that is: what incentives are provided to universities to make their campuses more congenial to students from underrepresented groups?" (Goodwin, 2006, p. 56).

Mitchell L. Stevens (2007) in his view inside the admissions department at an elite university entitled *Creating a Class: College Admissions and the Education of Elites* argues that affluent parents use formal education as a main way to hand down privilege to their children. Citing the notion of "social reproduction," he holds that formal education is part of a social process of passing on advantage that includes transferring knowledge, cultural perspectives, as well as social position. This social reproduction is such a strong driver for privileged families that the quest to get their children in the best schools is often all-consuming. Stevens claims, as others do, that education certifies privilege: "One answer, often called the reproduction thesis, holds that variation in education attainment essentially is a coating for preexisting class inequalities" (Stevens, 2007, p. 11). Steven's research conducted as a staff member and researcher inside an admissions department led him to believe that the result of increased access to higher education after World War II has been the construction of even more complex admissions practices: "My research suggests that one profound result of higher education's expansion has been the entrenchment of a complicated, publicly palatable and elaborately costly machinery through which wealthy parents hand privilege down to their children" (Stevens, 2007, p. 14).

Although college has become extremely competitive in the admissions game, the fact is that most students get into their first choice of college. Seventy-four percent of all undergraduates attend their first-choice institution and 20 percent their second choice. Therefore a total of 94 percent of applicants are admitted to their first or second choice in universities. This may mean that Americans have come to know, directly or intuitively, which universities will accept them. Low-income students understand the nature of the college class system and are not even trying to be admitted to many the elite universities. Joseph Soares, in his book *Power of Privilege: Yale and America's Elite Colleges*, remarks that, "It is not an exaggeration to say that college-bound youths in the United States know where they belong" (Soares, 2007, p. 11). In her book based on a study of high school college counselors and students, *Choosing Colleges: How Social Class and Schools Structure Opportunity*, Patricia M. McDonough argues similarly that through a process of "bounded rationality" students limit the number of alternatives colleges they might considered (McDonough, 1997). In this way, years of exclusionary admissions policies has led to widespread segregation of college choice in America by class and race.

The Questionable Role of Community Colleges

Perhaps college admissions policies at elite intuitions are the wrong thing to focus on in looking to better serve low-income students. Norton Grubb, in his book Working in the Middle, describes what he calls a sub-baccalaureate labor market, those who have finished high school, but not college (Grubb, 1996). According to Grubb, this poorly understood group actually forms fully three-fifths of the entire workforce. Corporate America often knocks universities for not teaching specific skills that can be used in the workplace while also complaining that college graduates lack broad critical thinking and communication abilities. Burton Clark's idea of the "cooling out" function of community colleges is disputed by Grubb, arguing that regardless of the design, two-year colleges in practice increase the number of students who would not ordinarily attend at college at all. The net result is that community colleges slightly increase the numbers of those who go on to get a four-year degree. Grubb summarizes what he calls the attitude of misplaced hostility towards community colleges and claims that there is no evidence of misdirection by counselors, or that those who attend community college are wasting their time. In Grubb's research, he found that many attend community college because they are unsure of their career path. For those in this situation, community college may be the cheapest way of finding direction.

However, many experts are more critical of the role of community college in meeting the needs of children from poor families. Steven Brint and Jerome Karabel's book on community colleges entitled *The Diverted Dream* introduced the notion of higher education as functioning in society to "manage ambition" (Brint and Karabel, 1989). The authors argued that the post-World War II demand for college education generated a calculated response from the social elite: the creation of the very large and "differentiated" higher education system that we have today. The design of this system, epitomized by the 1960 California Master Plan for Higher Education, was for the community colleges to function to restrict the number of students who have the opportunity to earn a bachelor degree. In this way, the California Master Plan was a direct response to the economic challenge of trying to accommodate increased higher education enrollment by forcing students into the much less expensive community colleges. There, the State pays roughly one sixth as much per student as in the University of California. The authors of the *Diverted Dream* make a political argument that the tiered higher education system creates "educated followers," not equal opportunity. The myth of the self-made man was supplanted in 1920s by the man who worked his way through college. However, California's three-tier system is essentially one that tracks students into careers, linked specifically to social origins: "The educational system in the United States plays an important role in the transmission of inequality from generation to generation" (Brint and Karabel, 1989, p. 224). They argue that although individuals certainly benefit from community colleges, the overall cumulative effect is a negative one on low-income citizens.

Financial Aid Policies are Inadequate

How does financial aid policy impact low-income students? In the past 25 years there has been an important change in financial aid policy which has directly impacted the enrollment in college of students from low-income families. Beginning with Ronald Reagan's election in 1980, the argument was made that investment in college aid was excessive, leading to a decline in federal grant aid for low-income students. Loans became emphasized over direct aid from the government. George H.W. Bush further cut federal grants to low-income students during his reign. In the Clinton years (1993-2000), the New Democrats took the centrist strategy of targeted tax relief for middle-class families with children attending college, rather than trying to regain the lost ground. In sum, throughout the 1980s and 1990s, there was a severe decline in college funding for low-income students. College grants dropped from 7.3 billion in 1980-81 to 1.4 billion dollars in 1990-91. Not surprisingly, there is a direct link between declined participation and reduced funding (St. John, 2003). The promise of access offered to low-income and ethnic minority students in terms of access to higher education through the Higher Education Act of 1965 and the subsequent 1972 Education Amendments was taken away by policy decisions starting in the 1980s (Mortenson, 1991). The overall result is that low-income students are applying to fewer colleges and enroll at declining rates. By the second half of the 1980s, the gap between black and white four-year college completion rates was wider than it had been at any time during the previous 20 years, a direct result of policies that began with the Reagan administration policies.

According to a Congressional report, almost one-half of college-qualified low-income high school graduates will not be able to attend for financial reasons. This amounts to an estimated 400,000 students per year. Low-income families on average need to cover two-thirds of a college education after receiving available aid equal to one-third of the total family income (United States Congress, 2002). In the first decade of the twenty-first century, the report estimates 4.4 million students will not attend a four-year college as a result of finances, and two million will not attend college at all (United States Congress, 2002). Michael S. McPherson and Morton Owen Schapiro in their book *The Student Aid Game* point out that the increasing cost of higher education has little impact on enrollment rates in high-income families, but a very significant effect on enrollment of low-income students (McPherson and Schapiro, 1998). In analyzing the way universities approach financial aid, they see the use of offers to students used strategically to further larger institutional aims: "Rather than viewing student aid as a kind of charitable operation the college runs on the side, most private colleges and universities—and increasing numbers of public institutions—now regard student aid as a vital revenue management and enrollment management tool" (McPherson, 1998, p. 16).

Certainly one factor that might influence attendance for low-income students at public universities is cost. Interestingly, while there has been much discussion in the media about rising tuition costs, the price for college attendance at public colleges when adjusted for inflation has not changed much since 1990. Low-income students pay approximately half as much as upper income students at both public and private four-year institutions (Figure 2.3).

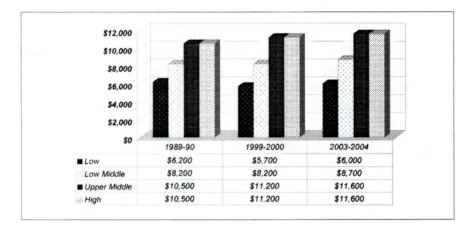

	1989-90	1999-2000	2003-2004
■ Low	$6,200	$5,700	$6,000
Low Middle	$8,200	$8,200	$8,700
■ Upper Middle	$10,500	$11,200	$11,600
High	$10,500	$11,200	$11,600

**Figure 2.3 Average annual price for students by public 4-yr university
and by income**

Source: Based on data from US Department of Education, National Center for Education Statistics, 2005 (presented in full in Appendix C); income listed by quarters.

In this way public higher education does seem to be succeeding at encouraging low-income student attendance.

What is the cost of attending college and what are the trends? According to the College Board (Baum and Lapovsky, 2008), over the past decade, published tuition and fees have risen at an average rate of 2.4 percent per year after inflation at private four-year colleges, compared to an average rate of 4.2 percent per year after inflation at public four-year institutions. Tuition and fees constitute 67 percent of the total budget for students enrolled in private four-year colleges, but only 36 percent for in-state students in public four-year colleges, and 17 percent for public two-year college students. On average, full-time students receive $10,200 of financial aid in private four-year institutions, $3,700 in public four-year institutions, and $2,300 in public two-year colleges. Overall, the trend then is for increased cost to students, rising more rapidly at public institutions.

The practice of "tuition discounting" at independent institutions wherein a large percentage of students are charged a lower rate than is listed, has become a topic of wide discussion. This practice which is especially used at lower-tier private institutions as a competitive recruitment tool is also used to a lesser extent by public institutions. According to a College Board report (Baum and Lapovsky, 2006), in the public sector only about 40 percent of the institutional grants are aimed at those documented financial need, while more than 60 percent of the institutional aid in the private sector awarded to those need-based. Furthermore, the discount rate has increased significantly in both publics and independents, but is leveling off at the public institutions. In this way according to one analysis (Davis, 2003), tuition discounting may actually be counterproductive in serving low-income students because it is sometimes applied to those without a demonstrated need.

Personal loans are another factor to consider in analyzing low-income student college attendance. Many have noted the cultural differences in attitude to taking on loan debt for students from low-income families. Additionally on a practical level, when one talks about bank loans that require some sort of security, low-income students often find it difficult to qualify. Data revealing student loan trends indeed do show that low-income students tend to take out loans less often and for lower amounts than middle and upper-class students. One remarkable point in data presented in the following figure (2.4) is the large increase in loans taken out by middle- and upper-class students, while at the same time the percentage of loans among low-income students remained flat.

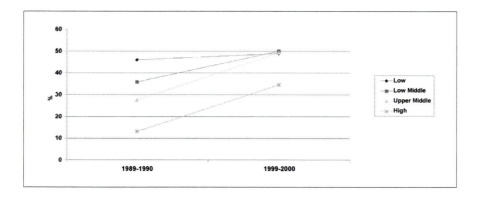

Figure 2.4 Percentage of students with loans by family income
Source: Based on data from Wei, Li and Berkner, 2004 (presented in full in Appendix C); income listed by quarters.

In fact, the upper-class student loan percentage increased by 21 percent during the 1990s.

Grants are another important type of financial aid, especially of interest at independent institutions because of the way they are used to manage the composition of the student body. Overall, the percentage of students who received grants in college increased from 44.8 percent in 1989-90 to 56.9 percent in 1999-2000. Who benefited the most from the increase in grant funding? Once again, supporting claims that the trend in financial aid is towards helping the middle and upper classes more than the lower classes, data collected for the 1990s show that low-income students lost ground in the amount of grants received. In fact, the students from the wealthiest backgrounds received 18 percent more grants over the ten year period (Figure 2.5).

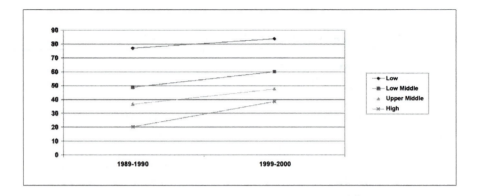

Figure 2.5 Percentage of students receiving grants by family income
Source: Based on data from Wei, Li and Berkner, 2004 (presented in full in Appendix C); income listed by quarters.

For private, independent universities, the financial aid game has become one in which the goal is to admit the best students while getting the most revenue from them. Consequently, they use the pot of university scholarship money from their endowment as a strategic tool to get the most academically qualified students who will be a credit to the university while balancing their budgets: "Instead of aiming to 'stretch' a fixed student aid budget as far as possible, the school sets out deliberately to shape a financial aid strategy that maximally advances the combined (and conflicting) goals of admitting the best students and gaining as much revenue from them as possible" (McPherson, 1998, pp. 16-17). Complicating the picture further, many private colleges are heavily involved in tuition discounting. According to the College Board, the real net price of attending a private four-year college in 2006 was $13,200 per year as opposed to the $22,218 average listed tuition rate. While over the past ten years public universities have increased fees by 51 percent, the net increase at private four-year intuitions has been only 27 percent (College Board, 2007). McPherson points out that in general financial aid approaches at individual campuses have led to creating less "suitable" college experiences for low-income students. He points to statistics of 41 percent of upper income, and 47 percent of the richest students, attending a university, compared with only 13.5 percent of lower-income students. Furthermore, low-income students disproportionately attend two-year community colleges at a rate of 47.3 percent; where as upper income students only enroll at two-year schools at a rate of 13.9 percent.

Consistent with the facts laid out above, Richard D. Kahlenberg (2004) notes a shift from an overall financial pie comprised of a proportion of 55 percent grants and 41 percent loans 20 years ago, to one made up now of 58 percent loans, while grants comprise only 41 percent now. A consequence of the past focus on affirmative action rather than class mobility, is that there is less representation from the lower classes than racial minorities at selective institutions: "The under representation of the poor and working-class at elite universities is far greater than the under representation of racial minorities" (Kahlenberg, 2004, p. 9). Statistically, the least academically qualified students from wealthy families have as much chance of going to college as the highest performing kids from low-income families.

Finally, McPherson and Schapiro suggest that there is an inherent hypocrisy in the rhetoric surrounding financial aid. While universities claim that they make admissions decisions separate from financial need, in fact financial need figures impact admissions decisions of those on waiting lists, in early admission, and for transfer students. Furthermore, the widespread practice of tuition discounting has in many cases become a game wherein low-income students are given financial aid awards that put attendance just out of their reach, while allowing universities to appear liberal: "There is a good deal of pressure on schools to maintain a claim to being need-blind when the reality of their policies is more complicated" (McPherson, 1998, p. 101). Furthermore, while the cost to students of public higher education largely stabilized, more affluent students are increasingly taking advantage of financial aid availability to continue and complete their college educations.

Sidebar Portrait: Lydia

Lydia is a university administrator whom I meet in her office in the old converted chapel on campus. She works in the Educational Opportunity Program (EOP) and sees first-hand the struggles and successes of first-generation college students. Lydia was raised by a single mother and describes her mother as neither for nor against her going to college. The resulting isolation drew her to her career: "I knew how lonely it was, I knew how difficult it was when you're out there on your own." Lydia married at a young age and luckily her husband was supportive of her educational pursuits. She attended a community college and then transferred to the University of California. The problems her mother encountered led Lydia to college: "I saw her struggle a lot and I knew that's not what I wanted." She sees herself in many of the young women she counsels who seek independence and better lives than their parents.

The Educational Opportunity Program involves all the campuses save one (Maritime College) in the California State University system. Begun in 1969 and once funded from the State based on overall campus enrollment, since the eighties has had no general funding. However, individual campuses decided to carry on with the program despite the lack of direct funding. EOP developed out of the Civil Rights Movement that called for greater access of minorities to higher education. Today over 30,000 students are in the program at 22 California State Universities. Services for students include advising workshops and a summer bridge program. Interestingly enough, EOP started as a minority-only program and then became based instead on household income level. Lydia explains to me that the economic criteria still means that the majority of the EOP students are from ethnic minority groups. Additionally, campuses have some latitude in admissions decisions and tend to give priority to those who have various needs characteristics of first-generation college students. The program includes supplemental instruction in mathematics and a summer transitional program the year preceding entering college. She identifies community or cohort formation as a key function of the summer "bridge" program. Although the EOP serves students for their entire stay in college, Lydia understands that the first two years are the crucial period for incoming students: "At that point after having the support of the academic program and two years of course work under their belt, they're well transitioned usually and can be more independent."

Lydia speaks about the challenges for college administrators to work with first-generation students, including their hesitancy to seek help and a general lack of understanding about how colleges operate. One strategy EOP uses is to try and involve faculty members. Of course, poor academic preparation is an on-going problem for underprivileged students, who typically enroll in remedial math and English courses. "Our students are immediately at a disadvantage because they come from different schools than those who come from high income areas." In some cases, the EOP program brings in students through special admissions procedures (this means the students have less than a B average in high school, the California State University minimum requirement.) Lydia sees students often coming into college not understanding that level of effort needed to do well: "They really underestimate the amount of work it takes." Typically, the first semester is the biggest challenge and often results in EOP students going on academic probation. The students don't understand in a concrete way what it takes to be successful academically in college. The EOP students also have social adjustment problems coming from close-knit families where they have rarely traveled or been away from their families. Lydia recognizes an ethnic- and class-related isolation that some of the students experience. Students in EOP have to specifically apply and by doing so set themselves apart: "In a sense when you say you are an EOP student you are saying, 'My family's poor, I came from an educationally disadvantaged background.'"

A primary challenge for students in the program is the lack of family support for them to continue studying. Many families rely directly on college-age students for financial support: "Not only do they go away, but now they have these tuition payments and housing payments." The families often plead with students to return home and help out financially. "The realities are that the families are preoccupied with surviving, being able to support their families—it's not a priority in a lot of cases. Survival is—you need to pay the rent. You need to do what you need to do, and in a lot of cases that takes all the members of the family contributing." Nevertheless, Lydia describes some encouraging families who still support the effort of their children to attend college regardless of the economic hardship to the family unit. She argues that there is a need to redefine what is meant by "parental involvement" when discussing first-generation college students: "I'm not talking about mom attending a PTA meeting every week. I'm not talking about mom volunteering in the classroom." Because of the extreme pressure on some low-income college families often just to survive economically, the involvement of parents needs to mostly be thought of as simply encouragement to attend school. They can't give their time to volunteer at schools, but they can emotionally and psychologically give support to their children and release them from the work of financially supporting their own families.

Lydia sees how some of the students feel a culture clash arising from their attendance at college. Especially for those students who live at home, they often live in two very different worlds: a traditional family life in the evening and the larger and foreign world of college during the day.

> They're coming here and they're starting to develop their own self-identities and in a lot of ways that creates problems because of the emphasis on tradition at home; versus here at the university with emphasis on critical thinking, creative thinking, and developing your own values, your own ideas. So you see a lot of conflict, especially for the young women.

Part of the tradition at home leads to pressuring students to marry at a young age, and for female students, keeps them from not leaving the safety of the home until married. Once married, attending college for female students is often dependent on the support of husbands. The EOP program is primarily filled with women students. Males often seem to be drawn to support the family economically, and in addition, may have trouble admitting so readily to needing EOP support. In Latino families especially, parents are hesitant to let females leave the safety of the house: "One thing you hear a lot is the fear that they will go off to college and get pregnant."

Lydia talks about the challenge of overcoming different cultural views of higher education: "In Mexico higher education is considered a privilege and not something the general public should aspire to." College is something only the upper classes participate in, and therefore working class families from Mexico have trouble understanding the function of college in America. Additionally, because there is little or no direct experience within the family of the American educational system, the practical steps needed to take to get into college and find financial aid are difficult: "If you look at the brochure and it says $1,300 per semester and you don't know what financial aid is, you say, 'forget it.'"

Regardless of the support from the university and the EOP program administrators, students do drop out. Lydia says that some families are upset when this happens, but others are actually happy to see their children drop out of school because it means that they can work full time and will not have more college bills to pay. For female students, dropping out often results from marriage or pregnancy, at which point the father often pushes the student to withdraw from school. On the practical end, Lydia views housing as a major obstacle for those from out of the immediate area. Financial aid doesn't generally cover housing completely and many of the students who come from poor families cannot secure bank loans on their own.

Lydia speaks of administrators struggling with the nature of low-income student motivation to succeed in college. In the application process to the EOP program, university administrators try to identify through the autobiographical statement those who seem the most driven. Over the years, the university has found motivation level to be key in the perseverance of students. Lydia typically hears from low-income students that they don't want to work in positions like their mother and father, and that they want to succeed to "make my family proud," and help out financially. There is also a larger racial motive that is described as breaking stereotypes: "I want to prove that a Mexican-American can be successful, can get their bachelor's, master's, PhD."

Lydia views the switch in policy from race to class-based admissions as being a "very touchy" subject. "Perhaps if you say it is along economic lines it elevates a little—what should I say—national guilt maybe." The thinking being that in the United States everyone has an equal opportunity to earn a degree and therefore there is no reason to single out a specific ethnic group. However, she points out that the reality is that the population served in EOP generally ends up aligning economic class with ethnicity. Lydia talks about defining what is meant for success in working with low-income college students. Grades are not alone a good indicator, and standardized tests are also less than effective for the population with which she works. She instead talks about identity formation, personal growth, and a connection to the university community as perhaps more important objectives: "They not only have to get used to college academically, they have to get used to interacting with different people." Lydia describes an extraordinary amount of change for students in the program: "It's such an exciting thing to see them come into the environment feeling self-conscious and maybe a little isolated, to get through that and some of the transition, and work through that." The impact of a college education on EOP students will be "incredible," according to Lydia, as it reaches beyond the individual student and influences subsequent generations in the family: "Even though their mom and dad didn't go to college, they did it, and so they will help their brothers and sisters." Grades do not tell the full story of both how much low-income students can change in college, and the very real subsequent impact of their extended families.

Conclusion

In this chapter I argue that a history of discrimination against low-income students continues today in subtle forms. Furthermore, statistics show a surprising pattern of second and third-tier independent universities actually admitting a higher percentage of low-income students than public universities. Given the land grant origin of public higher education with the charge of providing wide access to higher education, this finding is particularly disturbing. We found that the poor are affected by admission policies in a number of complex ways. The review of the history and practice of admissions at elite American colleges reveals consistent attempts to limit access to poor and ethnic minority students. The important changes in financial aid policy since the 1980s were charted and the devastating impact on low-income students considered.

The mythology of college and social mobility can be traced to the Enlightenment when the social ideas of doing away with advantages of birth and providing ways for the masses to participate actively in a democratic society first emerged: "Education has been seen as central to this agenda, in helping to provide the technical skills for modern society and in selecting the talented for upward mobility" (Halsey, Lauder, Brown and Wells, 1997). It is precisely because of its importance that education as an instrument of mobility that university admissions practices have so much symbolic meaning. The result has been that on the upper end of the class scale, both individual student applicants and universities engage in heated competition to leverage every advantage to stay on top. An article in the *Economist* expounded on the stark truth that, from the outset, low-income students are at an enormous disadvantage in this mad scramble: "America's great universities are increasingly reinforcing rather than reducing these educational inequalities. Poorer students are at a huge disadvantage, both when they try to get in and, if they are successful, in their ability to make the most of what is offered" (Staff, 2005, January, p. 22).

Responding to public pressure to support low-income students to a greater extent out of very large endowments, most select Ivy League schools have recently implemented financial aid policies that reduce or eliminate tuition costs for low-income students. At Harvard University, a financial aid initiative completely eliminates the cost of tuition for students whose families earn incomes of less than $40,000, and reduces the expected contributions for families with incomes between $40,000 and $60,000 from $3,500 to $2,250 on average (Staff, 2004). Yale, Princeton, Columbia, MIT, Brown and other universities are following suit with variations of this policy, no doubt partly to stay competitive for the most accomplished students (a point specifically mentioned by MIT administration) (Plotkin, 2008). It is difficult to assess the eventual impact of the change in this policy on the composition of the student body, or whether the intentions to economically diversify are genuine, but lacking different admissions practices I doubt that much improvement will be made. According to an observer at Yale University, one obvious advantage of the new policy for institutions is more flexibility to recruit athletes without offering scholarships per se (Fok, 2008). In this way, the factoring of financial need into admissions changes the long-held Ivy League's Statement of Principles around the recruitment of athletes and according to some analysts has shifted the balance of power further to those universities holding the largest endowments (Perlin, 2008).

Chapter 3
College is More Difficult for Low-Income Students

This chapter argues that children from low-income families experience college in very challenging ways because of a variety of factors that lead to higher discontinuation rates. While participation in college for students from poor families greatly increased in number at the end of the twentieth century, the overall percentage did not increase significantly. Affluent students still outnumber poor students in high school graduation, college attendance, and college graduation rates. Additionally, low-income students disproportionately attend community colleges rather than going straight into four-year colleges. Students from low-income families discontinue their studies in much larger numbers both in high school and then later in college. I've identified three main types of issues that confront these students: personal, family/cultural, and structural. The personal issues are those that often involve the individual human development and growth that is typical of college students, but perhaps more extreme in low-income students who carry the weight of additional stressors. Often the crux of the personal realm for these students has to do with self-image issues. I found conflict within the family to be a more important issue than anticipated. Finally, the larger socio-political structure has a direct impact on poor students through society's various systems, including higher education. I make the argument that although higher education can not be held responsible for every problem in society, it does need to adequately address the impact of these challenges for low-income students as they appear in college.

Low-Income Students Complete High School and College at Lower Rates

One indicator of moving up in society is the level of education one achieves. While the practical value of an education in the job market varies, a degree is typically seen as a symbol of social-economic class. During the twentieth century, especially after World War II, participation in college widened significantly. The percentage of college-educated citizens in the United States rose increasingly by almost four times between the years of 1940 and 2000.

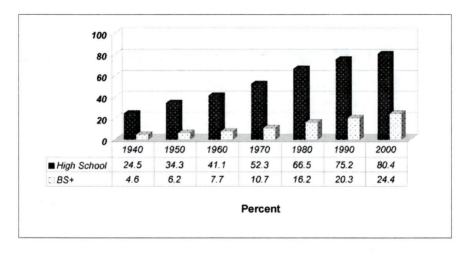

**Figure 3.1 Population 25 years and over who have completed
high school or college: 1940-2000**

Source: Based on data from Bauman and Graf, 2003.

As show in Figure 3.1, the trend in America the last 40 years has been towards an increased number of both high school and college graduates. However, who is it that is graduating from college in greater numbers? Has the increase in college been broad based across classes and ethnic groups? How does high school graduation differ among lower, middle and upper-class children? According to one study conducted at the end of the twentieth century, 19.9 percent of low-income children do not have a high school diploma eight years after they should have graduated (United States Department of Education, 2002). The middle class rate for the same group is 6.1 percent, with only three tenths of a percent lacking a high school diploma for students from the highest one quarter of the family income bracket.

The figures on the great improvement of college attendance by the children of the poor at the end of the twentieth century are deceiving because they don't account for the very high drop out rate in high school. The apparent rate of college attendance has improved substantially for low-income students since 1972 when it was only 26.1 percent. The following graph shows how the general rate of college attendance has increased broadly for all classes.

Nonetheless, these data are misleading because the percentage of high school graduates differs so greatly between lower and upper-class families. In 2004, 49.6 percent of students from lower income families were enrolled in college the October following high school graduation compared to 79.3 percent of those in high income families. Since Figure 3.2 does not represent all high school age children, but only high school graduates, the gap is in fact much larger than here represented. One can see then that the impression of a general rising of the tide of college attendance, and narrowing of the gap in attendance between low and high income families, overlooks the large discrepancy in high school drop out rates.

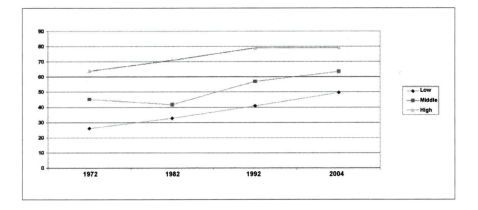

Figure 3.2 Percentage of college enrolled students in the October following high school graduation by income

Source: Based on data from US Department of Commerce, 2005 (presented in full in Appendix C).

Higher education in America is extremely hierarchical and simple college attendance alone is not terribly meaningful. Clearly, attendance at Harvard University is not the same as enrollment at a community college in terms of value to the student and subsequent life chances. In Figure 3.3 we see that low-income students disproportionately attend two-year and public institutions as compared to middle and upper-class students.

The data support the often-repeated point of view from experts that low-income students are more likely to drop out and not complete their college degree. We see in Figure 3.4 that only 15 percent of low-income students graduate within five years, as compared to upper-class students who earn a degree at a rate of 41 percent in the same time period. Furthermore, the pattern as represented over a five-year period in the 1990s shows a slight worsening of the situation for low-income students, while upper-class students made a minor improvement in their graduation figures.

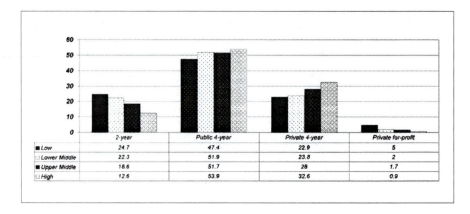

**Figure 3.3 Percentage of college enrolled students by institutional type
          and by income**
Source: Based on data from US Department of Education, NCES, 1989-90 and 1999-2000
National Postsecondary Student Aid Studies (presented in full in Appendix C).

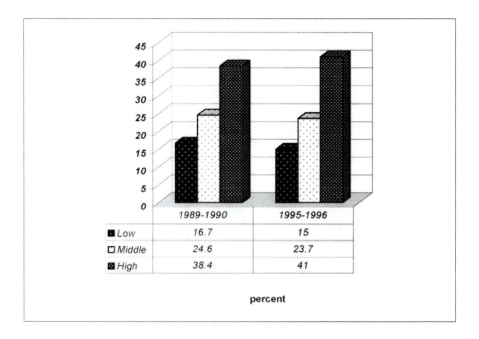

**Figure 3.4 Percentage of students graduating with BA/BS within 5 years
          by family income**
Source: Based on data from Horn and Berger, forthcoming (presented in full in Appendix C).

To summarize, participation in college of students from poor families greatly increased by number, but not overall percentage, in the later part of the twentieth century. Wealthier students still significantly outnumber poor students in high school graduation, college attendance, and college graduation rates. Additionally, low-income students disproportionately attend community colleges.

Issues

I found in the research literature and in my conversations with students from low-income families that their adjustment issues when attending college fell into four main domains of experience: personal, family, cultural, and structural as represented in the following figure (3.5).

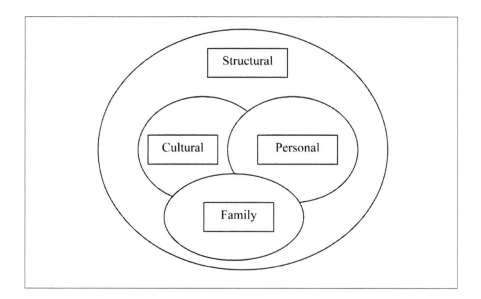

Figure 3.5 Low-income college student spheres of influence

The personal, family, and cultural domains overlap at times for students from low-income backgrounds. However, all three of these areas are influenced by a larger structure formed largely by the economic and political system. College for traditional age students is a place where significant human development occurs. The individual or personal level is characterized by students going through struggles of identity shaping and relationship forming typical of their developmental stage. In many ways this first domain is less controllable by educators and is a place where social and structural realities are played out and become evident. A student's family is perhaps even more central to the fate of students than is generally understood. The cultural background and context has a pervasive influence on students in college. Finally, the larger structure of society provides both opportunity and limitations for students. The political framework informs everything and is behind the social and personal experiences. Social inequality and public policy measures set the context in which individual students carve out their life chances.

Personal

In the personal domain, motivation is a key characteristic of successful low-income students. University administrators regularly talk about properly assessing the level of motivation in applicants because of a general perception that in addition to ability and preparation, perspiration is a key component of successful students. What is motivation and how is it evaluated in college students and college applicants? In these days of managed applicants especially for selective universities, ferreting out authentic drive in a student is difficult. Often for low-income college students, I heard the primary motivation for attending college tied to notions of socio-economic mobility. "I don't want to do what my mom and dad do" and "I want to make my family proud" are common types of responses. Additionally, women often comment on wanting the independence that college may bring them: "I don't want to have to depend on a man." Some ethnic minority students also focus on furthering their race through countering educational stereotypes: "I want to prove that a Mexican-American can be successful."

Faculty members told me repeatedly that they felt self-motivation is a required element of successful low-income students. While recognizing the obstacles first-generation college students experience, finally the responsibility lies with students who need to make necessary adjustments—and they do this only if properly motivated. Such students seek out additional university resources and persevere. Many students speak of the difficulty in adjusting to an environment of voluntary participation: "In high school they are more on top of you. If you don't go to class, 'Why didn't you go to class?'" Here it was easier for me to say, "'I don't want to go to class.' So that's what I would do for that class."

The context for individual motivation in college has changed. Charles Murray (1984) in his book *Losing Ground* notes that contrary to popular belief, the large increases in equality in education occurred before any of the significant civil rights legislation or court decisions. In point of fact, public K-12 education for the disadvantaged improved dramatically during the 1950s and early 1960s and had an impact because of the dismal conditions in many segregated school districts. As other scholars have acknowledged, the huge investment in the later 1960s in education for the low-income students subsequently had very little impact. Given this fact, Murray points to three associated popular myths about the low-income students that the American public has come to hold that are behind public policy measures in education.

Premise #1: People respond to incentives and disincentives. Sticks and carrots work.

Premise #2: People are not inherently hard working or moral. In the absence of countervailing influences people will avoid work and be amoral.

Premise #3: People must be held responsible for their actions. Whether they are responsible is in some ultimate philosophical or biochemical sense cannot be the issue if society is to function. (Murray, 1984, p. 146)

In his book written in 1984, Murray argues that status was withdrawn from low-income families with disastrous impact. Positive image, self-respect or even the opportunity for important perspectives has been lost because of changes in welfare policy and social attitudes. He notes that in the past, the poor could still work and thereby retain a sense of pride. The shift in policy led to the low-income students accepting a state of permanent unemployment: "For the first time in American history, it became socially acceptable within poor communities to be unemployed, because working families too were receiving welfare" (Murray, 1984, p. 185). In a practical way, someone who continues to try and work at a low-paying job given the social services available becomes laughable: "The man who keeps working is, in fact, a chump" (Murray, 1984, p. 185). Of course, welfare policies have changed since the 1980s and have tried in some ways to address the de-motivation to work implicit in some of the rules. Nevertheless, Murray's point about the psychological impact of policies towards the poor is important to note. In the education realm, this psychology of underachievement plays out in the pressure on low-income students to perform poorly and not participate in academic pursuits. As with the work game, one who plays the education game with few incentives is a "chump." In the larger ethical context of pinning social position to just desert, Murray points out that poor children suffer from these myths about low-income families:

There is no such thing as an undeserving five-year old. Society, in the form of government intervention, is quite limited in what it can do to make up for many of the deficiencies of life that an unlucky five-year-old experiences; it can, however, provide a good education and thereby give the child a chance at a different future. (Murray, 1984, p. 223)

Murray's insightful analysis of the common myths about the poor in America is important to understand because they are behind the altered public attitudes and subsequent public policy which are unfavorable to the poor. In essence the primary public belief here again is that the poor are responsible for their own disadvantage. In this way, the intense personal development that all college students go through at that stage in their lives is made especially hard for students from low-income backgrounds because they have been judged by society as coming from a community of underachievement and even immorality.

Family

One of the most important realizations I've had in writing this book is seeing the importance of families in the success or failure of low-income students. Those who seem to be doing well in college talk about the importance of their family and of receiving consistent support. The support comes in various forms, but primarily the support that matters the most is psychological and emotional encouragement. Family sustenance of this kind tends to encourage the development of the all-important confidence students need to persevere in the face of significant obstacles.

Table 3.1 Influence of low-income family on students

Positive	Negative
encouragement	questioning
college suitability	doubtful
understand value of college	question value of college
worldliness	cultural isolation
economic support of student	need to financially support family
equal support for males and females	male pressure to work; female pressure to marry
individual decision making	family-dominated decision making
talk about college experience	unfamiliarity leads to silence
relieved of family chores and sibling care	pressured to continue home responsibilities while in college
allowed to leave home	pressure to commute

In Table 3.1 one can see how low-income families can have either a positive or negative impact on their children in regard to going to college. The central concerns are both psychological and practical. The family is the central place of individual identity formation so that if a child is encouraged to attend college and is told he or she is capable, the student will begin to form a personal conception that includes "college student." If parents fail to understand the value of college or doubt the ability or suitability of their children for college, positive identity formulation is less likely. On the cultural level, if the family is culturally isolated, or adheres to rigid gender roles, then the students are hindered in their educational ambitions. How the family is structured influences the college going chances of children by insisting on the primacy of family over the individual, and the financial and family chore expectations. Once in college, the family's on-going encouragement, willingness to allow students to stay in residence halls, and engagement in active discussions about the college experience influence the likelihood of low-income students to complete their degrees.

The family influence varies by gender especially in particular ethnic minority cultures. I found with Latino families in Southern California a pattern of early pregnancy and marriage which often led to students dropping out of college out of practical necessity and/or the demands of male family members. I also heard disturbing tales of pressured marriages arranged by parents. Especially for close-knit communities, parents sometimes look to find financial security and cultural safety by making links to similar families. Once married, the husband then often determines that his wife should not be attending college. Education is empowering for many female low-income students, which helps build confidence and a less family-bound identity. Of course, this can lead to family conflict. While the family tends to emphasize traditional gender roles, the university has learning and developmental goals centered on critical thinking and development of personal values and perspectives. The further trend in higher education is that women are increasingly overrepresented on campuses, and this is especially true in programs for low-income students such as EOP where 80-90 percent of the students are female.

For those families that are less supportive of their children going to college in the first place, they are often relieved when students subsequently drop out: "The family is happy because the student can work full time and they may not have the school bills to pay anymore." In these instances, the negative impact is perhaps even greater on the student who has ventured outside the family and failed in the world of the dominant culture, and then finds that in some ways their own family is happy about their college disappointment. We see then in these ways the family itself is at times an obstacle for low-income students who attend college.

One clear obstruction for low-income students is their parents' lack of familiarity with college. For some parents the lack of knowledge is a passive hindrance which prevents them from asking questions or relating to their children's experiences: "We never really talked about it," was a common refrain. A 2001 report from the National Center for Education Statistics notes that those children with parents who attended college are much more like to attend post-secondary school themselves (82 as opposed to 54 percent) (Choy, 2001). The finding of the report points out low-income students are distinctly disadvantaged, even when controlling for factors such as education expectations, academic preparation, and support from parents and schools in planning and preparing for college. Furthermore, the disadvantage persists even for those low-income students who end up attending university and persist in attaining a degree. For others college was a sensitive topic both in terms of draining resources from the family and the ideas acquired. One former student remembered a professor recommending that students not talk about what they learn with their parents: "You'll only alienate them." Of course this truism is especially relevant concerning talk of politics, religion, and cultural values.

Additionally, many children from working-class families describe their individual college preoccupations getting lost in the family's daily struggle for survival: "They're always busy, always doing their chores, or at work. And when we're at home they are tired so they go to sleep." On a practical level, low-income students often have childcare and work obligations that pull them away from college: "I cook for my parents and cook for my sister. Although they tell me not to do it, because school is more important, but I feel I need to do it because I don't give them money anymore." Only marriage in many cases leads to young women leaving the home and the associated family responsibilities.

In this way, some undergraduates talked about separation from family as the biggest challenge, especially in the first year of college. As in Debbie's portrait at the end of this chapter, some students speak about the pull towards home being especially strong when there were problems with siblings and parents. For some of the students it is the first time they've ever been away from their families for any significant period of time. "So now you're not only away from home but you're living with strangers you don't know, who might have very different backgrounds. You grew up in a neighborhood where everyone looked like you and spoke the same language—now you're in a completely different environment." The tug from home can be very powerful, and students feel responsibility especially for brothers and sisters. The weight then of being a responsible older sibling sometimes is combined with the pull to take care of parents: "As far as financially, there was a while when my mom told me that she needed help financially."

Lacking a basic knowledge of college, many low-income parents can only focus on visible signs of school success such as time spent doing homework and grades. Students talk about how the parents are hard and demanding on them, even though parents often don't understand the college environment: "I don't really talk to them about, like if I'm having trouble in a class I don't let them know because my dad will be tough on me and bitch at me telling me what I already know." This student admits doing poorly the first semester in college and intentionally not talking to her parents about her problems. For parents of first-generation college, college attendance is out of the norm: "All the other families the kids they all dropped out or they had babies already." As a result, parents often question the reasons for attending college and the additional expense.

One professor I spoke with talked about the difficulty his family had in understanding his many years in college. When he made a transition to return to graduate school, the family was confused: "I had a job, a suit and tie job which for them was a big deal. It was a good paying job and I had been married for a year. They viewed it as almost a very irresponsible thing that I did. That I gave up the income—because I have a family now—I gave up the income, the security for my family for what they perceived I had already done." Attending college for four years as an undergraduate is often hard enough for low-income parents to appreciate, but the reasons for graduate school for many years more is a special challenge: "Even now my grandfather will ask, 'Are you done with school yet?'"

Cultural issues connected to the family arise in concerns over going away and leaving the home for college. "No, you're not going anywhere," was a common refrain heard especially from young women asking to be the first in their family to go away from home for school. Some students decide as a result to commute to college when that is feasible, in others to miss college altogether as a result of this limitation. For many I spoke to there was a pattern of eventually winning over the parents, with resolutions articulated as going away to college away from the family will "be good for her." At the same time, students speak with regret of the need to sacrifice both their time and closeness with their families: "We don't have time to ask about each, 'How are you doing?'" Family is still the main priority, but education for individual members comes in at a close second.

Ricardo D. Stanton-Salazar (2001) in his book *Manufacturing Hope and Despair: The School and Kin Support Networks of US-Mexican Youth* talks about Marx's notion that the wealth of an individual depends on social relationships and that the transmission of social networks and social ties are characteristic of the upper classes. An unequal distribution of opportunities results from this social network. An example of this notion given by Stanton-Salarzar is that Latino parents typically do not give specific direction in educational goals to their children, preferring to have children define their own direction. This "non-interventionist parenting style" is a handicap in educational environments: "This is to say that people make their way in the world by constantly negotiating both the constraints placed on them and the opportunities afforded them, by way of the social webs of which they are a part" (Stanton-Salarzar, 2001, p. 18). In this light, the apparent lack of support I found from some families is understandable. While parents may feel that college would be good for their children, in some cases culturally they are less willing to force their point of view on their children, something commonly done in middle- and upper-class families. Of course, motivation to attend college relates directly to having an accurate understand of the value of a degree and expectations of the effort needed and benefits accrued, which is less likely in uneducated parents. We see here then that the motivation that is identified as so important in the personal sphere is informed very strongly by the family.

Cultural

Beyond the immediate family, a primary aspect of adjustment problems for low-income students in college is the social fit for the student which can be difficult because of a lack of basic cultural background understanding or cultural capital. Peter Sacks (2007) in his book *Tearing Down the Gates: Confronting the Class Divide in American Education*, describes the dichotomy between two cultures: "Colleges and universities, for the most part, are 'rich-culture.' 'Poor culture' people often find campuses to be unwelcoming places" (Sacks, 2007, p. 264). Students I spoke with often revealed how their "poor culture" background left them out of step with the "rich culture" found in college. For example, one Latino high school student I asked about plans to attend the University of Notre Dame foresaw the adjustment in ethnic terms: "It will make me feel a lot more Mexican." A college counselor sums up the necessary cultural adjustment students from low-income backgrounds are forced to make: "You grew up in a neighborhood where everyone looked like you and spoke the same language—now you're in a completely different environment." Ethnic minority low-income students have obvious added social fit issues beyond those students who are white and poor because of their visible difference. Many of those I interviewed talked about being initially uncomfortable with the lack of color in the student populations on their campus, but how those that persevere adjust over time: "I'd look around in the classes and I was the only Latino person in there and felt uncomfortable. But after a while everyone is really nice, I made a lot of friends, and I don't feel uncomfortable anymore." Nevertheless, in the face of this adjust problem, students talk about retaining the culture to which they were raised while going to college: "Wherever I go, I'm going to take my culture with me."

Faculty and university administrators speak of the difficulty for middle-class students in adjusting and "figuring out" college, and how that initial difficulty is multiplied for low-income students, and complicated even further by gender and race. Students speak of having difficulty participating in conversations with middle-class students who are worldlier in many ways from travel and exposure to the larger world. Low-income students also told me about feeling regarded differently by faculty in subtle and not so subtle ways. Faculty members point to the socialization function of undergraduate education that results in an especially long road for those from divergent cultures required to meet certain standards of conformity.

Especially in parts of the country such as California which are culturally diverse, the ethnic adjustments are more complex. For instance, some low-income ethnic minority students talk about themselves as being bi-cultural thereby having an easier time with adjustment to the dominate culture found in college. One faculty member spoke about how Chicano students, who are neither Mexican nor American, come to college with a blended culture that has its own adjustment issues: "So their identity is this blended culture that is neither here nor there." Often these students were raised by parents who insisted that they speak English at home in order to better acculturate them. As a result, they speak Spanish poorly. Nevertheless, they still don't feel theirs is the dominant culture in America. The campus experience is thus very foreign to them and they don't have a distinct culture to fall back upon. Additionally, since the sixties, students talk about social activism and an environment where different cultures can be openly recognized and respected. "Everyone had a group," an alumnus from the 1960s told me. However, other ethnic minority students talk about not fitting into any of the distinct racial groupings formed on their campus. They identify the grouping as working against their more integrated racial interactions in high school: "Growing up, my best friends were Chinese, Muslim, Jewish, we had this very diverse group." Administrators and students talk about isolation in some cases felt by students from low-income backgrounds. By students accepting financial aid and scholarships and participating in programs aimed at lower-income students they identify themselves directly as low-income. Furthermore, when the ethnic dimension is added, there is sometimes a presumed advantage in admissions for ethnic minority and lower-income students which may further strain social relations.

Even so, many students express a confidence about their social skills and ability to fit in regardless of the college they attend: "I didn't think that I'd know where I'd be happiest just by the class of people that were at a school." As we saw in Rick's portrait in Chapter 1, college athletics can provide an in-road and smooths the transition for them. Athletic programs often help with practical issues of course scheduling and advisement as well as provide additional tutoring. The sports programs at many universities play the role of EOP programs and becomes a kind of home with its own culture: "I fit in that way." Yet, some I spoke with talk about the necessity for low-income students to give up their home culture in some sense by going to college. Of course when literally moving away from home as residential students, this sacrifice is material as well as cultural. For those students who commute to university while living at home, they face a bifurcated daily life where they move between their traditional accustomed parent's world, and that of their new and less understood world of the campus.

Gender differences are also noted in first-generation families with concerns for the protection of females: "I guess they were just afraid. Especially being a girl. They have that problem with girls; you have to take more care with the girl than a boy." Females remarked often about their lack of freedom, especially when coming home after being in college residence halls and apartments on their own. "When I went home I had to ask permission. They wanted me home at ten." This protective attitude towards females in some cultures further separates women from low-income ethnic backgrounds from the more affluent students who tend to be given more latitude by their families.

Generally, those I spoke with denied that they had to give up anything about their culture to adjust to college life. However, there were indications of a resulting distance from their immediate families.

> STUDENT: I think the only thing that I've given up is my family, because we don't really have time to bond. We don't have time to ask about each, "How are you doing?" I try to just focus on school and leave my family problems—not leave them behind, but kind of to the side where my education is more important.
> AUTHOR: What are the values of your family?
> STUDENT: Family.

Students describe the problem of communicating with their parents about their college experience. "We never talk about me and college. The only thing they ask is if I'm doing my homework. 'How are you doing?' 'I'm doing fine.' That's about it." The problem of relating to an unfamiliar experience exacerbates the typical communication problems that occur for parents and children in this developmental stage. Perhaps with even more pain and disjuncture, low-income college students returning home feel it is difficult to reconnect with old friends.

> I was different when I went back, for sure. I think there's a sense of that with my friends. I wasn't satisfied to hang out and do the things we used to do. We used to play a lot of cards. I remember sitting for hours with the guys, sitting under the light on the street. I would try to do that, but it was never quite as interesting to me as before.

In this way, low-income college students often feel isolated not only on campus but also when they return home.

Continually in my discussions with low-income college students I heard about how different the experience is for them, lacking immediate family members and relatives with college degrees. One person I spoke to described it directly as a mismatch where they, "may not understand or feel that college is for them," or recognize that it's an opportunity for bigger and better things. In contrast, those from advantaged families have numerous close relations with college experience; as a result students feel that "they kind of have the sense that this is the path that has been made for them." Black and Latino students come to college with the feeling of that their minority culture is amplified: "They come and see a primarily white campus with professors up there saying who knows what that has very little connection to their experience. I think a lot of them go through a deep exploration of themselves in the first year." Students I spoke with talked about at the beginning looking around in the classes and on campus and feeling self-conscious: "I was the only Latino person in there and felt uncomfortable." Others simply feel out of place in college:

> The first year it was very hard for me to get into ... I come from the San Fernando Valley and there's a lot of Latinos, and I came over here and there were Caucasians, and I was like freaking out at first because I've never been around so many people from a different background. I've always been around one set of people.

Students describe a basic suitability issue: "Although college is very important, it's not for everybody. Not everybody can be a college student." Some students expressed to me a lack in even a fundamental interest in reading: "Some people just aren't interested. Yes, colleges do have a wide variety of things that might suit your interest; maybe studying isn't your interest. I know reading isn't my interest. In school you have to read, and it's such a job for me."

The clash of the rich and the poor cultures in this cultural sphere is complicated further by race and gender. Nevertheless, there are clear commonalities through the poor culture background in the experiences of low-income students regardless or race or gender. For instance, the simple lack of college experience collectively in a family makes the first few years in a university particularly difficult for many students. Poor students in a rich person's culture in college often end up feeling outsiders on campus, and at home, where family members fail to understand the new world the young adults have tried to enter.

Structural

As represented in Figure 3.1, the structural level is dictated to a large extent by the choices our society has made regarding toleration for a high level of poverty in America. Poor students have adjustment problems in college primarily because of a lack of family and personal wealth. This lack of affluence affects their self-image and career goals from a very young age. The structure of schools with a focus on assessment of talent perpetuates inequality when low-income students are unable to keep up. If a student then manages by virtue of raw talent and perseverance to consider college, the economic reality of inadequate amounts of financial aid and a dependence on loans is another clear structural disadvantage. Finally, once in college the poorness of their families still influences college continuation decisions by students.

National statistics are clear in demonstrating how economics influence the college-going experience for students from poor families. Sixty-five percent of low-income students at four-year colleges and 80 percent at community colleges work between 24 and 27 hours a week on average. Additionally, one half of all low-income students in college live at home in order to reduce the cost of going to school (United States Congress, 2002). The following figure (3.6) shows how the concern over finances during college disproportionately impacts those students from low-income backgrounds.

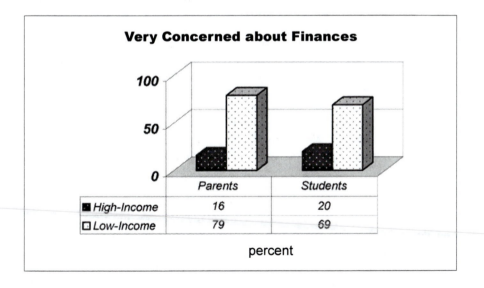

**Figure 3.6 Impact of high unmet need on high school graduates'
expectations and plans**
Source: United States Congress, 2002.

In this way perhaps the most important barrier for some first-generation college students is plainly economic. As one administrator put it to me:

> The realities are that the families are preoccupied with surviving, being able to support their families—it's [education] not a priority in a lot of cases. You need to pay the rent. You need to do what you need to do and in a lot of cases that takes all the members of the family contributing.

Low-income students report working to such an extent that it affects their studies. In most cases the students are not voluntarily working—the parents don't have the resources to support their children in college. The following is a representative comment from a student working too many hours while attending school: "It's kind of hard for me to work and go to school at the same time. I get home around 5:30 and then I have to do homework. It's kind of hard for me to concentrate, I don't have enough time to do my homework and study the way I'd want to." Faculty and counselors told me about students working "too much" to the point that their education suffers. Working long hours while attending college is generally not a matter of choice, but of necessity, one that is clearly more common with students from low-income backgrounds.

The basic economics of attending college should not be underestimated. Money is important in two different ways for college students: for the financing of their education and in terms of support of their families, or the lost income that is a result of attending college. The impact on low-income students of the changes in financial aid which has moved more towards a reliance on loans is great. Many low-income families cannot qualify for bank loans and furthermore are reluctant to take on debt because of negative cultural connotations associated with doing so. Low-income students talk about receiving various levels of financial assistance from their parents, from fully covering college costs, to more typically giving sporadically to their children. One student offered a typical response to my query about financial support: "My parents don't make that much money for me to continue with my education, but the little they make they give to me to keep on going to school."

The cost of housing is another key issue that comes up with first-generation college students because often it is not completely covered by financial aid. As an administrator told me, "For those students out of the area it's really difficult because they don't have the option of moving back in with mom and dad." Students from middle-class families easily qualify for bank loans to supplement regular financial aid, but many low-income students do not have this advantage. Personal loans simply aren't an option for them. The result is that even if poor college students manage to pull together the money to live in a residence hall their first year, there is continual pressure on them to move home. When students drop out of college, often there is a sigh of relief from their families because of the removal of the college expense burden.

Too often those looking at the public policy connected with financial aid overlook the sacrifice students make in lost income while attending college. Typically, this lost income is absorbed without thought for middle-class families. For low-income families dependent on the wages of all family members, the lack of a contribution from a young adult has a significant impact. Further, the more direct way that low-income students are impacted by economics is in the requirement that they give money to their families while attending college. For middle-class families, economic hardship means that families may not be able to completely support their children while in college and that students might need to take on a part-time job. The idea of college students actually sending money home to their families would seem extraordinary. Yet, I heard about poor students giving money to their families regularly. This is true for previous and current generations, from blacks, Latinos and whites, and from the eastern and western United States: "The whole time I was in college I'd send her [my mother] money."

The economic pressure then extends after graduation where the young adult is expected to support their family in a larger way. I found that low-income students attending college are under a great deal of pressure, both from parents and from themselves in a larger social context. Unable to let go of the challenge, students are the last to leave the library and fixate on tests and papers beyond what is healthy. As a result, these students become unbalanced in a way that often affects their performance: "It hurt us in the long run. But it wasn't going to be for lack of effort." One former student told me that the stress of college was so great it started to affect him physically: "I was losing my hair."

In sum, the larger structure of society puts immense financial pressure on students from low-income families. The individual, family, and cultural obstacles low-income students face in college are informed by this larger context of practical disadvantage. Financial aid and admission policies are directly informed by harsh perceptions that the poor in America are responsible for their own condition, and subsequently provide limited public support. The impact of America's ungenerous attitudes towards the poor has worsened the chances of students from low-income families to move up in society through a college education.

Sidebar Portrait: Debbie

Debbie is a sophomore business major. She describes herself as coming from a lower-middle class family and catalogs her father's career path: "He tried going back to school to become an insurance broker to kind of like work in the insurance business, but that didn't work out. So he ended up moving out of state to Arizona working in construction, not really construction. I don't really know exactly what he does." Debbie describes her parents as always talking about education to her as a child, looking at her grades to make sure that she had at least a C average. "My dad was the strict one on me, always making sure I did my homework." Debbie tells me that she loves to read and that her parents would buy her books often. Her father played a game with her wherein she read a book every month and then wrote a book report. As with many first generation students, Debbie describes how her parents consistently talked about college as a route to a better life.

The oldest of four children, her parents tried to motivate her to go to school "because growing up I saw a lot of the struggles of my parents financially." Debbie is the first in her extended family to go to college. While attending high school in the San Fernando Valley in Los Angeles, Debbie found out about college by becoming a peer college counselor to other students. Through that responsibility, she learned about college by filling in other high school students on the process of applying, and financial aid requirements. Leaving home and living in the on-campus residence halls has been an adjustment for her. "I actually expected to be in contact with my parents more, but it wasn't like that for me." At first Debbie tried to talk to her parents about what it is like at college, but learned to keep problems to herself: "My dad is really hard on me with classes and if I'm not doing well." She tells me about have trouble the first semester of college when she failed a history course. "The fact of being away from home, dealing with personal stuff with back home, it was a very hard time."

Debbie describes a typical adjustment problem with having to take more responsibility for her education in college: "I realized in high school they are more on top of you. If you don't go to class, 'Why didn't you go to class?' Here it was easier for me to say, 'I don't want to go to class.'" Additionally, she talks about the dependence of learning through textbooks in college: "Having to take a course and read off a book all on your own without any guidance or anything." Especially, for someone who is not a native English speaker, the pedagogical dependence in college on textbooks is a clear disadvantage. As Debbie told me, "It was kind of hard to go back to my room here and start reading out of a big textbook. The words were kind of out there."

Debbie felt that she had some cultural barriers to overcome as well in her first year in college. She is a student in EOP and was surrounded by Latinas from similar backgrounds: "I'd hang out with just them." Debbie describes coming from a predominately Latino community, typical of Southern California, to a primarily Caucasian university community: "I've never been around so many people from a different background." Although the California State University is one of the more ethnically diverse public university systems in the country, she felt isolated in EOP: "We felt so much out of place." The isolation in this case may have been more specifically about economic class and not race because of the already diverse student body. However, over a period of time, the members of their tight group made other friends and moved more into the mainstream of campus life.

Our conversation turns to her family. I ask about the plans for college of her 16-year-old sister. Obviously an emotional topic for Debbie, she describes how her sister became pregnant: "My 16-year-old sister is a mom now." Her sister still goes to high school, but is talking about going to a trade school rather than college. Debbie has tried to encourage her to go to college to no avail: "That's not what I want to do with my life," she tells Debbie. The situation with her pregnant sister has put Debbie in the position of holding her family together. As I found with many low-income students, family responsibilities, from economic to emotional, pull them away from their studies. Debbie tells me that she purposely decided to leave home for college in order to escape family stress, choosing a college 50 miles from her parent's home. Close enough to get to in an hour or so, but far enough away to force independent residence. Her first year of college was very difficult for her because of her family: "I was going through such a hard time." Her mother would regularly call her and talk about the conflict with her pregnant teenage sister: "She'd tell me, 'You need to talk to your sister. She doesn't want to talk to me. She doesn't tell me anything. I don't know what's going on with her.'" Debbie felt like she had to solve the family problem, which was perhaps unsolvable. Additionally, her mother asked her to help the family financially calling on the phone with a plea to, "Help her." As a result, Debbie felt forced to work while attending school and give her family money for support. "So that was a lot of pressure for me." She's now relieved that her parents have moved out of state and she no longer feels as much anxiety.

How has college affected her? Debbie talks about added maturity and independence. She phrases this as "leaning more towards thinking about myself than thinking about others." As with many of the college graduates I interviewed, Debbie talks about the empowering psychological impact of education, especially for women: "I used to have this problem where I'd put everyone else in front of me." Debbie tells me that she still "stumbles" at times, but that after college she wants to go to graduate school at Arizona State University, and eventually run her own business.

Debbie feels that the public universities do a good job of encouraging teens like her to go to college. However, she thinks the emphasis on SAT scores and grades in the admissions process is unfair: "I don't think just looking at SAT scores and grades tell you enough about the potential of students." Debbie's stress in talking about school and moving up in society is on the need to understand and allow for academic struggles for some students during high school. From her own experience, she sees students not understanding the importance of education to their future. For Debbie, everyone should have an opportunity, "No matter what happened in the past."

Debbie provides a vivid example of the pull of families on low-income college students, and the non-academic obstacles they face. Students coming from fractured and economically struggling families often pull on those young adults who have the ability to go to college. The weight on the student is both psychological and practical because of the need to support their family members emotionally and financially. Debbie, as other students in similar situations, ends by trying to separate herself from her family and asserting her independence. For young women from certain ethnic minority groups, this struggle for independence is especially difficult and often leads to the student dropping out of college. Additionally, we see here in Debbie's story that in her initial adjustment problems to the world of college, and in her need to separate herself from her family, she ends up with no anchor during her college years. Now out of place in her past family life, and feeling isolated at college, she is forced to form her identity as she earns her degree.

Conclusion

In this chapter I looked at how the experience of low-income students in college differs and argued that because of a variety of factors dropout rates are much higher. We began by examining statistics on low-income students in college and found that the chance of getting a BA or BS by 24-years-old has improved only for those families in the upper-half economically in America (Sacks, 2007). The increased public funding of higher education that occurred after World War II primarily benefited the children of the upper-classes (Machin and Gregg, 2003). I identified four main types of issues that confront these students ranging from personal or individual, to family, to cultural, and structural. The personal issues are those that often involve the important growth that is typical of college students but tends to be more pronounced in low-income students because of the problems in adjustment to a very different and unaccustomed environment. Additionally, the level of appropriate motivation to apply the extra effort needed to succeed despite obstacles is important on a personal level but influenced greatly by the larger family and social spheres. The wider cultural context and structure of American society has a pervasive impact on poor students, directly in terms of the economic realities for their life chances. The following chart lists the ways the personal, social and structural impact poor college students.

Table 3.2 Characteristics of low-income college students by domain

Personal	Family/Cultural	Structural
motivation	family needs	economic status
confidence	preparation	education system
work ethic	level of support	financial aid policy
worldliness	isolation	segregation
gender	gender customs	gender rules
race	race customs	race rules
personal development	restrictions	limits/opportunity
difference from parents	parents	income/occupation

The personal issues that impact student success in college center on self-image formation that expresses itself as a lack of motivation, low confidence, a poor work ethic, and an overall low amount of knowledge of the world. The struggle to separate from the parents, which is developmentally a common occurrence for young adults, is perhaps more extreme for poor students because of both cultural and practical attachments. On the cultural level, students are directly impacted by the needs of their immediate families seen vividly illustrated in Debbie's story of needing to intervene because of her teenage sister's pregnancy. The collective beliefs surrounding gender and other family-based restrictions strongly impact the students during college. The larger structural domain impacts both the individual and social levels specifically by setting income and occupational limits and social rules.

Although higher education is not the cause of the personal, family, or economic problems identified in this chapter, I contend that higher education has not done enough specifically to confront the problems of low-income students as they present themselves in colleges across the country. In her book entitled *Beyond the Open Door*, Patricia Cross (1976) argues that traditional higher education is not prepared to educate what she terms "new students," or those marginal ones who are the bottom one third of the entering class. In very poignant terms, Cross points out that the students from the bottom third tend to have different experiences when preparing for college. Rather than focusing on the learning, they concentrate on making the grade—literally:

> The lowest third are learning throughout the years of their elementary and secondary education, but they are learning different lessons from those intended by educators. Most are becoming students of methods to avoid failure. Some of these methods are ingenious; all of them, however, distract attention from learning and are therefore handicapping to future education. (Cross, 1976, p. 27)

How do students at the bottom of the college food chain react to the fear of failure? As I saw with many of the students I interviewed, they often over-compensate for this fear by having unrealistic aspirations of impossible, celebrity or professional careers, or dreams of graduate school at elite universities. Furthermore, students who have a history of poor or mediocre performance in school, according to Cross, have a tendency to protect themselves by not trying too hard: "Students seem to be saying that they cannot fail at what they do not try" (Cross, 1976, p. 27).

So we see that the emotional preparation for low-income students in college means fortifying and protecting the ego. For the very best students who have had repeated reassurances of their intelligence and skills, perhaps this is less of an issue. However, for the larger majority who has had at least a few educational performance failures, they understand that going to college is a risk to their ego. For them, learning equals a risk to their sense of self. Students new to higher education complain about the amount of work and the fast pace, are unusually nervous and introverted in class, and need more academic and personal counseling.

Cross notes that low-income college students are "pioneers" and as such are a combination of old attitudes and practices thrown into new environments that they aren't quite ready to adjust to in many ways: "Their parents and homes may present a way of life that is no longer adequate for them—and yet the new life promised by higher education is not quite ready for them" (Cross, 1976, p. 84). Furthermore, the educational establishment is generally not very flexible and willing to adapt to these new students. The result is that low-income students drop out, have trouble learning, don't try as hard as they need to, and often score low on traditional standardized tests. On the personal level, their home life has usually led them to non-intellectual preoccupations; they lack self-confidence which affects their ability to learn. Cross points out that low-income students are in the very difficult situation of desperately needing to succeed in college but not understanding how to do so. Interesting, she developed a profile for these "new students" and describes them additionally as preferring television over reading, learning through a presentation of knowledge rather than continual intellectual questioning, pursuing vocational tracks, and holding conservative values. I found in the interviews I conducted for this book many of these same indications in students from disadvantaged families.

Chapter 4

Gender and Race are Interlocking Categories of Inequality

This chapter argues that gender and race are interlocking categories of disadvantage with low-income students. I consider special challenges for women and ethnic minorities in college and how they have evolved over time. The chapter considers statistics showing that black and Latino students are far behind Asian and white populations in graduating from both high school and college today. Additionally, the impact on low-income students of the roll back of affirmative action policies is negative, and the outcomes of the new alternative method of comprehensive review in university admissions approach uncertain. The reality for many ethnic minority college students in America today is one of a web of disadvantage including limited progress in personal wealth, negative self-image, low academic expectations, and community segregation that perpetuate conditions. Additionally, the portraits of a current African-American student from South Central Los Angeles, a woman who returned to college in her mid-fifties, and a college professor who graduated from a Southern university are presented to deepen the discussion.

Affirmative Action Reversal Devastating

The *Gratz vs. Bollinger* decision which struck down point-based admissions at the University of Michigan led to Ohio State University, the University of Massachusetts and other institutions replacing point-based systems with policies relying partly on essays to gauge contribution to diversity. The Supreme Court's 2003 ruling in the Michigan law school case revealed that it was important to still have at least a symbolic nod to diversity, and that the argument that diversity was a valuable asset for an institution held weight in court (Schmidt, 2007). However, explicit forms of affirmative action are clearly under attack both in the courts and among voters. While the much discussed actions at the University of Michigan and in other states are still fluid, the examples where affirmative action policies have been rolled back show an immediate impact on the composition of university student bodies around the country. The banning of affirmative action in admissions at universities has had an immediately negative impact on enrollment at some of the nation's most selective universities. The first year the ban went into affect, the University of California at Berkeley law school had enrollment of black students decline from 20 to 1, while the number of Hispanic students dropped from 28 to 18. At the University of Texas law school, a reverse discrimination court ruling led to changes in admissions policies resulting in a drop to three black students from 31 the previous year, and 20 Latino students from 42 (Applebome, 1997).

When we look at high school and college completion more generally, ethnicity is clearly one link to low-income family status. The following figure (4.1) displays the United States Census breakdown of college graduates by ethnicity in the year 2000.

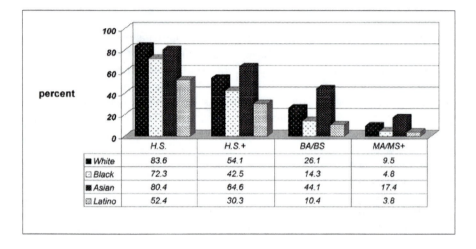

	H.S.	H.S.+	BA/BS	MA/MS+
White	83.6	54.1	26.1	9.5
Black	72.3	42.5	14.3	4.8
Asian	80.4	64.6	44.1	17.4
Latino	52.4	30.3	10.4	3.8

Figure 4.1 Educational attainment of the population 25 years and over by age, sex, race, and origin: 2000
Source: Based on data from Bauman and Graf, 2003.

By the year 2000 in America, the percentage of white college graduates approximately doubled those of both black and Latinos, while Asian-American students managed to approximately double the percentage of whites.

With the rise of the 1960s Civil Rights Movement, affirmative action was for many years the main way that social mobility was promoted in higher education. Public support for affirmative action has waned. A *New York Times* article notes this transformation in public attitudes and policy:

> With several populous states having already banned race-based preferences and the United States Supreme Court suggesting that it may outlaw such programs in a couple of decades, the future of affirmative action may well revolve around economics. Polls consistently show that programs based on class backgrounds have wider support than those based on race. (Leonhardt, 2005)

In 2005, a survey on the issue of class in America found that 59 percent still favor affirmative action programs, but are more inclined now towards programs based on low-income status (84 percent.) The impact of the roll back of affirmative action has not gone unnoticed. According to a report by the National Center for Public Policy and Higher Education, the discontent is particularly noted in African American parents of high school students (Immerwahr, 2004). "By the 2003 study, the level of concern among African Americans spiked, with 76 percent saying that many qualified people are shut out of higher education (compared to 51 percent among white respondents)" (Immerwahr, 2004).

The current conservative position on affirmative action is represented by such scholars as Thomas Sowell, a Stanford University-based scholar. In his recent book entitled *Affirmative Action Around the World*, Sowell (2004) argues that race preference programs around the world have not met expectations, and actually have been in some cases detrimental to the equal opportunity aim. He describes a "shifting effect" where affirmative action policy leads to mismatches throughout college system when the best minority students gain admittance in larger numbers to elite universities, thereby causing a chain reaction down the line wherein less prepared students end up at schools that are too advanced of a match for their background. These students, Sowell claims, would be better off at the schools a level down which better match their academic preparation. Thus affirmative action in his mind leads to an overall mismatching of students to institutions. The notion of one finding one's proper place among education institutions was examined in depth in the first and second chapters, and note here how this disturbing conception is at the base of Sowell's argument against affirmative action.

The debate on affirmative action has been most visible at the elite public universities such as the University of California. Beginning in the mid-1970s, the University of California became an increasingly selective institution because of a marked increase in qualified applicants. In the late 1980s, Jerome Karabel led a special committee to look into the admissions practices at the university. In its subsequent report (Karabel, 1989), the committee found that the University of California was becoming increasingly less open to ethnic minority groups. The committee concentrated on college preparation distinctions as a root cause noting that at that time only four and half percent and five percent of African-American and Hispanic high school graduates respectively met University of California eligibility requirements, while 15.8 of whites and 32.8 percent of Asian-Americans did so. Given these figures, one can see that it was no accident that the University of California saw an enormous rise in the number of Asian-American students at the end of the 1980s, and is steadily increasing to this day. As a result, the stated attempt to represent each segment of the California population in public higher education was obviously failing.

In his book *Two Nations: Black and White, Separate, Hostile, Unequal,* Andrew Hacker (1995) looks at the misunderstood advantages and disadvantages of being black and white in America. He points out that the long and short time impact of ethnicity in America is underestimated, partly because of a tendency of those with advantages not wanting to admit that they benefit from historical racism: "What white people seldom stop to ask is how they may benefit from belonging to their race" (Hacker, 1995, p. 35). Hacker argues that this unwillingness to admit advantage from racism explains the opposition to affirmative action: "They simply do not want to admit to themselves that the value imputed to being white has injured people who are black" (Hacker 1995, p. 66). Further, Hacker points to a continuing social isolation suffered by blacks in America, that is akin to the lack of "worldliness" I discovered in my interviews with students. An example of the impact of this social isolation, according to Hacker, is the poor performance on SAT tests, even among black students from middle class families. He cites the main reason for the poor performance as a social isolation which affects blacks from all classes. Cornell West in his influential book, *Race Matters*, argues that those in opposition to affirmative action fail to understand the deep psychological depression and negative identity issues that plague young black students in America. He notes viciousness in conservative arguments that deny the lasting effects of slavery in America. "In this way, crucial and indispensable themes of self-help and personal responsibility are wrenched out of historical context and contemporary circumstances—as if it is all a matter of personal will" (West, 2001, p. 22). Nevertheless, West seems to favor class-based affirmative action efforts.

Henry Perkinson (1995) in *The Imperfect Panacea: American Faith in Education* makes the important distinction between initiation and socialization. "Initiation" is what upper classes do in the education process, while "socialization" is the method that the lower classes experience. His analysis of education argues that education of children from low-income families has a distinctly different socialization purpose: "To make the masses industrious workers, loyal subjects, faithful church members" (Perkinson, 1995, p. 9). While there is a "messiah complex" or belief that education can fix social ills and be an "engine" for class mobility, the fact is that class background is a stronger indicator of school success than race or gender (Rothstein, 1995). Finally, Perkinson makes the point that the belief in education as a panacea for all of society's ills carries with it the assumption that people are the root of all social problems. Rather than changing the political system, the individual is the focus of change—a politically impotent position. In this way, the focus on the admission of students through affirmative action programs puts the onus on the responsibility of particular students and deflects the larger political context and history of inequality in America.

Recently, in what may become a widespread development, the University of California campuses at Berkeley and Los Angeles have begun to use the use "comprehensive review" in place of the forbidden affirmative action practice to consider student qualifications more broadly. While conservative critics have claimed that comprehensive review represents a resurrection of affirmative action, at least one study found that admissions results under comprehensive review are not linked to ethnicity (Hout, 2005). Nevertheless, it is probably too early to tell how comprehensive review will match up with previous affirmative action polices in effectiveness to meet admission fairness objectives.

Race Disadvantage

The relationship of economic class to race is complex, but clearly interlocking in some ways. In addition to the starkly prejudicial beliefs of the eugenics movement that claim scientific proof of racial inferiority for many ethnic minority groups (beliefs which in themselves have a unfavorable impact on college-going statistics), there is obviously a strong environmental impact. According to some experts in the field, the majority of black students report experiencing some sort of racial mistreatment during college and feel out of place in campus activities that reflect white traditions. Many parents of black children think that students pay a heavy price for going to white colleges, and especially struggle at large institutions where the sense of disconnection for minority students is heightened (Feagin, Vera and Imani, 1996).

Some scholars in the 1970s began to talk about the lessened relevance and impact of race on individuals in America. William Julius Wilson (1978) in The *Declining Significance of Race* argued that because of fundamental changes in race relations, the life chances of black Americans had more to do with an individual's economic class than his or her race. While not dismissing the continuing impact of racism and the alignment of race to class, he points out that a shift had occurred in America since the sixties, what he calls "different constraints," on the interactions of races so that racial antagonisms are displayed in new ways: "Class has become more important than race in determining black access to privilege and power" (Wilson, 1978, p. 2). In this way, overt economic oppression of blacks had been lessened according to Wilson. Nevertheless, the years of racial disparity created an "accumulation of disadvantages" by which each new generation is burdened: "The patterns of racial oppression in the past created the huge black underclass, as the accumulation of disadvantages were passed on from generation to generation, and the technological and economic revolution of advanced industrial society combined to insure it a permanent status" (Wilson, 1978, p. 120).

The conversation about the impact of race on individuals has become increasingly multifaceted. In *Being Black, Living in the Red*, Dalton Conley (1999) holds that in order to understand the "life chances" of children of a family or class one must take into account "wealth" (total financial assets or net worth) in addition to income, education and occupation. Generally, scholars, university administrators and policy makers use education, occupation, or father's occupation, and annual income as indicators of socioeconomic status, or class. This disregards the importance of net worth which is perhaps the most important factor in considering how parents pass along advantage to children. In point of fact, blacks in America as a whole have made almost no progress in terms of personal wealth. Conley cites statistics showing that at the end of slavery in 1865, blacks owned one half of a percent of the total worth of the United States, but by 1990 that figure had only risen to one percent (Anderson, 1994). "In other words, almost no progress had been made in terms of property ownership" (Conley, 1999, p. 25). Conley points out that in many ways race and class go hand in hand, but that what really hurts blacks is their lack of family wealth to pass along generation to generation thus keeping them generally disadvantaged. Rather than viewing education as an instrument perpetuating inequality, he sees inherited wealth as the primary culprit. Conley claims that when other factors are taken out, blacks are not any more likely to drop out of high school, and there is no significant difference in college completion: "Blacks are not disadvantaged in the education system; rather, they are disadvantaged in the resources they bring to the system. Race matters, but only indirectly—through the realm of class inequality" (Conley, 1999, pp. 80-81). As a result, Conley argues for class- rather than race-based affirmative action. To bolster his argument he cites statistics which show that blacks and whites benefit economically in similar ways after college, and that unemployment among blacks and whites from the low-income families is comparable. However, young blacks often start with severe disadvantages that are more economic than racial. Additionally, social problems such as unwed mothers exacerbate the economic disadvantage. He cites statistics showing that two-thirds of African American children are born to single mothers (Hacker, 1995).

> From the initial wresting of soon-to-be slaves from their families and possessions along the western coast of Africa, to the failed promise of land redistribution after Emancipation, to the dynamics of residential segregation and differential credit access that continue relatively unabated today, African Americans have been systematically prevented from accumulating property. (Conley, 1999, pp. 151-152)

The troubling facts are that African Americans score lower on vocabulary, reading and mathematics tests. The gap appears before kindergarten and persists into adulthood. While the gap has narrowed since 1970, the rate is still only 75 percent of white scores on average. When black or mixed raced children are raised in white households, their test scores rise dramatically (Jencks and Phillips, 1998). Scholars have also noted a "stereotype threat" which arises in ethnic minority groups that leads to poor performance on standardized tests (Steel and Aronson, 1995). The test taker's poor self-image and low expectations of performance end up impacting the ability to function well especially on difficult tests. Over time, the researchers argue that the response from minority students is often to remove themselves psychologically from investment in the test as a way of preserving their self-image. In this way, those from low-income backgrounds often don't see themselves as "students." In a controlled experiment on a group of college students, researchers tested black and white students and found that blacks with similar academic qualifications performed below the whites.

Finally, those students of color I spoke with talked about attending certain colleges because of the belief that they would be more likely to fit in: "One of the reasons I went to Fresno State is that I had the illusion that there were a lot of students of Mexican ancestry. I got there and there were very few." Once in college, ethnic minority students speak of sitting quite naturally at separate tables in the cafeteria populated by ethnic minorities. We saw in the last chapter how college choice is much more limited for low-income and minority students and this is partly because of a sense of comfort and lower academic expectations. The following figure gives a graphic representation on how the low position of ethnic minority populations in society leads to poor academic performance.

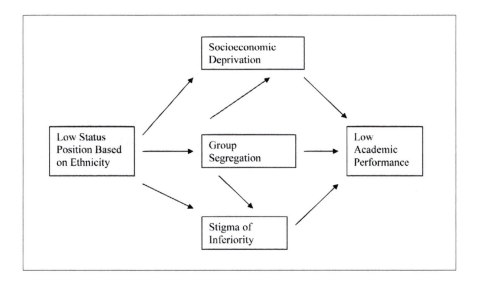

Figure 4.2 How low ethnic position causes poor academic performance
Source: Based on data from Fischer, Hout, Jankowski, Lucas, Swidler and Voss, 1996.

In this model, one can see how low status in society leads to deprivation, group segregation, and the stigma of inferiority. As a result, it is no wonder that low academic performance occurs disproportionately in ethnic minority groups.

We have seen that the environment for blacks in America today poised to go to college is one of compound accumulated disadvantages, including almost no improvement in average personal wealth, continuing and reinforced negative self-images, low academic expectations, and a continuing segregation that tends to amplify disadvantages. The persistent negative stereotypes about black genetic intelligence themselves are part and parcel of the negative environment in which they live.

Gender Disadvantage

Contemporary scholars looking at class and the social environment also often remark on how gender is different, but still interlocking. Pamela Abbott and Roger

Sapsford (1987) note that historically women and men form two different classes within the same family. For example, it is common to find that statistically the father's occupational advantage is more often passed along to sons, not daughters. Those women I interviewed from all age ranges made references to gender as an expression of class. One college graduate in her eighties described the common fate for women in 1930s rural America:

> Well, they didn't do much of anything, unless they took music or something like that. They ended up as farmer's wives, or with their husbands making all the decisions. They just followed what their husbands did. They didn't have money for themselves, the father decided what to spend money on, where to spend it. The wife didn't have much to say about that. It was just very boring.

According to many alumnae I interviewed from that Depression Era, women had very limited choices in careers; basically one could be a secretary, nurse or a teacher. One woman who attended college in the sixties spoke about common expectations. She reached a turning point in her life that coincided with the rise of the feminist movement:

> I remember going up the Janss steps at UCLA, I really didn't want to get married, I really didn't know what I wanted to do. And I saw these tables of women reading feminist books and I felt very relieved and excited, I felt not alone. The community I grew up in was conservative and it was an expected thing to get married after college. I saw a different path, it wasn't codified, but the feminist movement was emerging. I think my life would have been very different if I were two or three years older. I think I came of age right during that movement. It made a difference in my life.

She described further what many women experienced in graduate school, and doubtlessly still do, perhaps in less direct ways:

> I had another professor, a Southern gentleman, who told me point blank no matter what I did I wouldn't get higher than a B in his class because females didn't belong in graduate school. They were taking places that belonged to males.

Today students still face gender obstacles, as a university counselor told me:

> I have the students getting married because mom and dad want them to. Mom and dad spoke to so and so from their home town, 'we really think you should get married. But you have to stay at home until this happens. You can go to school as long as your husband supports you.' They're coming here and they're starting to develop their own self-identities and in a lot of ways that creates problems because of the emphasis on tradition at home.

One student described to me what might be characterized as arranged marriages where poor families plan for their daughters to marry sons of families from Mexico to lift economic burden and provide what they see as security for their grown children. Conversely, the gender roles in Latino society also end up influencing the educational options of men:

> In Latino families it is expected that a man will do what he has to do to take care of his family. The one who is the major bread winner. I don't think anyone actually told him, 'you don't have time for school.' It was more cultural. 'Oh, you're getting married, you're having a baby, you don't have time for school.'

In this way, men too sometimes end up with restricted options for higher education as a result of firm, traditional gender roles. Especially in particular ethnic groups, it is expected that males immediately go to work and continue throughout life to be the primary bread winner.

One young woman I interviewed has a mother who works in a factory and father who drives a truck. Neither parent went beyond a sixth grade education in Mexico. She tells me that her father doesn't want her to go to college because of the cost. Sadly, she tells me that she doesn't talk to her father: "We don't really have a father-daughter relationship really." She then reveals that her father wanted her to be a boy. Furthermore, her parents seem to believe that she isn't capable of going to college, that she isn't smart enough: "I'm not not worth anything." At the end of our interview she admits to me that she suffered from severe depression in early high school. When I ask her what happened she tells me, "my friends were not very supportive, they were trying to put me down. And I listened to them. Then I realized that they are useless. I was better on my own. That's how I got better."

In sum, although there has been a remarkable increase in the number of women in college, gender is still a strong part of the environment, the context within which low-income students interact with colleges.

Meritocracy in Admissions Ineffective

If affirmative action no longer has support from the American public, what impact might a meritocracy, or university admissions based purely on academic qualifications, have on women, ethnic minority students, and low-income student generally? Implicit in the support of a meritocratic approach to admissions is the belief that there is relative equality in our society. However, the low-income students I spoke with for this book talked about the lack of understanding in the general public about their efforts to survive and prosper in America: "They don't even know how it is to be like we are." Critics of affirmative action often do not understand the lack of resources at home, and something as simple as having a parent to help with homework questions. One young student interviewed argued, "I think they should see us first, and then they can criticize, they can talk about us. But not first." Conservative positions on affirmative action often assume that such policies serve to give ethnic minority students an advantage. However, when I posed this question to ethnic minority students they interpreted preferential admissions policies as benefiting middle-class and upper-class young people. In other words, the low-income students already assumed a formal or informal admissions advantage for children from wealthy families.

> AUTHOR: If you made admissions decisions at a university would you consider background?
> STUDENT: No, it wouldn't matter to me. Because, maybe because they have a single mother it's not their fault.
> AUTHOR: No, I don't mean that they would have a disadvantage, rather than you would give them preference if they faced more obstacles.
> STUDENT: What do you mean by disadvantage?
> AUTHOR: Obstacles such as poverty.
> STUDENT: Yes, I probably would. Because if they didn't do a crime, I probably would. If he or she is applying to college is because they want to know and it is fair to give them an opportunity.

As illustrated by this example, low-income families often assume there is a conscious effort to perpetuate an advantage for the upper classes in college admissions which stands in stark contrast to the middle-class assumptions about the legacy of affirmative action.

Furthermore, faculty members and students I spoke with did not like the idea of being admitted or hired solely because of the color of their skin. Some faculty and administrators see that there are two sides to the question. While one doesn't want a purely race- or class-based admissions decision, according to those holding this position, it needs to be taken into consideration somehow. Removing race completely from admissions decisions, as has been done at the University of California, leads directly to a narrowing of the types of students likely to attend college. In a general way, low-income students, faculty, and administrators tend to want to use a formula that would weigh more heavily towards admitting on the basis of academic merit, with a consideration of some undetermined weight for obstacles of race and class. When in interviews I bring up the notion of selective schools using a "character" evaluation in admissions decisions, almost everyone objects. It is interesting that the same general "holistic" approach elicits different responses depending on what is factored into that whole-person analysis. How do first-generation college students respond to the notion of class- rather than race-based admissions? Most I queried see the two as being closely related or interlocked. In concert with some of the experts in the field, many of those I interviewed talked about how focusing on class moves one conveniently away from the uncomfortable discussion of historical racism and slavery in America.

In my interviews, faculty and administrators often expressed great suspicion of meritocracy as an approach for admission practices. Words like "dangerous," "scary," and "terrifying" cropped up, fueled by a belief that "merit" has been historically defined by the empowered, dominant group. As opposed to those eugenics advocates presented earlier in Chapter 1, those I interviewed spoke of talent evaluation hiding behind a consistent lack of social support for low-income children. While many saw that there have been improvements in leveling the playing field, virtually no one felt that we had arrived to a point where everyone had equal life chances: "It's not about everybody getting what they deserve. To a certain extent it is who you know, who gives you the opportunity to go a little further."

Students know that there is a categorization and sorting function in education meant rhetorically to be an open meritocracy, but which in reality too often means placement based on class. This happens naturally through the location of K-12 schools in working-class or upper-class neighborhoods, and within individual schools. In this way, there can be a functional aspect of public education that routes children into paths that lead back to their class or origin. One can see this steering process in the data on low numbers of ethnic minority populations in professional careers. Many argue that schools in their sorting function are making career and life decisions for students. In this context, meritocracy only functions to evaluate those who have been sorted into the college track. Consequently, faculty and university administrators point to unequal preparation in K-12 as the primary reason that meritocractic admissions do not work.

The issue of meritocracy is especially interesting when one moves away from selective college admissions and looks instead at second- and third-tier institutions. As some scholars point out, there isn't really an admissions problem for low-income students at regional comprehensive institutions. If students meet minimal academic requirements (approximately a B average), they are admitted. Because of this fact, some feel on balance that the meritocratic approach at the selective colleges is more defensible, because a kind of college selection safety net exists. "Even though the upper classes are definitely getting into the better institutions, it's not so bad for the lower classes. They can still move up," is a typical response I heard from students. In this way, many I spoke with would prefer to define merit as effort: "I would select the ones that are going to work hard, more than the ones that have good grades." They note that native intelligence is no guarantee of success, and a work ethnic is more valuable: "If they really want something they're really going to fight for it." Those students I interviewed were often living examples of this drive and fight for a college education, regardless of innate talent measures: "I'm not the best student, I know that, but I never give up."

Sidebar Portrait: Anne

Anne is a black sophomore college student raised in South-Central Los Angeles. From a poor and notoriously gang-riddled section of the city, she describes herself as lower-middle class. Raised by a single mother from Detroit with a high school education, Anne was consistently encouraged to do well in school: "It was always school first." The story Anne repeatedly heard from her mother was that it was not important for previous generations to get a college degree, but nowadays it was crucial, that "you can hardly get anywhere without it." Her mother used to work in property management but is now retired. Anne talks about being read to as a child, but this did not result in her being a "reader." She also received encouragement early on from her older cousins who went to college. Nevertheless, Anne admits that she didn't even really know or understand what college involved. Once at the university, she changed her major from biology because of the difficulty of the hard sciences academically: "I watch *Animal Planet* 24 hours a day, but I can't go to class and do it. It takes it all out for me," she explained.

Anne tells me that she had great trepidation about going to college after hearing stories of strict teachers and high academic expectations. Nevertheless, as is true of many college students from all social classes, she talks with excitement about the sense of freedom and emerging adulthood she experienced in her first year. Oddly, Anne admits that she doesn't really like school and that it is not a top priority for her in life. She divulges being on academic probation twice, but likes the lifestyle college affords—not the academics. This is an attitude that leads to conflict with her mother. Anne thinks about a life after college that isn't dependent on good performance, and instead makes plans so she isn't "lost." When I ask her if she goes to college to prepare for a career, she hesitates and says that she just focuses on meeting people. Anne likes to work on campus and describes having too much free time as a student. She blames the excessive spare time in college life for leading her to distraction from her studies. Overall, she gives the impression of drifting interests in various different majors and careers from veterinary science to stand-up comedy. A sociology major now, she admits that she doesn't even know what "sociology" means, and really wants to be an actress anyway.

Anne is in the Educational Opportunity Program (EOP) and has found it useful in supporting her through the adjustment to college. When she struggled in her math courses in her first year, EOP provided a tutor for her. She has also found a network of friendships in the EOP program which smoothed her transition to college. In response to my questions about common problems low-income students have, she describes college as not "being for everybody." When pressed, she points to difficulties getting financial aid, pressure to go to college by parents, and other responsibilities at home that pull students away from the university. Mostly Anne talks about a general lack of interest in college shown by many students often because they don't want to study things that have limited practical application: "It's a waste of time" is how she summarizes their attitude.

For Anne it is clear that the attraction of college is more personal enrichment rather than career development. She talks about how students have a chance to "find themselves" and are shaped by their experience. "Just grow up. That's what I think it's there for." Anne also speaks about the importance of experiencing and knowing those from other cultures. When I ask her how her life would be different without college, she tells me that she would just be at home doing nothing at all. I then question her about public support of college education regardless of social class, and she revealingly confuses my question for advocacy of mandatory post-secondary education, responding that not everyone should be forced to go to college. Nevertheless, Anne feels that admissions policies are unfair. As with some of the other low-income college students I interviewed, when I ask about admissions preferences for disadvantaged students she misinterprets my question, thinking that I'm asking if disadvantaged students should be especially disadvantaged in admissions: "Like being in and out of jail, you don't want that. For instance in Compton, if you went to a school that was widely known for gangs, and given your background and where you are from, and they just say 'no.' What does that do? Just because you live a certain place and live a certain way, shouldn't make a decision on whether or not you go to college."

Anne does not think primarily of college as a way to move up the socio-economic ladder. In fact, after I mention money as a common motivation for attending college she challenges the notion: "Is that what college is for?" She then comments very directly on the lessened economic value of a college education at a state university such as the one she is attending. Anne tells me that she imagines someone with a degree from Stanford will get a job in corporate America much more easily and will move up in the world as planned by their families. As opposed to those who see college education as a great equalizer, she instinctively recognizes the hierarchy of prestige and value in college degrees. She knows she is not getting the same benefit from her college education in terms of future life chances.

In Anne I see an apt example of what will be termed later in the book as a "marginal" student who will become, even with an earned degree, a "marginal" graduate. While the use of the term "marginal" of course has derogatory connotations, it accurately describes the position of students like Anne within a university, and the impact of a college degree on them once graduated. I found it particularly intriguing that someone from a disadvantaged background would see the function of college in terms similar to those of the traditionally privileged, as a broadening opportunity for personal development. Maybe Anne is really talking about the need for "worldliness" pointed to regularly in my journey to understand the poor college student. Is Anne uninterested in getting good grades in college because she hasn't done well in the past, as a way of protecting her sense of self-worth? On the other hand, she admits not even liking to read and shows little real connection with the content of what she is learning. One imagines after years of forced public education, she regards education as a necessary evil, which is not for everyone, not for her.

Sidebar Portrait: Richard

Richard is a professor at a college in Texas with a long career in both the corporate world and academia. An athlete at a major Southern University as a student, Richard begins by talking about his background of growing up in the South in a working-class family, with farmers on his father's side of the family, and teachers on his mother's. Although his parents were high school educated, his grandmother had graduated from a historically black two-year teacher's college. Additionally, Richard's aunts on his father's side were both teachers, one eventually an elementary school principal. On his mother's side, no one in the family went beyond an elementary school education. "It was typical farm life. As soon as they were big enough to help out, they dropped out of school," he tells me.

Richard describes a bifurcated childhood influence, with on one side a country farm life, on the other a more intellectually stimulating life from his father's side of the house through contact with a boarding house of sorts for single teachers. "There were teachers, books, newspapers, magazines all over the house." Richard's father died when he was in the seventh grade, and as a result he always had dinner at his aunt's house because his mother worked until eight at night. "We usually had between two and four younger teachers boarding with us, and consequently around the dinner table there would be ten people nightly." He describes lively conversations about current events, religion, and politics; in fact, his aunt wrote a book on High Street Baptist Church, one of the central churches involved in the Civil Rights Movement. Richard explains the impact of attending the High Street Baptist Church on his eventual pursuit a college degree: "There had been more of a taste of it, more of an awareness of it at High Street. So that's the place that even in the generation before me there were black doctors and lawyers." Richard talks of a grandmother who only completed the third grade but who held a strong belief in the value of education: "Almost every day she spent with me she would say, 'I want you to get a good education.'" He tells me that her bedrock belief in education wasn't just about money and career advancement, but a basic desire for him to know and experience more. Here we see again the emphasis on worldliness through college.

A star basketball player in high school, as well as the recipient of a national scholar award, Richard had a number of college options. He did not feel limited in terms of college choices by his background: "I thought anything was possible," and describes an early life where "everything was going his way." Richard applied to primarily East Coast schools because of his knowledge of them, as well as his various connections through basketball. A Presidential Scholar from Virginia as a high school junior, he visited the White House when Lyndon Johnson was President and attended a reception on the East Lawn with celebrities Arthur Ashe, Bill Bradley, and John Updike.

Richard tells me of a difficult adjustment to college: "I didn't have any idea of what college was going to be like, categorically. And I certainly didn't have any idea of what the university was going to be like." Richard tells how his high school coach drove and dropped him off at the university: "Here's this gigantic place, I don't know anybody." He also talked about the academic challenge of going to the university after his high school preparation. "I remember the first Calculus class, the very first day, the guy holds up a book, 'How many of you used this in high school?' It was a big Thompson Calculus book. Usually you use it for two semesters for differential and integral calculus. Almost everybody in class held up their hands." Richard had never seen the book and had trouble adjusting when the professor decided to skip the first half of the text because the other students were better academically prepared.

Richard talks about part of the adjustment problem arising from the South in the 60s: "When I went to college there were a total of 15 black students, I think, in the entire university." He describes a very isolated existence on campus with five other male black students from his class (the black female students were separated), who all sat together in the cafeteria. Having been raised in the segregated South, Richard understood the general expectations and culture: "You kind of understood your boundaries; you did what was familiar; that was easy to do." He describes the joys of learning and expanding his knowledge of the world with simple cultural advantages such as listing to classical music. He also mentioned an art movie house that became popular in the 60s showing European films: "That was an eye opener."

Richard reflected on the difficult social adjustment to college, as well as the positive attention that made the students want to succeed. "It's like when you get some attention, you do your best." The flip side of being in the social and academic spotlight was that sometimes he tried too hard. "I wouldn't let it go. I was the last one to leave the library. I was the last one to leave the basketball court. And sometimes that level of fixating on things takes you out of the flow." As I heard from many low-income students, the immense pressure is a motivator to do well in school but isn't always productive: "It hurt us in the long run."

The experience of being a black basketball player at his college signaled a very important change at the elite Southern institution. In fact, the university was at first reluctant to grant athletic scholarships to black students and instead offered an academic scholarship to Richard who was gifted in both arenas. An all-white team, a perennial basketball powerhouse, had lost badly to an integrated team in the NCAA tournament. The conservative factions insisted on defending the old "style," which meant no black athletic scholarships. The university talked about not wanting to "lower their standards." It was another two years after Richard attended before the university gave out its first athletic scholarship to a black player. As evidence of the reactionary attitude of the university at that time, Richard described how the university was slow to condemn the assassination of Dr. King which led to large student demonstrations. The black students of his era were caught up in the slow transition of the university from a bastion of the old South forced to accept change.

As with many low-income college students with which I spoke, Richard felt a responsibility to help out his mother as much as possible. Suffering from chronic high blood pressure, his mother had become ill and could not work very much while he attended college. He sent her the $35 so called "laundry money" that he received from basketball: "I really didn't need it. I had my meals paid for, in fact I used to sell people food because I had my scholarship and I also had training table. I didn't have any money, but I had lots of food."

In his second year, his coach sent Richard to play basketball in a New York City summer league. He stayed in Connecticut with a protective family, but took the train into the city. Richard pauses as he remembers back to the first time he saw Grand Central Station and walked out into the loud bustle of the city. He describes making friends and running around the city until the last train left for Connecticut at two in the morning. "I think that exposure to the city really opened my eyes to a lot of things. I saw another kind of life than what I had been exposed to in Danville." Richard describes the familiar theme of students of returning home to find how much it has seemingly changed: "I wasn't satisfied to hang out and do the things we used to do." The university changed him. He even grew apart from the friends who went to other schools such as North Carolina Central, where his girlfriend attended.

Richard described a "preppy environment" at the university: "You were expected to have a certain kind of demeanor." The pressure to conform took on a very specific racial connotation on the basketball court. He had a falling out with his coach because he refused to cut his afro hair style, something that had taken on special meaning at that time in American social history, and was benched. Richard calls the action highly symbolic, that he was pressured to fit in. "Of course, this was a time when black folks in the country were saying, 'I'm not going to fit in.'" Richard faced other overt and more subtle racist attitudes at Duke. He recalled a professor who directly told black students that they would not get an "A" in his course. The intended lesson was to conform or fail: "We have to change if we were going to be successful." With peers, even informal discussions in the dorms often left black students feeling out of place because of the experiences of their affluent peers.

What was the impact of a degree on his fellow black students? Two out of the five in his immediate group dropped out. When I remark that given the obstacles, his classmates did well, he reminds me about the uniqueness of these students. The students who were fortunate to be the first to go to the university were exceptionally talented and clearly the academic best from their communities. "We hadn't been exposed to maybe everything we should have, but we were above average students."

The impact on Richard of his degree was significant. It was a booming time in America and engineers from good schools were sought after. He received three job offers from three interviews. However, I was surprised when I asked him if he felt that his social status had changed as a result of his degree: "Yes and no. We were still in the South, so there was status but no status." Richard talked about new respect in the black community, but not in the white South: "I don't think it mattered one hill of beans that I was an engineer in the larger community." He described the experience of being hired in Virginia for an engineering job along with a white man. At lunch they both went to J.C. Penny to open an account for household items needed for their new residences. "Two engineers, same place of employment, same salary, everything the same—they declined mine." He was forced to go home and use his mother's account to get the appliances he needed.

"You were only one step away from ever being superior to anyone no matter how much education you had—that was always true in the South."

Nevertheless, Richard believes in the importance of higher education. He talks about the changed perception where education has come for many to be regarded as not necessary. Richard identifies the concentration on money and link of wealth to success as part of the problem. When I asked about public support of higher education based on perceived talent, he became thoughtful for a moment. He then described a parable he had heard at a recent conference about someone who wanted to surf in Hawaii. "He made just enough money to live and spent all his time surfing." In contrast another man worked hard all his life and then retired. Then both happen to get ill and have to go to the hospital. Neither have enough money to pay their hospital bills, so they will have to be supported by the public. He asks, "Is one more deserving than the other?" In Richard's mind, they are equally deserving: "If this is a just and equitable society, you cannot make that distinction."

As an experienced professor, Richard describes college as functioning on one level to teach students how to conform before entering the larger society. He sees this function as being especially strong for low-income college students, as it was for him. Richard recalls one stuttering student in an introduction to business course who had trouble getting a full sentence out of his mouth. He did not have an affliction, he was just too afraid to speak. However, over the course of the college career Richard saw him grow to become an articulate young man and eventually a successful fashion designer.

Finally, Richard sees private education as doing many of the things that the publics should be doing. He describes his experience at a private university as a graduate student where the focus was much more on the individual needs of students. In public higher education, "there are more people, and there are standards that have to be met, it's not really about training the individual." He believes that society regardless of the type of college has lost sight of the public benefit of education: "It's not just making one person better off, that's the public piece, it's by making this one person better that we are all better off."

Sidebar Portrait: Karen

Karen is a woman in her mid-fifties who attended a Southern college for two years right out of high school. She received little support or guidance from her parents in regards to which college to attend or how to get in. As with many women from her generation, she describes delaying her education because of family responsibilities. Her husband's career came first and her economic fortune was tied to his: "Economically, my life depended on my mate. I did not create wealth for myself or my family." While Karen claims that she didn't feel any socially promoted limitations, she does admit that traditional male careers did not seem to interest her: "I don't think I lacked any options," she says in sum.

Karen's mother, who, like her daughter, left college to raise a family, said that she wanted her "youngsters" to go to college because it would lead to a better job: "I heard recently that people with a college degree make about $23,000 more than a high school graduate." She also pointed to the importance of college in providing the occasion for meeting "people of better backgrounds." Karen says that her mother always wished she had a degree and was very upset when her daughter left school, as she had done years before for similar reasons. A chemical engineer, Karen's father said for him it wasn't so much the money that led him to encourage his children to go to college, but to lead "a fuller, more satisfying life. Why not go to college?"

Karen raised a family and then returned to finish her degree at 50 years old: "I had to compete with younger brains, learn computer skills, and so forth." Additionally, she took a vocal minor and was "too old to begin much of a career using my body as an instrument," she tells me plainly. Nevertheless, with additional time and effort she managed to earn a 4.0 average and joined a local opera company. Although she did miss out on the extracurricular activities, Karen feels that she had an advantage over the younger students in relating on more of a peer level with the faculty and staff at the university.

Six months after graduation she summarizes her experience telling me that she did not seek a college education for employment: "I do not feel that I am qualified for any position I want to take, should I decide to seek regular employment." Her degree in communications has led to some freelance work as a "videographer," but the work is "irregular." College did benefit her career-wise by making connections with other students involved in her field, which led to two brief jobs after graduation. Karen sees the benefit in college from achieving training and education that is respected. However, because she picked an art-oriented communications field, she realizes that it requires her to promote herself and her work aggressively. "I haven't made the best transition," she admits.

Karen describes herself as a "home schooling mom," now retired since her kids are grown. Clearly much of her identity is tied up in her home schooling role. She speaks with pride about the pleasure of sharing her knowledge with her children. However, because she had not at the time earned her bachelor degree she was limited to an unofficial role in this capacity. Karen taught all four of her children in high school and successfully prepared them for college. Two of her children are now in graduate school. Karen points to the importance of college in teaching critical thinking, to "listen to both sides."

Karen is in many ways an example of a largely by-gone attitude by women towards a college education. Her college attendance was not motivated by necessity to find a high paying occupation or to move up in a general way in society. While she clearly expresses an understanding of the value of a college education, she knows how irrelevant her learning is to any practical application in the job market. For many women of her generation and earlier who deferred to their husband's careers, college represents an opportunity for enrichment and personal development.

Conclusion

In this chapter I show how women and ethnic minority students are interlocked in disadvantage with the more general category of low-income students. Statistics show that black and Latino students are far behind Asian and white populations in graduating from both high school and college. The disastrous erosion of affirmative action policies has forced a larger debate on meritocracy the future of which is unclear. Nevertheless, the environment for some ethnic minority groups, such as African-Americans, is distressingly negative in terms of economic mobility, improvements in self-image, expectations of college attendance, personal wealth, and integration with more affluent communities.

When one looks at group status and academic performance world wide, it is typical to find that those who are in lower classes predictably have lower standardized test scores and educational success, even among the same races.

Table 4.1 Group differences around the world

Country	High status	Low status	High test scores/school success	Low test scores/school success
United States	Whites	Blacks	Whites	Blacks
	Whites	Latinos	Whites	Latinos
	Whites	American Indian	Whites	American Indian
Great Britain	English	Irish, Scottish	English	Irish, Scottish
Northern Ireland	Protestants	Catholics	Protestants	Catholics
Australia	Whites	Aborigines	Whites	Aborigines
New Zealand	Whites	Maoris	Whites	Maoris
South Africa	English	Afrikaaners	English	Afrikaaners
Belgium	French	Flemish	French	Flemish
Israel	Jews	Arabs	Jews	Arabs
	Western Jews	Eastern Jews	Western Jews	Eastern Jews
India	Nontribals	Tribal people	Nontribals	Tribal people
	Brahmin	Harijan	Brahmin	Harijan
	High caste	Low caste	High caste	Low caste
Czechoslovakia	Slovaks	Gypsies	Slovaks	Gypsies
Japan	Non-Burakumin	Burakumin	Non-Burakumin	Burakumin
	Japanese Origin	Korean Origin	Japanese Origin	Korean Origin

Source: Fischer, Hout, Jankowski, Lucas, Swidler and Voss, 1996, Table 8.1.

Furthermore, one of the most important points the authors of *Inequality by Design: Cracking The Bell Curve Myth* make is that in America the poor are disproportionately represented by women. Since IQ men and women score equally on IQ tests—in fact the test was designed to find no gender difference—the claim that those with higher IQs are wealthy is simply wrong on the basis of gender alone. Finally, they argue that the United States does less than any other advanced nation to reduce poverty, and it is a clear decision by Americans choosing by policy to do less. In fact, pubic policy is full of examples of class bias exemplified by the huge and significant mortgage interest deduction in taxes which the poor typically cannot benefit from equally.

Universities through their admissions policies have "gamed" the system using students and student mix to their advantage, not to advance a social agenda (Kahlenberg, 1997). For instance, many selective universities rely on recruiting international students as a way of appearing diverse. Consequently, some critics now claim that affirmative action does a highly imperfect job of creating equal opportunity because not all minorities are disadvantaged, and others from lower class are disadvantaged but not minority. The unfolding argument holds that social class needs to be emphasized because a focus on race disadvantages only prevents us from understanding the deeper class context: "While the political argument is important, the ultimate reason for emphasizing class over race is that, on the merits, addressing race alone marginalizes larger and more fundamental issues of class" (Kahlenberg, 1997, p. 203). Certainly, there is a general awareness by experts and the general public of a chronic inability in our society to serve low-income students for recognizable reasons starting with a simple lack of family wealth. However, at the same time there is a reluctance to use strict policy instruments, such as affirmative action, to correct the problem. Again, we find in admissions policies the troubling indifference of the public to the fate of students from poor families.

Nevertheless, some recent scholars have commented on the impact of the rolling back of affirmative action in college admissions practices and have come to the conclusion that African Americans will continue to be "substantially underrepresented" at selective universities for the foreseeable future (Krueger, Rothstein and Turner, 2006). Using national statistics and predictive statistic formulas, these scholars argue that affirmative action in some form must continue to support the correction of the historical legacy of inequality. As opposed to what seems to be the prevailing opinion in the general public, predictive analysis leads to an argument against the use of class or family income supplanting of race-based admission preferences. In this way, support for affirmative action, or some other corrective policy, is needed because disadvantage for ethnic minority students persists.

Does the general public now have confidence in a meritocracy? The current college-going generation was raised on an active dialogue about civil rights and affirmative action. They are familiar with the debate and understand, at least intellectually, the arguments for past policies. This is a very different generation from my own, which was surrounded by often violent racial conflict, and certainly that of my parents where the first words in describing a stranger would usually involve an ethnic or nation of origin label. The public seems now to reject racial bias as a determining factor in an individual's success. This position says that the longer that colleges and the rest of society make decisions based on ethnicity, the longer racism will persist. It is believed that if everything were based on merit that eventually the whole social class and ethnicity problem would disappear. Nevertheless, what has been presented in this chapter, and book as a whole, clearly challenges the viewpoint that there is now a level playing field in society, or, more specifically, in college.

Chapter 5

Case Study: Recent Immigrants to America

This chapter argues that, in ways congruent with other low-income groups, educational institutions are inadequately serving the needs of immigrant populations. A case study of one group at a public university in Southern California illustrates this point. In my role at the California State University I have oversight of a special program to prepare children of migrant farm workers for college. In response to the dire statistics about large numbers of high school drop outs and miniscule attendance in college by the children of migratory farm workers, the local high school district requested the development of this unusual program which combines a university course in the afternoon (Introduction to Psychology the year of the study), with a morning of intensive study and language skills. Most of the students are foreign-born, and approximately one-third of the students lack proper citizenship documentation. The program ends with a culminating event held in our converted chapel auditorium on the grounds of the former State hospital upon which the university is situated. The event never fails to inspire and sadden me at the same time.

This chapter shows in the children of migrant worker population studied how educational institutions with the best intensions, often because of complex reasons, actually end up perpetuating inequality. For seven years I have watched students come and go each summer through this special program, which seeks to prepare as best we can some of the most severely disadvantaged students in our society for entrance to college. As the university administrator in charge of the program, I can tell the reader of a very specific example in the use of grades the way our educational system inadvertently perpetuates inequality. Each year school district and university administrators in the program are dismayed by the low grades students receive. Typically, a half dozen of the students out of the 30-35 students receive C, D, and failing grades. Additionally, A grades are rare. Over the six years the school district has worked to identify the best prepared students to participate in this program. Out of approximately 1,500 potential students in the County, 35 are identified. In other words, generally the students in this program are the highest performing at the secondary level. Nevertheless, the performance of the students measured by traditional college grades scales is disappointing.

In this way then, a program specifically designed by skilled and well-meaning K-12 and college administrators ends up in the case of a group of students within the program every year being potentially counter-productive. Instead of ending with a college credit, students have an unusable transcript. Additionally, even for the students who receive C grades, it is likely that many will now be even more concerned about their ability to perform at the college level. In this way, the grading system, even in a program specifically designed to bolster the chances of college success, serves to perpetuate and confirm fears of an inability to perform in college.

Each day I interviewed a different migrant student under a cluster of weeping willow trees far out on the South Quad of the campus. I use pieces of these interviews throughout the book, but want here to give separate time to the special group of students because of their broader significance. I also observed the students in the classroom regularly and those observations will serve as central vignettes in the larger story I tell in this book.

"Why is the university educating bean pickers and janitors?" a young Latino student reads out loud in front of a classroom with a shaking voice from a mess of single page notes he holds like a mirror in one hand. As the student continues to read the notes which are posts on a computer blog, I look around the room and see eyes welling up. A recent local newspaper article celebrating their success at attempting to move up in the world is under public attack. The university that has tried to help them is maligned. The Latino student continues to read the hateful, angry comments: "Educate them to do what?" and "Send the bill to Mexico!" he reads out loud. The built trust is gone in humiliation, replaced by the stark reality of bigotry and hatred. A Latina teenager with hair severely pulled back says softly, "We deserve a chance too."

The college experience of recent immigrants to the United States provides a powerful case study for a book about college access and mobility. The mobility issues are writ large in the immigrant population from Mexico that I have come to know in Ventura County through my job as an administrator at a public university. The all important functions of language, culture, and economics are clear, as well as the specific experiences the students describe with early pregnancy and marriage, alcoholism, and family violence. The obstacles that Mexican immigrants encounter are similar to the ones that other disadvantaged Americans endure. Additionally, what has become at times an ugly debate about immigration policy in the United States reveals shifting attitudes towards public education, and perhaps even a questioning of the responsibility of society to provide a pathway for moving up in the land of opportunity.

Some of what I found in this summer-long experience was expected, some not. I foresaw the importance of English language acquisition, but did not fully appreciate how utterly dependent success in school rests on this skill. I certainly understood the importance of culture, but did not see the more subtle ways that it would exhibit itself in forming barriers to college. One could predict an array of social problems among the poor, but I had yet to grasp the significance of the link to culture and family. Most of all, I was surprised by the extremely charged and tense family dynamics behind the students. Finally, one can read about economic depravation, but until seeing firsthand how it affects young adults one doesn't appreciate its significance. Some reading this book may criticize the approach as overly negative and dampening of the inspiration to go to college that we so often hear in education circles. However, I find the detailed appreciation of the obstacles students such as those in Summer College face moving. Those who do succeed in spite of a system that works against them are truly remarkable.

Classroom Observations

The university is built on the grounds of the former Camarillo State Mental Hospital. The mission revival style buildings constructed by the WPA in the 1930s are under a process of slow renovation that has left iron bars on many of the classroom windows, a reminder of the former residents. The Bell Tower building holds the majority of the classrooms for the university. Restored with unusual meticulousness for a state educational institution, the classrooms themselves are mostly long rectangles in shape, forcing the faculty members to decide between standing at one end or in the middle, swinging back and forth like a sprinkler head while lecturing. I join a morning session where the teacher assigned to help the students with language and study skills, discusses careers with the students. The teacher works with migrant students in the local high school and already knows many of them in this program. A student recalls a conversation she had with a boy her own age who she met working in the fields with her father. She asked the boy why he wasn't in school; he replied that it wasn't an option. "He had to work to get money for the family." The other students nod knowingly. This theme of both economic necessity and family as hindrance to college attendance is again one I consistently find in talking to college students from low-income families.

Despite the fact that these students obviously face many barriers, the teacher manages to engage them in a lively discussion of various careers. I suspect that many of the students never considered the possibility of working in professions common to middle-class families. Their ambitions have been dampened by low expectations and limited exposure to the professional world. Almost all of the careers mentioned in class would be a step up economically from working in the fields. A child of migrant workers herself, the teacher asks the students, "Have you seen how hard they work picking strawberries? I cry every time I drive through the fields." The reality for many Mexican immigrants is that they under constant fear of forced return to Mexico. Parents are understandably protective of their children, and the common assumption is that applying to college will somehow alert authorities. The students discuss how many who lack immigration documents, or "papers," are afraid of going to college. The teacher encourages the students saying that "education will be your passport."

The approach of the course is to tie the presentations back to the students' culture. While linking personal experience to the content of a course is generally a good strategy, this appears to be especially effective when working with first-generation college students who need to find a handle on the course material. They learn from this practice of bringing in their culture that their own experiences are valued in the academy and that they have personal knowledge which is useful in college. Because of language issues some students are uncomfortable giving academic presentations. The faculty member teaching the degree credit course encourages students to role play and dramatize the lessons from the psychology textbook. These presentations are powerful. The students present in groups on topics such as teenage pregnancy, divorce, alcoholism, human development, and family relationships. The role playing sometimes leads to students raising their voices in mock heated exchanges. While the student audience often giggles, it strikes me as the laughter of recognition. The tense situations the students portray are not new to them—they have seen family conflict, teenage pregnancy, family violence, and abuse in their own lives. I doubt that one would find such energized performance in a psychology course with middle-class young adults.

Family

'At some point you disappoint yourself or your parents.'

I saw deep love in these students for their parents, as well as dismissive and even resentful attitudes. Many of the students talk about needing to pay their parents back for the struggle they've had in their lives and the sacrifices they've made for their children. Others talk about parental alcoholism, abuse, disregard, and overbearing control. In many cases I was struck by the look of distain and even hatred for their parents in the students' expressions. In some cases the students feel grateful for the struggle of their parents on their behalf; in others they blame the parents for not providing a better life.

In one skit the students present a story about a teenager who is accepted to Harvard University but whose single mother does not want the child to leave. This skit turns into a violent argument with the mother saying the student is selfish and that she needs help at home with her other children. "You want to leave and have me do all the work," the mother says. An older sister intervenes and says, "I quit school because I had to work for you and I got pregnant. I don't want the same thing to happen to her." I look around the classroom and see that the other students are riveted—this conversation is all too familiar. Afterwards, the students who did the presentation explain that parents only know to work hard to survive. They don't understand school as work. Furthermore, female students often end up choosing a father-figure boyfriend which leads them away from school because they are too often raised by single moms.

This skit points out a reality I've come to understand very clearly in the group of students I studied—they are in deep conflict with their parents. This conflict is complex and multilayered. Recent immigrant families from various places often have a culture which puts extreme importance on the family. Additionally, the years of struggle for survival have led to an increased focus on the immediate family. However, the tensions pulling this unit apart are great. Children from these low-income families either are dissuaded from going to school because the family needs their income to survive, or when encouraged to go to school are put under enormous pressure to succeed in order to "save" the family. The future of many of these families is completely dependent on how well these students do in school.

Symptoms of the deep family divide were found everywhere. One day in class students act out a skit with an Oprah-like talk show format talking about the generational divide. A mother complains, "She doesn't speak Spanish anymore." The daughter replies, "I speak English at school with my friends. Why shouldn't I speak it at home?" Another time, the students present a skit on illegal immigration. The daughter doesn't understand her parents. When she is given $20 for her birthday she erupts, "Twenty dollars? It's my 18th birthday, I'm expecting a car." She continues viciously, "You never have money. Why did you come over here anyway?" And then mirroring what she has heard repeatedly from some conservative Americans, "We're in America, we need to speak English."

Culture

Social institutions can be said to have a culture, a set of beliefs and standard forms of behavior. Those who are aware and expert in this culture are likely to be more successful and respected by others in that same culture. College is a culture with perhaps unusually strong rules of behavior. The standards expressed in the SAT test might best be portrayed as those of a proper preparatory school teacher leading an English composition course in an elite school in New England. With approximately four thousand colleges in America it is hard to generalize, but the college prep school teacher definition of the cultural bias is pretty close to the broad truth about culture and higher education. If one thinks, talks, and studies like a student in an upper-class college preparatory school, the university experience will fall into place. However, if one only recently has learned to write and speak English, has not be surrounded by the canon of Western European literature in a home library, and does not think or behave in expected ways, college appropriateness and success is in question.

In one classroom session the students perform a skit on human development that reveals the cultural clash in attitude towards school. They portray a child growing up at various stages in an American family. In one scene student actors show a parent teaching children "Itsy Bitsy Spider"—something that makes the students laugh loudly at adopting what seems to them a very odd Anglo song. The skit ends with the child graduating from high school and rejecting the parents, preferring to celebrate with her Americanized friends. Later, although they don't really understand the world of education, her parents encourage her to go to college. The story ends before a decision by the daughter has been made. The student narrator then tells us that the reason the group didn't portray a decision is that "everybody has a different destiny." While in this instance the parents ended up encouraging their child to go to school, the value ultimately expressed is that not everyone has to go to college. This skit seems to me to indicate an attitude change in progress in the Mexican-American culture. There is a clear conflict between older Mexican views of college for low-income children, and the new American belief that college can be for anyone. Young adults in the current generation are caught up in this no-man's land with perhaps the somewhat empty assurance that college isn't for everyone. This lukewarm support for students to go to college was something that I consistently saw in the low-income college students I interviewed, especially with Latino children.

The cultural misfit with American higher education also functions in a very practical sense with the students who become young parents. An example of this is when one group does a skit on infertility. We see a couple receiving counseling because of difficulty getting pregnant, and then learning that they will have a baby. At this news the other students in the class clap loudly. I suspect that an upper class or middle class group of students would not have responded with such approval, revealing a very different attitude towards pregnancy and children in their culture, especially among the low-income Latinos. The privileged have long believed in the need for birth control and understood the economic handicap that unwanted/ unplanned children bring.

While I saw expressions of pride and familiarity with their own culture, I also saw understanding of the perhaps unfortunate impact of practices derived from their common culture. In one presentation on Erickson's stages of human development, students explained that "In our culture people have babies when young and leave them in bad places, and they grow up insecure." Also regarding their physical selves, the students stated: "In our culture we don't exercise, we're lazy. We eat at McDonalds and In-'N-Out." According to the students who were presenting, "Hispanics have low self-esteem, especially females. Consume the highest percentage of fast food as an ethnic group." Low activity rate leads to obesity: "50-60% of Latinos are physically inactive" they say. In another skit on eating disorders students tell their classmates that Latin women see models on TV and in magazines and try to look like them. Generally, I surmise from the skit and the reaction from the students in the classroom that there is a very different response to eating disorders in Latin culture, with overall less sympathy and than one would find in middle-class Anglo communities.

Another major thread I discovered in observing Latino students was a lack of confidence or even belief in their cultural background. In an orientation session for freshman students in the special EOP program they learn about "self-assertiveness." Mostly Latinas, some wearing wedding rings, sit upright, alert and look like they are trying hard, but lack confidence. The presenter tells them that they are to learn to be "responsible" for their actions in college, and that aggression is not the same as assertiveness. In general I can tell from some of the verbal expressions used by the students that they have been already somewhat schooled in the dominant culture. The lesson taught to these female low-income students is that they need to be more assertive in certain ways than their culture generally dictates.

Remarkably, the students in the Summer College program expressed a pretty complex understanding of the role of culture in learning. For instance, one day the students did a dance routine outside on the broad lawn where commencement takes place. With spinning, colorful skirts, they perform traditional Mexican dances inviting the other students to take part. The students in the group then teach the other students a contemporary Mexican dance. Afterwards, the students explain that their psychology topic is long- and short-term memory. They show how it was easier for the students to learn the new dance because it was based on other traditional Mexican dance steps. "Because the steps are part of our culture, it was easy for you to learn." The lesson: specific cultural knowledge is an advantage in learning if yours is the dominant culture, the one used in university knowledge.

Social Problems

Throughout my observations and discussions with students I saw direct and indirect evidence of families suffering from various addictions and forms of abuse. While I made no attempt at statistical comparison of frequency of these disorders in this migrant population to the general public, it is logical to expect that the pressure of such hard lives and generations of bottom-class dwelling have led to a greater tendency towards alcoholism and other psychological problems. Nevertheless, the prevalence of signs of such social problems in these young adults surprised me.

One day in class a group does a skit on young marriage that plays like a Greek tragedy. The storyline follows a girl who marries at a young age because she apparently is looking for the father figure missing from her life. The family's fortunes take a very bad turn when the mother reaches menopause and begins rejecting her husband. The husband turns to his sister-in-law for sexual pleasure and this leads to the tragic drug abuse and overdose of their daughter, divorce, and finally suicide. The skit is acted at a very high level of drama with the actors yelling and screaming like fighting parents. Administrators down the hall are disturbed by the loud acting. The young sister of one of the students used as an actor in a previous skit is so distressed by the acting that she leaves the room crying.

On another day, the students present a skit portraying an argument about money at home between parents and children, and mother and father. The mother in the play claims that money is a "man's problem." Finally, one of the children asks for help and goes to a psychologist to discuss the family arguments. This scene seems more prescriptive than descriptive of what would normally occur. Afterwards, the students in the skit note, "In our culture, people get married early, so they often fight in front of their children. The children grow up and do the same thing." In this way, the students describe how social problems are passed on from generation to generation in their culture.

The students exhibit signs of understanding culturally dependent definitions of psychological disorder. For example, students play a scene representing domestic violence. The focus is on the effects on children. At one point a counselor tells the parents, "Your daughters are learning exactly what you are doing." Afterwards, a tall, thin Latino states that "Machismo is part of our culture." Furthermore, a student reads out loud from their report, "Smoking and alcohol abuse are more common among Latinos." The students explain how alcohol has become the number one problem for Latinos: "Latinos culturally have alcohol at celebrations, but such traditional use has expanded over to daily life."

Economics

On the first and most basic level, low-income students don't go to college because they cannot afford to do so. Despite what is popularly understood, the issue isn't only the cost of higher education and financial aid, but the simple need to spend time working for the survival of the family. Financial aid cannot replace foregone wages. Repeatedly, students I talked with described severe economic need which forces child labor, dropping out of school, and for those few who do go to college, the concurrent financial support of their parents. The students repeatedly talk about how hard it is to work and go to school. For those who are lucky enough not to have to work, the pressure of succeeding at school is immense: "Our parents work so hard, working hard at school is the least we can do," one student told me—a common refrain.

Sadly, the students display a worldly understanding of the base unfairness and inequality in the world. One day in the classroom, students present a parable comparing an upper-class family to a struggling Latino family. The wealthy family is characterized as jaded and spoiled; the student actors have fun taking on affectations of the rich such as greeting each other with "Ciao." The skit contrasts two teenage students specifically, one from each family. The wealthy teenager is an arrogant, undisciplined student who takes drugs, and ends up getting a Latino maid fired unfairly. In contrast, the Latino teenager tries hard in school and is good to his parents. The skit strikes me as a morality play with the root meaning being a tragic parable about the unjust fate of humans on earth. People do not get what they deserve—this is the experience these students have learned in life. After the skit, the students comment on the story. "We're not poor Mexicans. We have clothes, just not the clothes we want." They explain with wisdom beyond their years, "It's not just about money. Some people don't have a father, or don't have love." I see here that the students identify their social status as being linked not only to money, but to social and family problems.

Sidebar Portrait: Juan

Juan is the most popular boy in the class. With the other students he is lively and quick to joke, to laugh. He is a star actor in class skits, hamming up parts from an abusive husband to an attentive boyfriend. Juan walks out across the long lawn with a female student after lunch. I can see the two have become fast friends. He approaches me with trepidation, shakes my hand weakly, and lowers his eyes. Juan is nervous, but curious. As with the other students I interviewed, Juan appears to me to be older than his years, suspicious, worldly, but not in a positive way. Juan knows things about the world most children his age in America can't even imagine.

Juan describes himself as "middle class," though from what I learn this is an optimistic description. Everyone in America seems to claim to be middle class. His parents do not speak English and had very limited elementary school education in Mexico. "They can write. Not that much, but a little bit," he says. When I ask about their attitude towards education he says with a soft voice, "They want me to get an education and have a better life." How do they support him in his pursuit of education? Primarily by not insisting that he work in the fields: "Most of the people my age are working." Juan reflects on his difference from his brothers and sisters who were put to work at a young age: "It's really hard when you have nothing at all and you have to work. You have to give up something."

As with most all of the students I interview, Juan talks with conviction about the necessity to go to a good college. At times, this belief in the college good is that of a religious zealot with unquestioning belief: "If you don't study there is no way that you are going to be someone in life." This is another part of the education zeal—college education is directly linked to self-worth for many of these students. I then see a glimpse of the visible world weariness of these teenagers in Juan. "I see most of my family, the other relatives, they have a sorry life. It's really bad because sometimes they don't have enough to eat, they don't have anywhere to live." Juan has a direct view of the bottom of our social system. "They can only wait for a better life by getting an education and going to college."

When I ask Juan about his image of college life he searches for the right words. "It will shake my life." He tells me he wants to study architecture, yet he cannot name an architect. Furthermore, he is strangely unembarrassed by this fact. Juan explains that he likes to draw and is always scribbling home floor plans. I think about his general naiveté about college and professional careers. It also is not lost on me that he is drawing pictures of stable and elaborate homes that he has never lived in.

Going into his junior year in high school, Juan is starting to prepare for college. Along with other students in the migrant program, Juan went on a special college tour and visited the campus of Stanford University, where he dreams of attending. (I feel bad for thinking to myself during the interview that he has no chance of getting into Stanford.) Why Stanford? "I just want to do it to show that I can do something that some people think is impossible." Yet Juan's family resources are very limited. When I ask him if there are books and magazines at home, he tells me matter-of-factly, "No. At home we take care of the house, working, take care of the babies." The second youngest of a family of six, none of whom went beyond elementary school, Juan is aware that it is difficult for young students like him to stay in school, let alone attend college. He tells me that the most difficult part of going to college will simply be staying in college, "It's too much, they can't handle it," speaking of other migrant kids who drop out of high school and college. I later learn from an administrator of the migrant program that they face staggering drop-out rates in high school, let alone college. "Kids just disappear," the administrator tells me.

Juan talks about basic survival and his own struggle. "We've gone through a lot. Just to get here and have a life. It's a different society. In Mexico it's completely different. You have a better chance here to survive." Survival, not success, is in his mind. Unlike many Americans who are convinced about the openness of our society, Juan is aware of his class ceiling. When I ask him to compare his potential benefit of education to someone from a wealthy family, he instantly recognizes a difference: "I don't think it will be the same because of the way my parents used to live. It's very different. You go up just a little bit. I can give my child a better life." This child of migrant workers does not repeat the common American belief that anything is possible in our society—not for him.

Juan reveals the immense pressure to succeed, something that many students from low-income families describe. The family is depending in many cases on the graduates to support the family once they earn their diploma: "I feel like I have to support them financially." He ends by admitting to me the obvious angst he feels to succeed in college: "I feel like if I don't go to college I'm going to fail my family. It's really tough being the first one because you get all the pressure coming from everywhere. Your parents expect a lot from you so it's really hard. They expect you to get the education and be successful. It's really hard because you got the pressure. You have trouble concentrating when studying. You think about telling your family. You're not going to be able to concentrate when you think about the pressure from the family." I ask him when the pressure will end and he replies, "I don't think I'll get rid of the pressure until I graduate from college." Our interview ends and Juan walks slowly back across the wide Quad, wading through the deep grass.

Sidebar Portrait: Maria

Maria is simply an exceptional student. She is the kind of pupil that teachers immediately recognize as talented and very likely to succeed in getting in and staying in college. Maria is one of the rare exceptions of someone from an extremely disadvantaged background who will succeed no matter the struggle. She is that gifted. Less than five feet tall with Indian features, like John Irving's character Owen Meany she TALKS IN CAPITAL LETTERS with a booming, yet raspy voice. Maria is remarkably well spoken considering she has only been using English for a few years. She has four sisters and a brother, with an older sister at California State Bakersfield, the first in the family to go to college. Maria's parents never went to school and are illiterate in both English and Spanish. She describes a sad home life with her mother, brothers, and sisters all working in the fields, and an alcoholic father who stays at home, no longer able to work.

Maria describes a hesitant attitude towards education in her family. The surprising ambivalence towards education is one of the truths I've uncovered in my research. Often low-income families are disinterested in education. In her case, Maria talks about the different perspective in Mexico towards school and the emphasis instead on work, usually manual labor. Now in the United States the choice is between performing well in school and working in the fields picking strawberries. Maria bitterly replays her father's taunts of her, "No, you are not going to make it. You're going to be like everyone else. You're going to get pregnant." She tells me with steely conviction that she will persevere, and I can't help but believe her. Maria's vehemence and the obvious conflict with her father are something that I found repeatedly with the low-income college students I interviewed. College is often a point of conflict in families, and parents are an obstacle to the success of their children. Maria talks about a push and pull between the parents and her older sister over going to college: "It's kind of complicated to understand. But at the end they knew that was best for her."

Maria uses the word "hard" repeatedly, saying it like it has two syllables. I ask her what it was like for her older sister to be the first to go to college. "It was hard because it was something different. It was hard because she was working at the same time as she was studying. It was so hard for her." She says that her parents supported her sister with a little money, but that they had to focus on the other children: "There was me and my little sister, and I don't work, so she has to contribute to the house too. It is hard." As a result, her sister helped support Maria's family while in college: "Some times she gives a little something to momma, just to help her." Maria too expects to be required to help her parents out financially when she's in college.

Harvard, like Stanford for Juan, has taken on a symbolic meaning for Maria. "I have other options, but my first option is Harvard. It seems like a dream." When I point out to her that Harvard is very different culturally from what she's experienced thus far in her life, she brushes it off: "Yes, everything is hard. We have to get used to it and adjust. It doesn't matter if you fit. It's something I really want and I've been working so hard for it. So if I get into to Harvard I'm going to just do what I'm supposed to do and live with it." She's heard these words said before, and I believe she not only will get into Harvard but will survive the experience regardless of the difficulty of adjustment. I just hope the reality is as meaningful to her as the dream.

Maria's motivation to take advanced placement courses, courses at the community college, and participate in school activities comes from a sense of family responsibility and a need to bolster her self image.

> Everything I do is for me, but at the same time I'm thinking of them [my family]. All the sacrifices that they are giving to me in order to have the education that I have, that makes me work harder. I see them telling me, 'I love you. You did it. I'm so proud of you.' That's something that keeps me going. That's my motivation. For some people they don't have it, but I have it and I take advantage of it.

Maria tells me about how she relies on motivational books by popular authors, such as Anthony Robbins, to keep her working towards her goal of going to law school at Harvard and become a public defender. "I know it is going to be hard, but if I really want it, I can do it."

I ask Maria what she'll put in her application essay for Harvard University. She describes life with an absentee and alcoholic father, and the family's plight immigrating to the United States. "So basically it was about how hard it was, being over there and being here. And being without a dad—I never knew what it was like to live with a dad. And he being an alcoholic and seeing all the suffering of my parents. My brothers and sisters trying to continue living and surviving." Maria talks about the discrimination her family faces: "It's something that's so hard. You want to give everything you have and then they destroy your feelings. And there's people that can get rid of it and continue their lives, and there are others that are hurt and can't go on. And sometimes you don't expect it from other people and you get it. It makes some people stronger, and others weaker." What is her response to the negative comments in the newspaper blog? "We are uneducated, they are probably educated and they have everything. They haven't gone through what we had to go through so they probably don't understand because they aren't in our shoes. I just hope God blesses them and I will see them later," she tells me with a flash in her eyes. Maria walks with short, rapid steps back across the lawn to class.

Culminating Ceremony

The final night of the month-long program arrives. The students bring their mothers, fathers, brothers, sisters, cousins, and grandparents. I greet the students and their families at the entrance. They look down and nod. A father offers his hand in silence.

The university president and other officials speak. Two students rise and read speeches in English and Spanish. The students are awarded certificates by faculty. I rise to give the closing remarks. "We put on many wonderful programs that serve the community various ways, but nothing matches Summer College," I say. "This program strikes to the heart, to the soul of the University and its mission. In America we are fond of talking about the land of opportunity, and education as a main pathway to that opportunity. And for many this opportunity through education is a reality. I'm sure there are many in this room with stories of their own success through education. But for some, such as students like you, our educational system fails." I see the eyes rise from the school officials on the left of the auditorium realizing now that I'm not going to give the expected perfunctory speech.

"A child from a wealthy family is many times more likely to attend college than one from poor family," I say, gaining momentum. "A child with parents who went to college, with tutors, computers and books at home is more likely to go to college than those students without such advantages. Although educators work hard to provide opportunity for all through education, the reality is that too often our educational system reinforces advantage, and reinforces disadvantage. As students move from kindergarten through college, the gap between the advantaged and disadvantaged grows larger. This is the horrific failure of American education and why programs like this one for children of migrant workers are so important. We need programs like this for the university, for the school system, for our society."

I look down at the students at the table in the front row—I have their attention. "In the past few weeks I have had the opportunity to observe and talk to the students in this program on an individual basis. I can see in your faces that you are probably wondering why I asked such strange questions, and what I think of what you said and what I saw." Two young students respond with open-faced smiles. "I will tell you. First, I am amazed and humbled by your perseverance given the enormous obstacles you've faced and will face in the future. Many of you are clearly on a mission to go to college and be successful. And this mission is not just for yourself, but the fate of your entire family is often riding on your individual success in going to college. You carry an enormous weight. And what you pursue is not just money. While studies such as the UCLA Freshman Survey tell us that students are primarily motivated to go to college to attain high paying jobs, when I asked you about your reasons for going to college you gave me a different answer. Certainly, economic stability was part of your motivation, but you talked more often about attaining respect and a desire to do something to help others. Virtually all of you have your eyes on helping careers such as social workers, doctors, nurses, therapists, and public defenders. This motivation to go to college is unique for you as a group and will serve you well in your pursuits because your ambitions have substance."

"Finally, I want to say if there is one thing that I wish I could give you it would be more confidence. School has a way of hurting self-esteem for some. You need to understand that if you get a C in a class it does not mean that you are a C person. You simply earned a C in that class—you need to learn from that and try to do better next time. If you receive a poor score on the SAT test that does not mean that you are a flawed human being. You simply didn't do as well as you would like on the test, and should learn what you can from the experience, retake the test, and move on. It is vital that you protect that core belief in yourself, that sense of your own value. When you go on to college, and graduate school, the work will get harder and you are bound, no matter how smart you are, to encounter criticism and poor marks. Maintain your confidence and sense of self. Believe in yourself." The room is silent. With my hands wide, palms up, my voice cracking noticeably I say, "I believe in you."

As I walk alone later across campus in the warm summer night, the head of the migrant program at the local high school stops his car and leans out the window. He thanks me and there is a look of recognition in his eyes. I understand now what must be reinforced for him on a daily basis working with these troubled children—the system mostly fails them.

Chapter 6
Erosion of the College Image

This chapter argues that public attitudes and popular images as seen in popular newspapers and fictional accounts have perpetuated stereotypes of low-income students and assert an ideal social mobility function for higher education that now shows signs of fading. American beliefs about college have changed and are in the process of changing further. The public is increasingly aware, as has been shown throughout this book, that the traditional image of college as an instrument of mobility in society simply does not fit the reality. As seen earlier, there are two major beliefs about the poor in American society: first, that their position in society is a result of a combination of inadequate talent and flawed values. Second, that the individuals themselves have primary responsibility for changing their condition. We have seen throughout this book a long history rationalizing this view of the poor and see the specific ways the collective attitude is expressed in practical ways in college. Now we turn to the rhetoric of the college myth itself.

Public media both inform and reflect social attitudes of a specific time period. American perceptions of college are complex, varied, and often linked to class, ethnic background, geographical region, and time period. One particularly rich way of exploring changing public opinion, especially about collective mythology, is through analyzing media representations. In this chapter I examine the public image and the collective myths about college as seen in newspapers, novels, and films in an effort to understand how the image of the low-income in American colleges has changed. I believe many will be surprised to see that the poor in college have been a topic in popular culture for two centuries, and most importantly the function of college itself has been a major theme in novels and films. In this section of the book, I also trace the more explicit thinking about the purpose of college, especially as it relates to broader democratic participation through newspaper editorials over the same two century time period. While opinion pieces in newspapers are certainly different than novels and films, they express the evolving public thinking on college and often evoke collective social mythology in their arguments. I end the chapter by considering the perceptions of previous generations about the college mobility myth.

Early Popular American College Images

From the beginning of America's history, the impetus for establishing colleges has been based on populist ideals of broader access to better jobs and to instill values of good citizenry. Ben Franklin's *Proposals Relating to the Education of Youth in*

Pennsylvania (1749) and William Smith's *General Idea of the College of Mirania* (1753) expected education to include preparation for a vocation, use of English rather than Latin, emphasis on citizenship rather than religion, and education of the many. Furthermore, alongside the elitist experience in American colleges, there is a tradition of college students working while going to school. At Dartmouth for instance, student employment was regarded as part of the education, not just something done by less fortunate, poor students.

Nevertheless, social distinctions clearly existed at places such as Harvard University, where students were listed by the rank of their families, those from the upper-class had the best rooms and were first at the table for meals. It was relatively easy to discourage admissions to select colleges because the required Greek and Latin were not taught at most high schools. When low-income students did gain admission to elite institutions they were often isolated. For example, Hastings Hall at Harvard for many years was known as "Little Jerusalem" because of the number of Jewish students residing there. Fraternities and clubs controlled access by class creating one university for the select and the other for the so called "fruits." Prep-schools fed upper-class students into elite colleges, and then connections made at those colleges linked them to successful connections after college. The standard for connection and success at institutions such as Harvard in the nineteenth century was not academic performance. In fact as late as the end of the nineteenth century, only a minimum of a C grade was required in one third of Harvard courses.

A search through the archives of American newspapers over the past two hundred years reveals a unique sense of how college came to be represented over time, a richer picture in many ways than gleaned from academic books on the history of higher education. Opinion pieces repeatedly raised debates over college content, who should attend, and the larger function of higher education in society. Between the type-set lines, evolving attitudes as especially represented in opinion pieces about the education of the poor in America clearly emerge. In the nineteenth century, America went through a public debate and struggle over the fate of its colleges. The limitations of traditional higher education in terms of who it served, what was considered proper subjects of study, and where learning occurred was challenged by an America with growing populist attitudes on a headlong machine-powered drive towards the emerging modern world. In the midst of the Industrial Revolution, the resistance to incorporate engineering and agricultural sciences into curricula showed how far out-of-step colleges had become with the needs of the rapidly developing country. The Morrill Act of 1862 establishing the land grant, or public university system, and the Chautauqua Movement, which led to the university extension programs, were both major milestones in this general revolution in American colleges. A *New York Times* editorial written in 1871 gives a flavor of the public debate that occurred throughout the nineteenth century over the fate of higher education:

> The worthy Professors, who, in the seclusion of academic halls and class-rooms, have paid too little attention to the needs of the busy world about them, have

awakened to the importance of other things than Greek roots and the mysteries of the calculus, and have discovered that as the world is making progress in educational matters as well as in the economic arts, they must meet the demands of modern minds, or be left behind in the educational race, only to be consulted on by-gone matters, like the dusty books of reference which crowd their library shelves. (The "new departure" in colleges, 1871, p. 4)

Newspaper editorials of the time repeatedly question the practical use of college. Well-know railroad magnate Henry Huntington expressed his opinion on a college education in an interesting article published in the *Los Angeles Times* in the year 1900:

Mr. Huntington, who is know to have entertained very radical ideas on this subject, expresses regret at the increase of higher education for the masses in the United States. He believed that the vast majority of our young people spend too many of their vigorous years inside the school room and not enough in the practical work of life. (Education and labor, 1990, p. 16)

Huntington further complains that the values of traditional college are to create "sterling qualities," or in other words, impractical traits for gentlemen who have no intention of working. Print media's consistent concern also encompassed the influence of the wealthy, such as the Rockefeller and Carnegie families, in the endowment of universities echoed in its affirmation of the need for intellectual freedom divorced from political or religious support of the institution (Education and labor, 1900).

Americans at the end of the nineteenth century looked to Europe for models of higher education which in turn influenced its popularization during the twentieth century. In a *New York Times* opinion piece, the author noted that broader public access to college in both England and Germany, had mixed results, claiming that in both countries it appears that demand for college education had outstripped supply or need in society (Too much higher education, 1883). The author of the article argues that America has even a lower tolerance and need for college-educated men than in Europe. Nevertheless, by the end of the nineteenth century and the beginning of the twentieth century, the traditional American colleges expanded who they served to include some women and middle-class students, to offer applied sciences such as engineering, and to establish opportunities beyond the Ivy-walled campuses for the larger American society, thus creating a generally more educated society.

The college novel is a fictional genre that includes popular forms, as well as some well-known literary efforts. Novels about college both help form public opinion and reflect the realities of the times as seen by the authors. Often loosely autobiographical in nature, these novels tend to focus on coming-of-age stories and the extracurricular side of college, especially football and fraternities. From the first college novels, students from poor families were standard, often stereotypical, characters in stories set on campuses. In most cases these students followed a typical arc of development from being out of place and socially rejected, to finding success, usually on the football field, and then becoming accepted by their more affluent classmates. In this way college provides more a setting where one proves socially acceptable rather than a place to demonstrate academic skill which leads up the social ladder. In fact, most of these college novels rarely spend time on academics, and make fun of those who study and do well in school—typically unpopular poor students.

Kramer's annotated bibliography of the American college novel (1981) lists hundreds published over the past two centuries, especially numerous at the beginning of the twentieth century. The generally recognized first novel set at a college was Nathaniel Hawthorne's *Fanshawe* published in 1828. However, this was a very early effort, one from a literary author that separates it from the majority of the college novel genre. One of the early novels dealing expressly with a poor student attending college was *Nelly Brown* published in 1845, which tells the story of a student's tribulations adjusting to college with two wealthy roommates (Whippoorwill, 1845). A stereotypical character often found in these early college novels is of a student from a poor family who is serious academically, but has trouble adjusting to the advantaged culture of college. Generally, a sympathetic character like this is surrounded by wealthy and silly roommates for contrast, as in the 1886 *Two College Girls* by Helen Dawes Brown.

Sometimes the poor student is represented as someone from the American frontier. An example of this type of college novel is *A Princetonian: A Story of Undergraduate Life at the College of New Jersey* published in 1896, and which featured a former sheriff from Nebraska enrolling at Princeton (Barnes, 1896). As is common in these novels, he has problems fitting in until he becomes a football star. *Boys and Men: A Story of Life at Yale* is another version of this youth from the frontier at an Eastern college motif, this time with a poor student from Arizona (Holbrook, 1900). A different version of this rags-to-college story is in the 1901 novel *For the Blue and Gold*, which portrays a non-traditional 23-year-old freshman at the University of California Berkeley (Lichtenstein, 1901).

In the nineteenth century, the American mythology of college concentrated heavily on the extracurricular side of college with coming-of-age stories of poor students who are initially outsiders, only to win acceptance through athletics. Newspaper editorials and fictional representations reveal a questioning of the purpose of higher education, application to the practical world, and portraits of social climbing primarily for the wealthy, save the occasional poor student struggling from the bottom. In an era where for the majority of the population college was a mysterious world, a romanticized vision was popularized and the college myth formed.

Twentieth-Century Popular College Images

The debate about how wide the access to higher education should be made continued into the twentieth century and was directly linked to controversial American immigration policy. In a 1916 article reporting on a National Conference on Immigration and Americanization in Philadelphia, a delegate argued that it was a mistake to expand higher education to accommodate the huge influx of foreign-born new citizens, but instead recommended supplying only rudimentary education necessary for Americanization (The immigration problem, 1916). After World War I, articles began to appear which discussed the first standardized intelligence test. These columns point to the extremely low level of general public education in America and the subsequent need for schooling in a democratic society (The status of education, 1922). At the same time, others noted the low test scores coming from immigrant groups, and used such statistics as rationale for limiting immigration before America experienced a general "dummying down." As presented in earlier chapters, the devolution of the population is a constant concern first seen in the eugenics movement tying genetic ability, education, and immigration policy which informs policy up until the present.

An intriguing opinion piece in the *New York Times* from 1926 reports on a study conducted by the relatively new American Association of University Professors regarding undergraduate admissions policies; it lays out two opposing camps in the admissions debate: one described as "aristocratic" concentrated on limiting access to higher education, which insists that not all have the ability to enter into a demanding course of college study; and the second described as the "democratic school" which insists that college be available to all and stresses vocational and practical application of knowledge. "Maintains that the chief end of education is to give as many men and women as possible power to lead useful lives, contribute to the welfare of the community and enrich their own inner experience" (Aristocracy and democracy in education, 1926). The author of the opinion piece argues that the aristocratic view is open to criticisms of snobbishness, while the democratic position may lead to a mediocre American higher education system. The solution offered: meritocracy or admissions based purely on academic performance and standardized intelligence tests. In this way, the aristocratic ideal of quality and limited populations in college is maintained, yet the democratic impulse to make education available to all finds an outlet. Thus we see reflected 80 years ago a position on meritocracy which still preoccupies us today.

While meritocracy was touted by some, others decried the practical problem of supporting elite colleges without the aid of wealthy American families. Such articles in the early twentieth century point specifically to the problem of stiff academic admissions requirements leading to a reduction in students from wealthy families. A 1927 piece entitled "The Deadly College Bookworm" portrays a group of non-academic minded students who can profit from college: "boys who are 'none too good' in studies, but who nevertheless benefit greatly by four years at college" (The deadly college bookworm, 1927). The article points out that it is not the "bookworms" who end up financially supporting the college, but those that are none too good: "The boys who merely plugged along are now the ones who make handsome endowments. If they cannot get into college at all, what will the colleges do for money in another decade or two?" the commentary asks. This quotation is a stunning summing up of the financial forces driving the admissions policies of private universities then and today.

By the end of the Depression, newspapers ran articles questioning both who should go to college and how much the education of individual students should be subsidized by the government. Over 65 years later, American society still wrestles with this central debate to some extent. In a 1939 article, the author quotes a study funded by the Carnegie Foundation that found a very large increase in college-going young people from one in 24 just after the turn of the century, to one in seven almost 40 years later. Additionally, funding for college had reached modern standards of one-third government, one-third private endowment, and one third from individual families. However, the column condemns statistics which show that many talented individuals do not attend college, and many less gifted but advantaged attend in their place: "We send many to college who ought not to be there. Many who ought to be there are unable to go" (How good are colleges?, 1939). The article concludes that society cannot accept a system where collective resources are put to educating the "less talented." One can read this argument as either an attack on the wealthy who do not perform well in college, or an assault on prying open the doors to college more broadly to include some of the "less talented" poor students. Either way, the analysis uses meritocracy again as the ideal for deciding who goes to college.

Women were another historically excluded group of students and the attitudes towards them in popular media are in some ways more complex than that towards students from the low-income families generally. Nevertheless, newspapers at the end of the nineteenth century and beginning of the twentieth century reveal mixed attitudes towards the education of women that are largely consistent with attitudes towards low-income students. The *New York Times* in 1873 described the education of women at Cambridge University in a positive light and comments that some falsely think that educating women is like "training dogs to walk on their hind legs" (Higher education of women, 1873). In a kind of competitive spirit, the author of this editorial argues that if England is educating women to the college level that America should certainly educate women as well: "There are no women in the world so quick-witted and clever as American women. With the development of our society, the time has come when the highest standard ought to be reached" (The education of women, 1873). The doors of the academy were slow to unlock to women students, but throughout the twentieth century, they were persistently forced open.

In 1935 James Rowland Angell of Yale University reportedly made a speech at Bryn Mawr in which he described the important change that had occurred for women in attending college:

Unquestionably they are made less docile, for they are now fully aware of the vigor and integrity of their own thought processes, while the simultaneous opening to them of practically every door in the world of business, the professions and politics, has robbed them forever of any disposition to accept the male as an inevitably superior person. (Higher education of women, 1935)

Newspaper editorials reveal similarly negative attitudes about college educated women: "There is a widespread prejudice to the effect that the average college girl is too 'up-stage,' feels too superior, resents office discipline and routine and all that sort of thing" (The college diploma, 1922). But the plain prejudice towards college graduates wasn't limited just to women but also to middle-class men as well: "After all the ridicule that has been heaped upon the poor fellow, he has come to know that it may be all right to hold a college degree, but it is not at all alright to talk about it. The intellectual snob is no more sought after than the social snob in the business world" (The college diploma, 1922). Newspapers and popular media generally are consistent in perpetuating this suspicion of academia and are direct in showing a public attitude of anti-intellectualism.

Generally, newspapers in 1920s America reveal changing attitudes about women in college and the workforce. A 1923 article in the *Los Angeles Times* begins with the common portrait of privileged young women attending college with little effort to take their studies seriously. It then explains that this perception of women is changing and that in fact many of the female students at the University of California, Berkeley work part-time while attending school.

At that, they have snatched another treasured laurel from masculine brows. Many are the self-made men who tell with unction the story of how they worked their way through college and wax complacent on the attending applause. Hereafter the girls will be able to emulate them and bask in the public approval. (College girls work, 1923, p. 114)

We see here in this bitter-sweet commentary that college has become a Horatio Alger-like route for women as well as men.

Published in 1912, *Stover at Yale* is one of the most famous and influential college novels. Owen Johnson, the author son of the poet and editor of *Century* magazine, Robert Underwood Johnson, achieved his greatest success in this collegiate work. While the novel doesn't focus on a poor college student, it does directly deal with the turning of the main character, Dink Stover, against Yale social snobbery. College novels such as *Stover at Yale* deal head-on with meritocracy, summarized by the main character, "'It's the one place where money makes no difference,' Stover said, with a flash—'where you stand for what you are'" (Johnson, 1968, p. 8). Dink Stover became the archetype of the college man of the era. Ideas of privilege and open competition are in the forefront of this novel: "For the first time, a little appalled, he felt the weight of the seriousness, the deadly seriousness of the American spirit, which seizes on everything that is competition and transforms it, with the savage fanaticism of its race, for success" (Johnson 1968, p. 63-64). Predictably, despite Dink's acts of non-conformity, he ultimately wins the highest honor of membership into the famous Skull and Bones club. The novel portrays confusion about the position of college in society, but seems to support the right of the individual to express dissenting opinion and go against the conformist high society as represented by Yale. Nevertheless, one senses that this is an argument within the wealthy class, not the larger society. A Harvard version of *Stover at Yale* was published in 1917 under the title of *The World and Thomas Kelly*, and focused on how snobbery in Cambridge initially excluded the main character from clubs (Train, 1917). Once again, as is common in college genre fiction of the time period, Thomas' athletic talent as a tennis player ensured his social acceptance.

The growth of college enrollments after World War I and the increasing public debate over the standards and content of higher education accounts for the great number of academic novels published since the 1920s (Lyons, 1962). An interesting reversal of the usual rags-to-college story is the novel *High Hurdles* (Husband, 1923), which follows a wealthy undergraduate who leaves school after failing exams in his sophomore year only to work in a coal mine to regain his work ethic. The story ends happily when the main character becomes the business success he was apparently meant to be. Another notable novel is *Not to Eat, Not to Love* (Weller, 1993), which deals, remarkably for the genre that usually ignores the content of higher education, with some academic concerns in its portrayal of a football-playing art history major at Harvard.

As early as the 1920s, novels begin to emerge which dealt more realistically with the circumstances of being poor and in college. *The Western Shore* (Crane, 1925), was written in the emerging social realism style and portrayed a group of students attending the University of California at Berkeley. This unusually well-written novel features working-class students, portrayals of clumsy, ambivalent youthful male-female relationships, Jewish and gay students, and no football. Credited as one of the first realistic looks at university life, the author has some of his characters question the relevance and importance of college, as seen in the following passage: "The prospect made him infinitely weary, for would he be any better off when he had a degree?" (Crane, 1985, p. 290).

How are low-income and minority populations portrayed in film during this period? Although both novels and movies are popular art forms, American films have had historically a more low-income audience, and rarely had any artistic ambitions. As a result, the portrayal of poor students in films is perhaps more stark and obvious than in college novels. In the necessarily stripped down and simplified storylines found in film, the social tensions between groups and the challenge of individual characters to overcome the obstacles of being a poor outsider are flatly represented. Nevertheless, we'll see that there are many parallels between the two popular forms, especially in the way they reflect changing attitudes towards the function of college in American society.

As early as 1914 in D.W. Griffith's 1914 *Strongheart*, which dealt with the college experiences of a Native American student at Columbia University, American films have depicted low-income outsiders in college. As with college novels, films often depict poor students who are inclined to books and academics as social outcasts. According to one observer,

> Higher education as an elitist institution emerged as the most significant aspect of college films of the 1920s and 1930s. Plots often deal with the attempts of an outsider (usually a poor student from a humble background, contrasted with the rich society kids) to join the elite through success in college. (Hinton, 1994, p. 4)

On this point we see a strong parallel between college novels and films of the period. College became a regular subject of American films starting early in the silent film era, where, like the college novel, they both formed and reflected the image of higher education of the specific time period. These films since the 1920s indicate that the social side of college life was viewed by the public as the most distinctive and interesting aspect of the collegiate experience, the one most worthy of their attention in public entertainments. Wiley Lee Umphlett, in his book *The Movies Go to College* (1984), argues that college was used as a setting in films because it provided an environment where individuals have the opportunity to revitalizing or remake themselves—a characteristically American preoccupation. College films often show the social tension of youthful idealism faced with the reality of the world, which then leads to individual transformation. Characters in college films find their dreams don't match reality. In this way college is portrayed finally as a place for intense socialization.

The overall plotline of college films often involved a transformation of the main character through revising an innocent idealistic self: "The representative college-life movie reveals that a student's ideals and dreams often do not measure up to the realities created of our system of higher education" (Umphlett, 1984, p. 18). A good example of this point is the popular *The Freshman*, portrayed by the comedian Harold Lloyd as "Speedy," a young man desperately trying to fit in. Speedy makes one social blunder after another as he attempts to present a successful social image of himself, a particularly American obsession according to some observers: "This perception of Americans' basic fear of being unpopular reveals both a clue to understanding a dominant side of our nature and the key to interpreting Hollywood's cinematic version of our collegiate traditions" (Umphlett, 1984, p. 16). *Naughty but Nice* (1927) is a female version of *The Freshman*, and shows a naïve country girl attending a fancy finishing school that ends with a better understanding of herself. Overall, both films reveal an anti-intellectual message of the individual versus the dominant system.

Elizabeth Ewen and Stuart Ewen (2006) in *Typecasting: On the Arts and Sciences of Human Inequality* point to the powerful image from *The Jazz Singer* of Al Jolson sitting at a mirror putting on black face before a performance. A fantastically popular film with an early star of stage and screen, it provides a poignant image of the meaning of inclusion for immigrant populations into larger culture in the early part of this century. *The Jazz Singer* is a story about Jews becoming white by acting black, or by ridiculing blacks. The key scene in the movie shows Jolson applying blackface makeup in his dressing room. By doing so, he takes on a white, not Jewish, identity. Assimilation was thus what Ewen and Ewen call a Faustian bargain that many immigrants faced: "In order to truly become an American, one needed to internalize the notions of racial inequality that had, for so long, been implicit to the American heritage" (Ewen and Ewen, 2006, p. 435). This kind of assimilation process presented in *The Jazz Singer* is not unlike what was seen in college films of the time period such as *The Freshman*. The 1930s were the most popular decade for college films and featured the wildly popular sport of football as a chief topic. One notable film of the period is *College Holiday* (1936). This musical featured Jack Benny in the role of a hotel manager who is convinced by a eugenics professor to help study a set of college students with the objective of scientifically determining which ethnic group is smarter.

In the early twentieth century, the popular images of college and depictions of low-income students came to full fruition. The real life increase of both women and Jewish students in college life was combined with fictional representations employing plotlines involving the plight of outsider low-come students who often confront broken dreams. Stories of assimilation and trivialization could not hide the start of the unraveling of the popular college image.

Mid to Late Twentieth-Century Popular College Images

During World War II, patriotic articles decried the destruction of the world-leading research universities in Germany now reduced to instruments of the Nazi state. Free thinking and intellectual dissent were replaced by insistence on loyalty and the indoctrination of students into fanatical Nazism. In contrast, the authors of opinion pieces of the period assert the democratic approach of American universities beyond the reality on campuses of the time:

> Here in the United States we have clung tenaciously to the ideal of an education open to all, with no restriction on opportunity or college attendance. The emphasis remains on mass education, with the widest diffusion of knowledge and understanding. Some educators have begun to worry about the handicaps imposed on self-supporting students, and where possible they are being relieved through scholarships. But there is no tendency to create an elite class. Higher education in America is still unshakably democratic. (Educational ideals, 1941, p. 16)

In this way, World War II seems to have led American public opinion, from the radical thirties and eventual conflict with fascism, to an insistence on "democratic" approaches to higher education in America. Yet not all articles during the war were so self-congratulatory. One piece written in 1942 about the changes during the war in elitist universities in England, pointed out that American higher education wasn't so different. Although Americans had long regarded Great Britain as a country of hardened class positions, the more global view in the post-war world made many more aware of the similarities in social systems. The article points to President Conant of Harvard's public speeches about the need to change admissions practices at the Ivy League schools so that they were less geared towards preference to legacies: "He advocated 'a well-supported educational system by which talent reaches the college level irrespective of private income'" (The education of the free, 1942, p. A4).

After World War II, newspapers began to include editorials which expressed fear that the generous G.I. Bill would result in too many college-educated Americans. The implementation of the Bill had encountered widespread opposition from some in higher education when being considered in Congress, and this strain of popular opinion continued well after the war ended. In one 1949 opinion piece, the author claims that the rise of Nazism was partly a result of too many educated citizens:

> These are displaced persons in a very literal sense. They feel that their education entitles them to places of preferment, but they are an educated surplus; all the places are filled. So they become malcontents, furnishing the intellectual material for revolution. The higher echelons of the Nazi organization, for instance, were filled with down-at-the-heel Doktoren who could not find suitable positions in the republican regime. (Buyer's market in college graduates, 1949, p. A4)

The article continues with an argument that if people attend college primarily to move up in society that there are too many pursuing this same objective to be handled by the economy. Instead the author suggests that college needs to be reserved for the most talented. In the post-war economy, the fear of a class-less society was epitomized by the image of a world full of college graduates all struggling to make their way in the new world where traditional barriers were removed.

In the same vein, from the late 40s through the 50s, there were many editorials about the fear of broad access to education "watering down" the quality of American education at all levels (The quantity of education, 1952). Articles began appearing which express concern that the explosion of access to high education after the war had hurt those students who were most talented by dragging down or "leveling" the quality and academic expectations—what one article called the "glorification of the mediocre" (A "perversion of democracy," 1959, p. B4). These opinion pieces began to assert the distinction between equal opportunity and equivalent talent:

> Having acknowledged that all men are created equal before God and the law and having nobly inferred from this that all men should have equal opportunity, we

assume by some of our acts that all men have equal capacities or talents. And this is as self-evidently false as the first proposition is self-evidently true. (Equality and equal education, 1953, p. B4)

The author states plainly that not everyone is intellectually capable of earning a college degree. While it is true that American post-World War II policy led to the opening of college doors and subsequently forced the colleges to teach high school level courses in the first two years of college, this is an old argument that can be traced back into the late nineteenth century where colleges complained to secondary schools about poor academic preparation. Finally, the editorial article points out the excesses of democracy which eventually lead to the disadvantaging of the talented: "The tendency to disable the superior in pursuit of the delusion that equality can be achieved only through the dominion of mediocrity" (Equality and equal education, 1953, p. B4). In this 1953 editorial we see an assertion of meritocracy in higher education.

A more positive refrain in the 1950s in America, was a discussion of how broader educational access now powered the economy: "The economic value of the American individual has risen largely because of the growth of opportunity, the rising educational level and the marked increase in the productivity of the whole community" (Education and the rich life, 1954). Additionally, there was an increasing appreciation for rapid advances in the modern world resulting in reduced work weeks and more leisure time. College education in this type of dream post war world was seen to enrich graduates as much as to ensure high paying vocations. Talk of college creating "rounded individuals" became more common in the public mind than ever before.

By the mid-60s, articles once again appeared describing the over-educating of Americans and the absence of enough skilled blue collar workers. One article in particular cited an American Council on Education study that found four million unemployed with, coincidentally at the same time, four million unfilled blue collar jobs (A vocationally deprived generation, 1964). The claim was made that the educational system was geared for all to go to college when only approximately 20 percent at that time had such ambitions. References to college in newspapers to the Free Speech and anti-war movements dominated in the 1960s, but in the 1970s and 1980s, there began talk about the right of citizens to go to college and how to balance merit and access (The 'right' to go to college, 1979, p. C4). Since the 1980s, articles largely focus on both the struggle to get admitted to top colleges and the subsequent benefit. One piece claims that the impact of an Ivy League degree is short lived for those without family connections. The corporate world seems generally dismissive of educational pedigree and instead looks with a cold eye at results: "The name of the college you attended might be a factor in your first job, but after that, it's performance" (Smetanka, 2007, p. 1A).

Novels set on college campuses became increasingly realistic during and after World War II. James T. Farrell wrote two novels that were evidently quite autobiographical, including one set in Chicago about a commuter student in the late 1920s (Farrell, 1943) and another about its central character attending University of Chicago while working at a gas station (Farrell, 1963). Books about outsiders to the college world were common in such as *The Corpus of Joe Bailey*, which tells the story of a poor student from San Diego attending the University of California at Berkeley who never adjusts to middle-class life in or after college (Hall, 1953). Non-traditional students became more commonly understood by the public in the later half of the twentieth century and were portrayed in novels such as *Continuing Education* (Weil, 1979) about a 38-year-old woman with three kids who returns to college to study art, and *Night School*, which profiles an evening education program in New York City (Cassill, 1961).

In the early 40s, campuses also became a favorite setting for MGM musicals such as *Girl Crazy* (1943) and *Bathing Beauty* (1944). After World War II, college films shifted their focus to depict college as the ticket to success in life; this shift, of course, coincided with the G.I. Bill and influx of middle and low-income students into post-secondary education. Veterans going to college became topics in *Apartment for Peggy* (1948) and *Yes Sir, That's My Baby* (1949), and by the 1950s, college isn't seen as so elite in Hollywood films. "There was no guarantee of the results, of course, but the inevitable democratization of the college experience had now become more pronounced in our society, and the movies did not hesitate to reflect this change" (Umphlett, 1984). Movies of that period such as *Hold That Line* (1952), featuring the Bowery Boys of Dead End Kid fame, show how far colleges had opened their doors. However, women didn't fare as equitably; in the fifties and sixties the myth of women going to college only to get married was perpetuated in various Hollywood romantic comedies.

This decade and a half of images presenting the American Dream in college was followed closely by a more realistic portrayal in the 60s, 70s and 80s. *The Young Lovers* released in 1964 is one of the first films to offer a truthful depiction of college life. In fact, some have noted that American cinema from the sixties on reveal a stark decline in the belief in the education myth: "These three decades ring a death knell to the mythic dream of higher education; in film after film, we see faith in a previously unquestioned myth seriously undermined. Students in college question why they are there and parents wonder why they are spending the money to send them" (Hinton, 1994, p. 30). Perhaps as college became more common place it lost some of its mythical power in the collective American imagination. Films such as *The Graduate* (1967) and *Carnal Knowledge* (1971) are prime examines of the changed public image of college presented in the 60s and 70s. In *The Graduate* the young scholar from an affluent family, played by Dustin Hoffman, is asked by his perturbed father, "Would you mind telling me then what those four years of college were for? What was the point of all that hard work?" Hoffman's, as Benjamin, thoroughly 60s response: "You got me." In *Carnal Knowledge*, Sandy played by Art Garfunkel, explains to his roommate: "I feel the same way about getting laid that I do about going to college—I'm getting pressured into it." Reflecting the historical era evolving out of the Vietnam War, these movies epitomize the rebellion of middle- and upper-class students to the role college seemed to play as an instrument of conformity and path to affluence. The general tenor of college films of this era is exemplified in *Animal House*'s clear example that undergraduate education is irrelevant to later success in life.

Films such as *Breaking Away* (1979) and *Educating Rita* (1983) deal head-on with the class issue in college. In perhaps the most touching moment in *Breaking Away* the father walks with his son across the beautiful university campus and talks about cutting the stones for the buildings: "When they were finished, the damndest thing happened. It was like the buildings was too good for us." The resolution of *Breaking Away* addresses the question of who should go to college. The plotline illustrates how poor students feel the need to assume another identity to be accepted and do well in college—better to be an Italian bicyclist than poor American if you want to attend college. *Educating Rita* was one of the first films to tell the story of non-traditional students in a story about a British student at the Open University who tries to make good through education. Other notable films of the time include *Soul Man*, released in 1986, which tried to make a comedy out of affirmative action by featuring a white student at Harvard Law School who pretends to be black to avoid paying tuition. In *Good Will Hunting* (1997), Matt Damon as a janitor at M.I.T. is discovered as a mathematics genius, showing how a poor but talented student is exploited by a professor. Note in this film how irrelevant college is to the innately talented main character.

Books such as *The Case Against College* (Bird, 1975) in the 1970s present a rather strident case against the value and function of college in America. While this and other similar books are sensationalistic in style, they nevertheless found a popular audience attracted to a critical view of higher education, especially during periods of downturn in the economy. The book criticizes the class basis of college: "In our supposedly classless society, the diploma is our class distinction. By giving it to everyone, egalitarians hope somehow to make everyone upper class" (Bird, 1975, p. 116). The author of this book derides colleges as "finishing schools" for the gentlemen, not unlike what the newspaper articles in the last chapter reflect, and that it is irresponsible for American society to delude low-income citizens into thinking that they too can become upper-class by going to college: "No one likes to say it out loud, but in America we have cruelly deluded the lower middle class into thinking that they can gain access to power by studying, in formal classes, the arts, amusements, concerns, sentiments, and conventions of the 'gentleman' who are the successors if not the descendants of the 'gentlemen' who inherited power along with their land" (Bird, 1975, p. 119).

Post-war America and the entrance of returning soldiers into the academy exploded the myth of higher education, as it demonstrate concretely its promise. A population now to a much larger degree had some experience in college and the mystique began to wear off. As a result fictional depictions of college became much more realistic and presented more rounded portrayals of students from low-income families. Additionally, a cynicism crept into the national dialog in newspaper articles, as well as fictional representations.

Contemporary Popular College Images

In current times, when one does a search on references to colleges and universities, as a clear sign of the times, the majority of articles are on sporting events. Additionally, articles on public policy and funding issues for public universities are common. Nevertheless, I did find articles specifically on the issue of access often having to do with the impact of policy on individual students. An example of such stories is about a young man named Mitchell Owens in the *Amarillo Globe-News* relates his tale of dreams of attending college and moving up in society. He describes a senior year in high school spent gathering information: "The summer after I graduated, I was calling WT's financial aid office every day," he said. "I didn't really know what I should do as far as financial aid" (Newman, 2007). The article then gives the context in which increasing university expenses combined with less public funding have led to increased costs to the students. "As a result, college students like Owens will continue to wrestle with how to pay for higher education: grappling with the price, searching out funding resources and realizing the worth of a college degree." Articles such as this one show the increased public concern over access to higher education caused by changes in financial aid policy that we saw from chapter two began in the 1980s. Newspapers now increasingly tell stories of non-traditional students returning later in life to college. In an article in the *Longview News-Journal* in Texas, a 40-year-old man working as a blue collar repair man returns to school to study electrical engineering. "'It's a big challenge, trying to have family time and get my homework done,' he said. 'I try to take time out for my kids'" (Phelps, 2007). He talks about a supportive wife and family but admits the fear of an uncertain future after college: "'It's scary being 40 and facing having debt, but I know it's worth it,' he said."

Contemporary newspapers also tell stories of struggles by minority students to go to college. In a Washington State local newspaper, students talk about being "lucky" to go to college. This piece also reveals that for many minority students going to college goes against social and family expectations: "Rosales didn't give higher education serious thought until the final trimester of his junior year at Davis. That's when he began to realize how an education could benefit him" (Cole, 2007). Rosales talks about limited options in his small town of Yakima, Washington and how he expects his college education to expand his opportunities. He chose the University of Washington because it was close to his home, where he earned a BA in Ethnic Studies. He is now a graduate student at San Diego State University. Voicing a typical inclination of first-generation college students, Rosales talks of "giving back" to his community by becoming a school teacher. Revealingly, he talks about the benefits for him of attending college: "'It's difficult to see many of the immediate benefits ... but I think I really grew more through the trials and tribulations faced throughout the entire education process. I feel progression is based in each of our collective experiences,' he says."

Continuing a custom in journalism from the past, many present day accounts identify the failure of the primary and secondary schools to prepare students for college. In this vein, an article in 2007 noted that half of Boston public high school graduates were required to take a remedial class in math upon entrance to community college, a quarter of which then promptly failed (Bombardieri, 2007, p. 1A). A school superintendent was quoted in the article as saying that renewed focus needed to be on college success, not just graduation from high school. Finally, in a tradition that dates back to the 1950s which makes fun of the inability of college students to answer seemingly simple questions, a recent report queried 14,000 freshmen and seniors at colleges and universities nation-wide and found that more than 81 percent of the students surveyed knew generally about Martin Luther King Jr. and his famous "I have a dream" speech. However, the students thought that in it he was arguing for the abolition of slavery, which of course had occurred a century earlier! (Staff, 2007, p. B3).

In a way that, to some extent, mirrors the change in American attitudes and sensibilities as seen in fiction and film, newspaper articles about college in the past 20 to 30 years are more grounded in reality. A result of college attendance becoming a more common experience and because of a more realistic review of the college myth, college isn't represented so much as an individual's way up but as a complex institution that provides television programming through athletics programs, research for the corporate world, and degrees. Clearly this review of newspaper articles on the subject of college over the past few hundred years in American reveals a consistent concern and debate about who should go to college, how they should be admitted, and what sort of financial support should be provided by the government. In this way, the popular image of American higher education is brought down to specific public policy issues and values in this collection of newspaper columns as seen over time.

In the late twentieth century, college campuses became frequent locations for biting satires on academia, signaling a more mature and critical understanding of the university. Literary critics have noted that one reason the college campus provides a perfect setting for satires is because its strong hierarchy is well-suited to humorous situations (Lyons, 1962). In *Me and the Liberal Arts* (Morrah, 1962), a boy from a small town in the South tries to enroll in college but gets in the wrong line and is instead employed by the college as a groundskeeper. In this satirical commentary on the poor in college, underprivileged students are admitted but only to work, not study.

In contemporary novels, college often serves as an ironic and titillating setting. Novels such as Jane Smiley's *Moo* (1995) use the modern university as an absurd Kafkaesque location, in this case an agricultural university, for a plot full of intrigue and lust. In Tom Wolfe's *I Am Charlotte Simmons* (2004) we find a rather sensationalistic depiction of three converging scandals. It portrays a fish-out-of-water story of an academically gifted freshman from backwoods North Carolina who is shocked by the liberal lifestyle she finds at prestigious Dupont University. She takes up with a predatory fraternity boy but ends up with a star basketball player who is under investigation for having an academic tutor ghost-write his British history assignment. A subplot involves a scandal about an ambitious California governor's secret affair with a co-ed on the eve of his commencement address. One interpretation of this satirical novel is as a commentary on the fate of a low-income young woman at an elite university who is naïve enough to believe the college myth. She finds exploitation and disillusionment and general mistreatment throughout. The theme presented in this book is that college is not for the likes of a poor girl from North Carolina, no matter how gifted academically. On the other hand, those privileged children of the wealthy attending Dupont on reflection don't seem that well off either.

Generational Perspectives: Where We Have Been

How has the image of college changed for students? For this book I interviewed a group of older first-generation college students, primarily connected to a senior citizen group taking university courses for enrichment purposes. The difference in attitude from today's students towards college is clear from the start when one listens to past generations. Although often their struggles to get and adjust to college are similar to those experienced by today's students, the attitude toward that struggle and position in society is markedly different.

Older first-generation students, for whom going to college was more unusual, didn't waste a moment too long in school and getting a job that would occupy a lifetime: "My family's work ethic was to find a job, work hard and stay with it." Perhaps even more than today's students from low-income families, many past generations spoke about parents who did not understand the value of higher education. Males in particular were expected to find a good job and to support a family. Parents of first-generation college students today hold often almost a blind belief in the importance of education for their children, regardless of their own level of educational attainment: "I was raised almost entirely by my mother, who had a high opinion of education even though she had only completed the sixth grade." Some talk about not only the general importance economically of pursuing a college degree, but of the subsequent "respectability" gained. The following description is typical of what I heard from the older generation of first-generation college students:

> My mother was convinced that higher education was essential to success. She had only completed the sixth grade before her mother died in childbirth and she was forced to stay home to care for younger children. She never had the opportunity to further her education in any formal sense, but she worked hard at being a waitress, which allowed her to support her and me.

Books around the house and role models in relatives and family friends appear to have been important resources in the past as they are today for first-generation college students. Living at home without parental financial support and working at part-time jobs were also all common experiences in the past.

In a more important way, I heard something from past generations that has become an important discovery in my search for understanding low-income college students, which is that the deprivation is not just about being formally educated, but one of worldliness: "The adult people in my life did not have many worldly life experiences. Many were first-generation born, did not have any more than a high school education and did not travel." One older first-generation student aptly described the importance of this broader knowledge of the world to success in school:

> Looking back on it now, the key difference between me and the more advantaged classmates was having a perspective. Perspective is key to making decisions. If the young adult doesn't have it, then it is important for the network [parents, friends, mentors] to provide it.

The all-important web of relatives, friends, and business associates who support privileged children was missing then as it is now for first-generation college students: "I just was not able to get any perspective from this network." One man from the Middle West spoke about this chasm of influence and knowledge of the world as because of being raised in rural areas, not the "big city." "Coming from families that were advantaged (professional parents, wealthier, well traveled) allowed them to have more and different encounters/experiences that I did." He spoke about classmates in college having fathers who were doctors and lawyers who would help them with good advice on their field of study, applying for graduate school, and finding good jobs after graduation.

Students from previous generations, especially in college in 1950s and 1960s, talk in many cases about an easy transition from college to successful careers. Unlike today's graduates who often first have trouble finding a job, and then typically change careers many times, they had less employment transitions and lived securely: "I was able to provide for my children without difficulty due to the salary I was able to receive due to my education." Earning a degree had more importance to former generations, especially for first-generation students. Many noted a watering down of the prestige and impact of an undergraduate degree: "Today a BA degree is only a stepping stone to an MA or similar degree." In many cases, attending college is more socially expected now according to those I spoke with. Especially for females in previous generations, college was a route to personal independence and security wherein some met with resistance from parents, while others enjoyed supportive families: "My father especially was proud to have a daughter in college." One retired woman told me about being accused of cheating when she scored well on a math aptitude test which showed she should pursue engineering. Nevertheless at the end of World War II, she said that women were actively recruited by universities for typically male majors.

Previous college-going generations speak of many of the same adjustment problems students today experience. They pointed in particular to poor academic preparation and in general "fitting in," and many talked about the heavy reliance on the fraternity and sorority system for social life at that time.

> All social life on the campus revolved around the fraternity/sorority system. They gave the parties, they visited each other for exchange dinners, they sponsored their members for offices in various campus organizations, and they provided the campus leaders. If you were on the outside of this system it was difficult to blend in.

For many, the difficulty of adjusting had to do with moving from a rural to an urban setting, or large college, and a modern world. For instance, one woman told me that she was used to only handling cash at home and had trouble with paying tuition and rent in this manner.

Low-income college students from previous generations also pointed to financial need as an obstacle: "Money was a problem and scholarships were not as available as they are now, nor were the subsidized lending programs." This lack of money led to some not adapting to the campus life because of the need to live off-campus or at home, and missing out on opportunities to join fraternities. Those who attended college in the 1950s consistently commented on the lack of financial aid, loans or scholarships. Some of the students found special employer sponsored programs for more applied majors such as engineering. For instance, one spoke of a program at General Motors that helped fund his engineering degree.

Overall, previous generations seem to note more direct impact from their college degree than seen in today's graduates. Especially for the post-World War II college generation up until the 60s, the economic and career benefits were clearly identified. Additionally, those I spoke with who now are retired, and perhaps have a broader life perspective, often discussed the psychological and personal longtime benefits of having a college education: "It gives you confidence." The retired college graduates I interviewed talked about their education leading to a lifetime of cultivated interests, the ability to think analytically and have a curiosity about the world around them. Additionally, they often remark about how broadening it was to meet people from different backgrounds as well as nationalities: "to interact with a diverse population of students from all over the world. This helped shape values such as empathy, acceptance of others." In this way, many in earlier generations focus on learned tolerance as a benefit of college education. "A college education provides the student with knowledge of other cultures and ways of thinking which creates greater tolerance for differences in society."

In terms of the social mobility function, those from previous college going generations did indeed see a way up the social ladder: "Education tends to bring capable people from original lower socio-economic level up to place where they can contribute." However, some noted that in order to earn their degree they had to give up a few years of earnings. Additionally, the education they received was not always directly related to the careers they pursued: "My college education did not prepare me for the business aspect. That I had to learn from observation and experience."

It was interesting to see how older, pre-affirmative action generations viewed equity issues in college admissions. Some simply believe that if there is an opportunity to go to college, regardless of the obstacles, then the equity social aim is met: "Lower-income students are given the opportunity to enter the middle and upper income classes as a result of education." Others point to a work ethic and positive attitude as being more important than providing a level playing field. In general, the pre-affirmative action era students often seem unwilling to accept corrective measures that were not used in their era. Nevertheless, they do often realize that inequity existed at the time. For example, one told me that he was denied entrance to medical school because at 26, he was considered too old.

Some doubted that education or college would in itself lead to greater social equity. One older woman argued for a larger understanding of the "system" of education that includes more informal kinds of learning occurring with family, friends, and mentors in various capacities: "I think unfortunately, too many students take classes to get a degree and forget to learn along the way." Education for many former college students means discussion and encountering divergent points of view that prevent the kind of narrowness that many without college are hindered by. I saw in this group from previous college generations an acceptance that there are "natural" limits in ability and opportunity in society, and that college for them and others was important in their lives, but had distinct boundaries.

Conclusion

College in America for at least the past two centuries has been emblematic of central beliefs in our society. From the "college man" at the turn of the nineteenth century to the images of hard working minority students in the 1960s, the popular image of the university as seen in college novels, films, and in the popular imagination form evocative patterns of meaning. In this chapter I reported on what I found in looking through newspaper and film archives and at college novels with an eye towards seeing how the college-going experience for low-income young adults have been portrayed over time. One can see that the popular images over different eras of American history as seen in newspapers and fictional accounts has perpetuated images of low-income students, asserting an ideal of social mobility that has faded. With students today, I found collective descriptions of college as a route to easier work, better living conditions, and a place where individuals can succeed with enough effort. Low-income students also talk about college as a place where they gain an important worldliness. While college for the past two centuries has been a symbol of American belief in boundless opportunity, many speak about college as a place that is not for everyone.

The students I spoke with about images of college were consistent in many ways with those found in popular media including newspapers, novels, and movies.

The following table contrasts the idealist college myth perpetuated through the beginning of the twentieth century with the realistic/critical image more typically found at the end of the last century and today.

Table 6.1 Comparison of old versus new images of college

Old college image	New college image
College is a path to moving up in society	Sometimes a path
College is open to everyone with ability	Impractical for some
Merit-based admissions correct inequality	Advantages perpetuated by system
Financial aid corrects inequality	Partially helps, but too dependent on loans
Family background does not matter in college	Family background matters
IQ and academic success linked	Environment counts
There are no genetic differences in talent/ability	There are differences, but individual effort, self-image, and family background impact
Women and ethnic minority students face few barriers	Larger social structure still has impact
Elite universities look for diversity	Want to appear diverse
College success and subsequent economic mobility linked	Privilege and connections matter
Degrees for low-income students have equal impact	Family wealth has long-term impact

In many ways the distinction between the old and the new public images of college have primarily to do with an increasing appreciation for the complexity and variation in college-going experiences. Media images by their nature tend to reduce portrayals of institutions to a few key characteristics in order to carry greater symbolic meaning. Clearly, the one-note type of rags-to-riches-through-education stories of the early twentieth century no longer suits the twenty-first century audience. The primary change in the public images show that we no longer believe as a society that college is a consistent and broad-based way up in society for all. Additionally, the more realistic popular understanding of college sees that admissions and financial aid do not completely level the playing field for poor and ethnic minority students. Overall, American attitudes towards higher education reveal an acceptance of differences in talent and position in society that perhaps would not have been acceptable to articulate a century ago.

In sum, the history of the college novel reflects attitudes towards the poor student as deserving, but out of place. The poor student character is inherently ridiculous in many of these stories because he or she believes that college is about studying and social mobility, while the wealthy students know the hierarchal truth. The post-World War II novels express a deep disillusionment with the myth and become mainly realistic in style, or bitingly satirical. Like the novel, college films primarily focus on student life as a setting for romantic comedies often set in fraternities and sororities. In the last 40 years representations of college in American film have become more realistic telling stories of characters learning the irrelevancy of higher education to their lives. Movies often depict college as a place where personal issues take precedence over studying for the main characters. In recent times, filmmakers have turned a critical eye towards higher education and created an image of mistrusted institutions failing to adequately prepare students emotionally and intellectually for the real world.

American views of college, as reflected in the extremely popular representations of college students in Dink from *Stover at Yale* to Benjamin in *The Graduate*, have come a long way. Instead of being a place, as Dink says, where "you stand for what you are" college has become in the jaded eyes of the graduate from the 1960s a meaningless diversion representative of a world with twisted values. In this context, the notion of the poor characters striving for the college degree in the belief that it is a route to upward mobility is increasingly ridiculous. In fact, the characterizations in popular media today rarely represent college in the simple terms found 100 years ago.

In examining how the images of college have changed over time, I found an increased sense of the variability of college-going experiences. Americans are less confident of the simple college myth, that education is a sure way up in society, or that there is in any sense a real level playing field. Apparently, from all the evidence we've look at in this book, Americans are comfortable with this reality of the limited impact of college on individual fates and by extension on our society. The equal opportunity rhetoric does not deter Americans from understanding and accepting the limitations of admissions and financial aid policies to help poor and ethnic minority students. Finally, American attitudes towards higher education have become in some respects cynical, revealing an acceptance of differences in talent, position, and inequality in society that is deeply disturbing.

Chapter 7

As a Group, the Poor Benefit Less from a College Degree

This chapter argues that the impact of a degree on college graduates from low-income families as a group in terms of subsequent wages and other indictors of social mobility is less significant than for those from more advantaged groups. This is not to say that individual students from low-income families do not experience sometimes great direct financial benefit from a college degree only that as a group the real mobility is not as advertised. Critics of higher education have for many generations in America doubted the value of a college degree. I've been surprised in my own work at a college to find so many in the academy and in the community who minimize the practical impact of a degree. Especially within the corporate world, I find that it is very common to hear a refrain that it is not where and if you went to college, but what you can do. However, throughout the twentieth century as the doors of colleges were opened wider to the general population, there have been warnings of a watering down of the value of a college education.

In a recent report from the College Board (McPherson and Schapiro, 2006), the editors note that educational opportunity in America is in fact "spectacularly unequal." They claim that it has become a common understanding in America that the poor are largely uneducated and less able to go to college: "For reasons most people could easily name, students from impoverished backgrounds are less well educated and less well prepared for college than are those form more favored backgrounds" (McPherson and Schapiro, 2006, p. 6). We have reached a point in American higher education where admission to some college for the minimally academically qualified is open. While this is true in a strict sense, the practical impact of financial necessity becomes the real limit to access. The report points out most private colleges ration access to their resources based on a student's ability to pay high tuition rates. A result of changed finances in higher education and perhaps a greater sophistication in administration, has led independent universities to recruit upper-class students with more vigor in order to raise revenue. For instance, at 28 of the most selective private institutions, the so-called COFHE schools, only 10 percent of students come from the bottom 40 percent of the United States income distribution (Hill and Winston, 2006). As discussed here earlier in the chapter on admission practices, there is no practical advantage to universities in admitting poor students despite stated purposes of diversity. The report points out that if the result of these policies is to increasingly force low-income students into two-year and third-tier regional comprehensive institutions, then the quality of these lower-level institutions needs to improve in order to better address the education of the poor.

In the last chapter, where college as represented in popular media was taken up, we saw that since the end of World War II that there has been a broad discussion about the over-education of Americans; this widespread perception has continued. Richard Freeman's trendy 1976 book entitled *The Overeducated America* points to the powerful image of access to higher education presented in the well-know TV commercial from the 1960s for the Negro College Fund of a woman scrubbing floors so her son can go to college. This image epitomized the great growth in college enrollment that occurred in the 1950s and 1960s when the number of college students tripled and the number of bachelor degrees earned increased by 91 percent. Yet in the 1970s the percentage of college students declined for the first time in American history, signaling for some an educational oversupply. Freeman felt that this downturn was a watershed event, "likely to alter the degree and form of social mobility, the distribution of income, the rate of economic growth, and the link between schooling and work" (Freeman, 1976, p. 188). In response to the believed decline in the value a college education in the 1970s, he predicted that people would search for other ways to move up the socio-economic ladder. This natural attempt to look at other routes for advancement could lead to great social unrest if those from low-income groups saw that the myth of mobility through education was no longer accurate.

Before looking at data it is important to point out that statistics can be misleading when looking for causes. Some social science scholars note that superficial or surface causes appear responsible for a given outcome when there are more "basic causes" which are really behind the scene: "Empirical data can tell us what is happening far more readily than they can tell us why it is happening" (Lieberson, 1985, p. 219). In what follows the reader should keep in mind that the numbers describe what has occurred better than telling us the cause.

People on the Bottom Do Not Often Move Up

Many scholars point to two different ways of measuring how often people move up in society, either by income or occupation. Generally, the recent consensus is that there has been a slowing of mobility in the United States since the 1970s. According to one study (Beller and Hout, 2006), using either measure of income or occupation, only 30-40 percent stays in the same income or occupational bracket as their parents. The following table (7.1) shows economic mobility in the United States between 1979-2000. Note that while the majority does move to another general class, the persistence within the specific class is highest among the rich. In other words, the poor and the rich are the ones most like to stay in the class to which they were born.

Table 7.1 Intergenerational wealth mobility, 1979-2000

Origin quintile	Destination					
	Poorest	**Second**	**Third**	**Fourth**	**Richest**	**Total**
Poorest	45	27	11	9	9	100
Second	24	35	20	14	7	100
Third	11	20	35	21	13	100
Fourth	7	11	23	33	25	100
Richest	5	6	9	25	55	100

Source: Keister, 2005.

Increases in economic inequality during the 1980s made social mobility more important. Furthermore, despite the myth of greater mobility in America, the United States today only ranks in the middle internationally in terms of mobility. Additionally, 12.4 percent of the population or 33.9 million people, in America reported living in poverty at the end of the twentieth century (Bishaw and Iceland, 2003).

Some scholars find no evidence of social fluidity in industrial societies worldwide. Mobility rates seem to fluctuate slightly without any constant pattern of improvement or worsening in modern society. In their book *The Constant Flux: A Study of Class Mobility in Industrial Societies*, Robert Erikson and John H. Goldthorpe (1992) trace the belief in unusually high rates of mobility in America to Tocqueville's well-known studies conducted during the nineteenth century. In the same time period, Engels, in his work with Marx, also added to this perception by proclaiming that the United States was a country where everyone could become an independent capitalist of sorts. The reality is that the rates of mobility in America today are no greater than those in Europe, and the pattern internationally amounts to fluctuation or variance without a clear trend up or down. In this way the stratification of society into different classes is characterized by a powerful self-maintenance tendency. Those in power tend to try to maintain their status regardless of the country. Put another way, those people who create the rules write them so that they can continue in power. Finally, statistics repute the notion that America is a country of great social mobility. Instead, there appears to be a great churning of society primarily among the middle-classes.

Less Impact of a College Degree on Lower-Class Students

How does a college degree impact the lives of children from poor families? Generally, there is a correlation between a college degree and higher levels of income, and the economic gap between those with and without degrees increases over a lifetime. However, data indicate that people overestimate the real value of college and its impact on occupations and financial status. Additionally, there are indications of differences of impact based on class and ethnicity.

United States Census data reveal that those with college degrees in fact do have a higher annual income, with the difference in average income between a bachelor degree and a high school diploma amounting to a doubling of income over a work life. However, a closer look at these data reveals that the impact of a college degree at earlier ages is less in real dollars: $7,518 dollars annually for those 18-24 years of age, and $18,576 per year for those 25-34. In this way, the association of a college degree with income increases over a lifetime (again, this does not demonstrate that education causes the increase in income).

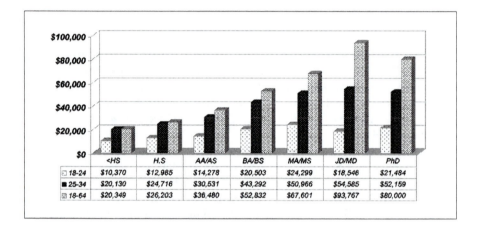

	<HS	H.S	AA/AS	BA/BS	MA/MS	JD/MD	PhD
18-24	$10,370	$12,985	$14,278	$20,503	$24,299	$18,546	$21,484
25-34	$20,130	$24,716	$30,531	$43,292	$50,966	$54,585	$52,159
18-64	$20,349	$26,203	$36,480	$52,832	$67,601	$93,767	$80,000

Figure 7.1 Earnings of the civilian population 18 to 64 years by educational attainment, California: 2000
Source: Based on data from US Census Bureau, 2000.

Indeed, if one calculates the cost of going to college and the lost wages while in school, it will take approximately nine years on average for a student with a bachelor degree to break even (figuring $20,000/yr. for college expenses and $25,000/yr. in lost income).

Two different national data sets give us an idea of the benefit of a college degree. In the National Center for Educational Statistics study *Where Are They Now? A Description of 1992-93 Bachelor's Degree Recipients 10 Years Later* (2004), approximately 90 percent of those queried 10 years after receiving their degree felt that their undergraduate degrees were worth the cost, time and effort required. Furthermore, 57 percent felt after ten years that their college degree was very important to establishing financial security, and 78 percent indicated that it was important to their work and career. Another look at how college graduates view the benefit of their degree through the United States Census gives us a more complex impression. Ninety point four percent of those surveyed nationally agreed that college was worth the financial investment. Contradicting the belief in this benefit is the fact that only a little over half of those surveyed credited college with leading to their current occupation and financial security. Furthermore, the link between a college degree and financial well being is not significantly different for women or ethnic minority graduates. What does one make of data showing overwhelming belief by the public of the financial worth of a college degree, yet at the same time admitting that for only some of the students the degree has given them economic security and prepared them for their current position? Apparently there is a disjuncture between the belief about the benefit of college and the reality as it is applied to all students. Additionally, the economic impact of a college may be indirect in some cases and therefore difficult to measure.

Furthermore, when trying to summarize the economic benefit of a college degree, one must balance increased lifetime income and position with lost income during college and acquired debt. According to the institutions in the table below (7.2), we see that greater access means greater debt in many cases.

Table 7.2 Institutional type example and low-income student indicators in 2004-2005

Institutional type example and low-income student indicators				
Institution name	Dependents: % applicants below $30,000 (2004-05)	Pell grants: % of 12-month enrollments (2004-05)	Percent of graduates with debt (2004-05)	Average debt of graduates (2004-05)
Florida State University	10	24	52	16,597
Princeton University	5	8	26	4,370
Santa Monica College	19	8	*	*
Spelman College	22	38	82	16,700
University of California	17	29	47	13,171

Note: * Not available at this time.
Source: Economic Diversity of Colleges.

While both the historically black college (HBCU) Spelman College and public universities Florida State and University of California at Berkeley attract far more low-income students, the resulting amount of debt collected by students at these institutions for individuals is significant. At the same time, the elite private institutions are in the fortunate position of being able to subsidize the financing of the select and very limited population of students they accept who are from low-income families. In addition to individual student debt, one also has to add the many years of lost income forgone by students who are taken out of the full-time job market while making progress towards their degrees. At an average of five years of study and an income of $25,000 per year, $125,000 of salary has been sacrificed by a student. In total then the real cost of a degree for student attending Florida State University, for example, is approximately $142,000.

The financial impact of a college degree as measured by average income differs significantly by ethnicity, used here as an indicator of class. Ten years after graduation, while a white graduate averages $61,200 per year, a black college graduate averages $53,500 (United States Department of Education, 2004). Unemployment ten years after college graduation is almost double for blacks as whites, 6.6 versus 3.5 percent. This measure based on US Census data indicates that blacks do indeed benefit less economically from a college degree.

Furthermore, one needs to look more closely at types of degrees and majors, and the characteristics of the graduates. Norton Grubb (2001) sees a fundamental difference between the labor markets for college graduates and those with partial higher education, especially two-year and vocational, and a large difference in benefit of college for men versus women, as well as for African-Americans. For example, men earn $29,652 annual earnings after graduation, while women average only $13,632. Despite the trend towards adult education, degrees received later in life generally do not provide economic advantage. Additionally, not all degrees are created equally. Since 1972, returns on attending elite colleges have increased as they have become more selective (Soares, 2007). Overall, there is decreased opportunity for low-income students to earn a degree, and lessened impact on their class position if they do earn one.

Despite assertions that the field is leveling allowing colleges to use a purely merit-based approach to admissions, many experts in the field are suspicious. In *Power and Ideology in Education*, Jerome Karabel and A.H. Halsey argue that despite common perceptions otherwise, the educational system in America often works to harden class positions: "It seems likely, then, that schools at least reinforce the inferior position of disadvantaged children with respect to education opportunity" (Karabell and Halsey, 1977, p. 21). They point out that the clear demand for education does not necessarily mean that social mobility will result. On the contrary, one result of the increased access to higher education in America has been a defensive tendency by the middle- and upper-class to protect their educational advantage through seeking additional degrees and by emphasizing the prestige of colleges they attended. This point was driven home earlier chapter two in the discussion of admission practices at elite universities. Karabel and Halsey further point out a number of myths of education. First, while Americans like to believe that there is a natural democracy of natural gifts, scholars generally agree that at least to some degree IQ is inherited. At the same time the great belief in education's ability to cure social problems is exaggerated. Second, the notion that college teaches career-specific skills is largely inaccurate; graduates acquire these on the job. A Marxist analyst of education, the authors claim, predicts an overproduction of college education which may in fact have occurred in America at the end of the twentieth century. Society has deflected the problem of an overabundance of college-educated students entering the workforce by putting the blame on individual performance. Finally, Karabell and Halsey claim that a college education removed from the specific social context is in fact a "weak currency." For the privileged, college education is simply added to the other forms of capital they already possess, it does not in any way replace that wealth. Norton Grubb concurs with Karabel and Halsey's assessment of the impact of college degrees. While 29 percent of jobs in 2000 required education beyond high school, higher education does not guarantee access to a good job. He points to the difference between education as a necessity and its sufficiency to ensure higher salaries and prestige: "Despite its popularity, the naïve version of human-capital theory has never been quite right" (Grubb, 2004, p. 156). Therefore, Grubb argues that to recommend college to all students is a correct general truism, but simply does not necessarily apply to all.

In sum, national data indicate that there is an association between a college degree and higher levels of income that increases over a lifetime. However, it is more difficult to firmly claim that the college degree causes the higher income because although there is a general belief among graduates in the benefit of college the actual impact on occupations and financial status is uneven. Most importantly to our inquiry, there are indications of differences of impact based on class. There is a conflict between the belief about the benefit of college and the reality students from poor families.

America Suffers by Comparison Internationally

In Europe, where there is a long tradition of class analysis, reviews of data disappoint in trying to show progress in class mobility through education. Especially in the United Kingdom, where there was a very large shift towards public post-secondary education in the 1960s and 1970s, the social mobility results are not what many expected. Surprisingly, American and European systems, notably that of Great Britain, show similar results while starting with very different approaches. Both systems function in a way that leads to tracking of students into distinct vocational or higher education routes. Kerckhoff (1974) presents the notion of "contest mobility" in America versus "sponsored mobility" in England. In this model, American education concentrates on making mobility an open contest, while in England the educational system recognizes a need for the government to directly support mobility.

Public policy internationally has displayed consciousness of class, while American higher education has relied on a less centralized and more privatized non-system. Only with affirmative action policies implemented at the end of the twentieth century did American higher education become directly purposeful in addressing inequality in educational opportunity. While most Americans believe that one of the ways that we promote the values of democracy and equality is through education, the United States shows less real mobility through education than is commonly believed.

The issue of social mobility is probably an even greater issue of attention on the international scene than in America. In a wide ranging analysis edited by Yossi Shavit and Hans-Peter Blossfeld (1993) published in book form as *Persistent Inequality: Changing Educational Attainment in Thirteen Countries*, the authors asked the primary question of to what extent socio-economic characteristics and education changed over time. Studying data collected in 13 different countries, they found that "In most cases, expansion has not entailed greater equality of educational opportunity among socioeconomic strata" (Shavit and Blossfeld, 1993, p. 15). In other words, except for Sweden and the Netherlands, the authors found that there still exists a clear connection between social class and educational attainment. These data are particularly surprising in that many of the studied countries went through a kind of radical restructuring which would lead one to predict measurable changes in socioeconomic inequality. Nevertheless, they found: "Even in extreme cases of industrial transformation (such as Taiwan, Japan, and Italy), and radical changes of the occupational structure (Israeli Arabs), the parameters of the education stratification process remain stable" (Shavit and Blossfeld, 1993, p. 19). One pattern the authors pin-pointed as a reason for this continued inequality was the increased vocational education options rather than college in order to accommodate the increasing numbers of low-income children. In addition, the example of Sweden shows that there can be multiple causes for class equalization outside of education, including family structure, labor market, and workplace conditions. In that society, experience showed that educational reform does not guarantee equalization (Jonsson, 1993).

Some scholars have looked at the overall international economic impact of education in relationship to class. Alison Wolf claims that the sorting function of education is important for businesses needing quick ways to place new employees (Wolfe, 2002). Contrary to popular belief, she argues that increased public education does not always lead to better economies. In fact, those countries which have concentrated most on elevating the education levels of their population have grown more slowly than those which have devoted less attention to education. Skilled workers are less important to economic growth than other factors making up the total economy. In those more liberal-minded countries that have concentrated on education as a way of lifting the standard of living for all, the result too often is over-educated employees and ineffective economies. Internationally, the increased investment in higher education has led to higher participation among the upper and middle classes. The impact of broader higher education is particularly evident in England where the upper classes increasingly participated in higher education: from 33 percent in 1960 to 79 percent in 1994. At the same time, those from low-income family backgrounds increased involvement from only four to 12 percent. In Japan, from 1961 to 1976 participation of those in the top 40 percent of income class rose from 72 to 76 percent.

In America, those from the top 25 percent family income and lowest 25 percent in school achievement entered college at the rate of 57.9 percent, while in the same year of 1972 the highest achieving lower 25 percent economic class went to college at the rate of 69.7 percent. In 1992, the rate of low-achieving high-income students rose to 77.3 percent while high-achieving low-income students entered only at a 77.6 percent rate. Thus by 1992, those from upper-class families who performed poorly in secondary school entered college at the same rate as those from poor families who performed well in secondary school (Wolfe, 2002).

So we see the American approach has not led to the increased mobility or participation of its low-income citizens over other countries internationally. Sadly, very different systems, cultural institutions, and class systems have not produced significantly better results in achieving mobility through education for low-income citizens. Nevertheless, Illich puts the American experience in an international context: "Whatever his or her claims of solidarity with the Third World, each American college graduate has had an education costing an amount five times greater than the median life income of half of humanity" (Illich, 1983, p. 49).

Student and Alumni Impressions of Social Mobility Function

Low-income students I interviewed were aware that college would not benefit them in the same way that it benefits upper-class children. Some see education as the only way up, save luck. Others believe that for most students college maintains their class position, echoing the belief of many economists. Low-income students also recognize that not all colleges are created equal. They understand that some are harder to get into, more expensive, and have predominately upper-class students. Students also talk about the advantage of already having money in their family, the inherited wealth benefit, which already positions them in the upper-class after college. Finally, they appreciate the nature of college prestige afforded by expensive college degrees. Many low-income students believe that they themselves may not benefit much from a college education, but that they will impact their descendants in a bigger way.

Some low-income students speak about relatively easy transitions to the job market. Other alumni talk about a direct career benefit from college, as one woman from a Southern university told me, "I'd probably still be working some meaningless job instead of having a career that I love." Some graduates point to very tangible economic advantages of college: "I would not own my own home, car, or be able to live life as I do know." The impact on college graduates was clearly a movement up in class from lower to the middle class for many. One woman in her late thirties from the South described college as a way out of a suffocating small town life. One single mother attending college later in life spoke about finding "adequate employment" but more importantly gaining self-confidence that led her to leave an unhappy relationship. Finally, a woman in her late thirties with lupus describes pursuing her dreams through college, and founding her own non-profit organization. She told me that college "opened doors" and that she was "catapulted" to a higher class because of her education.

Many college graduates have more difficult transitions from college, such as a recent graduate in her early twenties from a regional comprehensive university in the South, who described the transition from college as "rocky." She now works at Starbucks and laments not having a specific career goal: "You have to build your own bridge to a career and sometimes that takes a while to figure out," she tells me. Even so, she feels her degree will give her more choices in the future and that she has developed as a whole person. Another young woman in her early twenties tells of taking a few months off after graduation, doing temporary work, working as a substitute teacher and now pursuing work as a special education teacher. She denies that there is a mobility function in college, unless one picks a "profitable field"—evidently not teaching. Others speak about universal young adult type of experiences involving trouble adjusting to uninteresting and unchallenging jobs: "I can't do this for the rest of my life." Many speak about college itself being a limiting factor in that it directs one along a certain career route that may not suit the individual. Some non-traditional students in particular note little career impact to their degrees: "I don't think it changed anything." But in this case the student instead focuses on self-esteem gains rather than importance to her career. Another non-traditional student summed up the same sentiment: "I have completely benefited more than others because I have taken my time through school and have completed my education for myself and not for anyone else." Low-income college students are aware of their own uniqueness in surveying the overall social mobility function. They know that simply because they personally may have been successful it does not mean that their class as a whole is moving up in society. "I'm one out of 100," one told me.

Sidebar Portrait: Cindy

Cindy describes herself as an example of "downward mobility" in society, coming from an upper-class background but now living among the lower-middle class. Returning to college later in life, Cindy's husband and parents discouraged her warning of depriving her children of needed attention: "They never once believed that I would finish and be able to support myself." She saw college as a way out of an unhappy marriage with a depressed and abusive husband: "Choice, a very powerful word. I never felt I had choices before I completed the BA."

Cindy tells me about the emotional toll her struggle took, both in terms of her conflicted family life and the obstacles encountered as a non-traditional student. She worked part-time at a local nursery while attending college where she "hauled dirt, cow manure, plants and created terra cotta statues for retail sales." Working all day three days a week she was worn out and struggled to study and take care of her children: "Often my daughters would find me passed out with my psych book on my face!" A non-traditional student, she talks about feeling separated from the general college population: "Non-traditional students reflect a more serious side of obtaining an education." Cindy talks about feeling immense pressure to finish her education before time runs out on her to make important changes in her life. In contrast, she saw younger students who squandered their time, who were completely supported by their privileged families: "I did not learn to enjoy campus life."

After earning her degree, Cindy successfully made a career transition into management. She started as an administrative assistant, but eventually became a supervisor and manager. College for Cindy, as with many first-generation college students, provides a much needed confidence boost. In her case, Cindy also credits education with realizing the need to leave an abusive marriage. She points to the importance of learning critical thinking in college, an ability that can be applied to other areas of her life. Additionally, she appreciates the broadening impact of college exposing students to different social groups. When I ask her about whether her college education moved her up in society, she claims that she was not looking to move up: "I never wanted to be the golf club, tea, and crumpet type." Cindy argues that to pursue mobility in society is a value choice that she has rejected: "I felt a drive to a peaceful joyous life and I have found it."

As is common with non-traditional adult students, a university education often represents a personal turning point in life and enabler of change. As a way to a career and to make an important personal transition in her life, college was successful for Cindy. I do note however that Cindy's view of college is consistent with a more realistic or critical view of the function of college in America—she doesn't expect or want college to be an avenue to moving up in society. Instead, Cindy sees college as serving a very specific and limited, albeit important, function enabling her to transition personally out of a bad marriage and practically into a living wage.

Sidebar Portrait: Regina

Regina is from the generation who went to college in the early post-World War II Era. She describes herself as coming from a low-income family where she was told very directly: "Our family cannot afford to go to college." She followed the vocational track in high school: "I did not choose the college preparatory courses such as languages, higher math, etc. This was because of the guidance my parents provided to me."

Regina says that women in her time had very limited career choices: secretaries, nurses or teachers. While jobs were widely available for men, women had few opportunities and faced prejudices of all sorts. In high school, a counselor identified Regina's potential and pressed her to apply for college; a teacher encouraged her to take Ohio state English exams for a scholarship competition. Eventually, Regina attended Ohio State University and trained as a teacher: "I lived in Columbus where Ohio State was located, and could live at home, thus cutting expenses." Ohio State was, even at that point, a very large university, with mostly residential students. Regina describes the population as mostly middle-class from the larger towns who enjoyed many of the student activities for which she had limited time—sororities, student government, and sports. As with many of the low-income college students, Regina describes how her family issues conflicted with her studies. Her father's cancer drew both emotional and financial support away from her. While in college she "got by" financially on two scholarships and a part-time job. "Without the encouragement of two special teachers and a desire to be a teacher myself, I would never have gone to college." Regina took on a heavy load of studies, part-time work, riding the bus back and forth to Ohio State from her home. She pushed herself to graduate in three years in order to enter employment earlier: "At times, I did not know if there would be enough to pay the next quarter's fees." Although the first in her family to attend college, Regina's sister and cousins followed after her and completed college.

Conclusion

This chapter illustrates the lessened impact of a degree on college graduates from low-income families compared to more advantaged groups. Overall, what the numbers tell is a complex yet stark story of not only lessened access, but a lower impact for low-income students when they do manage to overcome poor preparation, lack of financial assistance and other types of cultural capital and earn a degree. The stories from alumni demonstrate how college degrees during the decade following World War II were valued and benefited students in direct ways. Their lives contrast sharply with the stories of current students found throughout the book who recognize differences in the values of degrees based on social background and college attended. These contemporary students also speak of the gap between expectations of the benefit from a degree and the reality they face, as well as the psychological damage incurred by poor students who leave college prematurely.

Data show that American social mobility is limited and not markedly higher than in other industrialized countries. Different cultural and political systems internationally using different approaches have not produced significantly improvement of mobility through education for low-income citizens. In America, the chance of getting a college degree has increased in recent decades only for those families in the upper-half economically. Wealthier students still significantly outnumber low-income high school and college graduates. Although national data indicate that there is an association between a college degree and higher levels of income, it is difficult to claim in broad way that a college degree leads to higher income because the actual impact on occupations and financial status is uneven. Furthermore, the impact of a degree varies based on the social class of a graduate. Thus, there is a conflict between the belief about the benefit of college and the reality for students from low-income families.

Economists and sociologists have looked at patterns of social and economic mobility and ways to predict the "life chance" of a child based on assorted variables. Mayer (1997) in her book *What Money Can't Buy: Family Income and Children's Life Chances* argues that once basic needs are met that the specific characteristics of a family are more important than income or wealth in predicting social position. She describes two basic theories for predicting life chances for children: the investment theory and the good-parent theory. Contrary to popular opinion, family income only serves as a "proxy" for important characteristics of families such as an emphasis on a work ethic and developing cognitive skills that positively influence children. Although linked to income, the family characteristics, according to Mayer, are more primary in determining a child's life chances.

Given these facts and perspectives, it would appear that simple financial investment in college by government and/or individual families does not alone have a positive impact on low-income students. The negligible benefit of a college degree, especially for students from low-income backgrounds, led John Ashworth (1998) to coin the phrase "marginal graduates." He cites figures indicating that 30 percent of college graduates report being over-educated for their current positions and questions whether there really is a positive return-on-investment for public higher education if the data on these marginal graduates are fully recognized. Ashworth notes that as increased participation has led to more marginal graduates, the social rate of return has dropped considerably. Consequently, a further public investment in higher education may be a waste of resources: "… the social rates of return to higher education for the marginal graduate appear low enough to suggest that investment elsewhere would seem a better proposition" (Ashworth, 1998, p. 33). The ineffectiveness of simple educational expansion to meet the needs of poor students can be further characterized by a theory known as "maximally maintained inequality," or the idea that lower classes only move up when the needs of the upper-class are completely met first. In this way, the growth of secondary and higher education capacity in America from 1920s to 1980s led to a narrowing of the gap in educational achievement from underrepresented groups, especially women, but did not have a large impact on the plight of the children of the poor (Hout, Raftery and Bell, 1993). In the next chapter, I consider the significance of the data presented in this chapter and implications of the argument that has been made throughout this book regarding the way American higher education perpetuates inequality.

Chapter 8
Conclusion: We Can Do Better

Review and Summary

This book follows a linear progression from the academic and social preparation for college of students from low-income families through experiences while in college and revealed how students as a whole are prepared for failure. In the first chapter I took up the controversial topic of the impact of natural ability and environment on low-income students, and the degree to which society purports that individuals are correctly sorted. Thus, people are poor simply because they are intellectually less gifted has been the argument made by the eugenics proponents over the past two centuries. I also explored the fascinating history and function of standardized testing and exposed a link to the disturbing eugenics movement, as well as their practical utility in restricting enrollment of "undesirable" applicants at elite colleges. Obstacles for low-income students surrounding language proficiency and the limited availability of Advanced Placement courses were investigated. The lack of social preparation for students from low-income families was illustrated by the front of the classroom experiences of faculty members. This is in many ways the most difficult obstacle to overcome for students because poor self-images reinforced by school performance, parental education limitations, and low expectations handicap students. Although students are encouraged by the rhetoric of our culture to pursue their educational dreams, at the same time they often carry with them negative self-images. As a result, students from poor families are inadequately prepared for college and set up for failure.

The second chapter followed the history of calculated discrimination against low-income students in admissions practices. The hugely unequal statistics on the admissions of low-income students to American universities are detailed, as well as the mysterious practices of elite universities. Furthermore, I explored how the important changes in financial aid policy since the 1980s, which put more of an emphasis on loans rather than scholarships, had a devastating impact on low-income students. Current financial aid policies were found inadequate to encourage and support low-income student enrollment in college because of the larger economic context.

The next chapter contended that children from low-income families confront many challenging obstacles in college leading to higher stop-out rates. Statistics showed that while American society as a whole is increasingly college educated, low-income students are not rising in educational attainment at the same rate for multiple reasons including a significantly larger high school discontinuation rate. I categorized adjustment problems for low-income students attending college fall into personal, family, cultural, and structural categories. The personal issues that impact student success in college center on self-image formation that expresses itself as a lack of motivation, low confidence, a poor work ethic, and an overall limited knowledge of the world. The struggle to separate from the parents, which is developmentally a common occurrence for young adults, is perhaps more extreme for poor students because of both cultural and practical attachments. The level of appropriate motivation to apply the extra effort needed to succeed in college is important on a personal level, but influenced greatly by the larger family and social spheres. On the cultural level, students are directly impacted by the needs of their immediate families seen vividly illustrated in Debbie's story of needing to intervene because of her teenage sister's pregnancy. The collective beliefs surrounding gender and other family-based restrictions strongly impact the students during college. The wider structural context has a pervasive impact on poor students in terms of the economic realities for their life chances, and impacts both the individual and social levels specifically by setting income and occupational limits and social rules. Overall in this chapter, I discovered the importance of the family in encouraging children to attend college. Furthermore, if the family is culturally isolated or adheres to rigid gender roles, then the students are hindered in their educational ambitions. The way the family is structured affects the college-going chances of children by, in some cases, insisting that students make choices benefiting the family over the individual.

The fourth chapter considered the interconnected challenges for low-income women and ethnic minority students in college. The chapter looks at how public institutions have struggled with changes in policy regarding affirmative action, as well as more recent efforts to use more complex admissions models. The prospects of college admissions based purely on academic merit was analyzed and found to be unpromising because of the larger social-political context. I learned that race and gender still have a strong and complex impact on college-goers. The fifth chapter is a case study of one group of students, children of migrant workers, at a public university in Southern California. Drawing on numerous interviews with students, as well as classroom observations, I described their often poignant stories showing what it is like to be an outsider in college.

In the sixth chapter, I argued that the college myth of social mobility has persisted but is now fading. By analyzing images of college in popular culture, I tried to better understand higher education's articulated social purpose in America and how it has changed over time. College movies and novels present intriguing representations reflecting collective attitudes about the role of higher education in American society. From early characterizations in novels and film, the poor have consistently been portrayed as outsiders in college. This attitude mirrored the debate in newspapers in the last two centuries of the function of college and how wide the door of the academy should be opened to the unwashed masses. Contrary to unchanged American political rhetoric, fictional representations at the of the twentieth century show a much more realistic and cynical view of how colleges in reality benefit children from low-income families. I also gathered the perspective from older Americans which shed particular light on the changing reality of women and ethnic minority students in college. While their stories are quite different from the current students, the knowledge and attitudes gained from the Depression Era, wars, years of work experience, and just living, provide depth to our examination of class in America. Past generations of college graduates talk about barriers, especially for women and ethnic minorities, but in a time when degrees were more unique speak of greater personal benefit. Overall, American attitudes towards higher education reveal an acceptance of differences in talent and position in society that perhaps would not have been acceptable to articulate previously.

The seventh chapter showed the generally low rates of mobility in the United States and the weaker impact of a degree on low-income students. Overall, what the numbers tell is a complex story of not only lessened access, but reduced impact for low-income students. Alumni stories illustrated how college degrees during the decade following World War II were greatly valued and benefited students in direct ways, contrasting with the stories of current students who recognize differences in the values of degrees based on social background. International statistics reveal that American social mobility is not as high as in other industrialized countries.

Finally, in this chapter, I reflect on the findings and their implications and consider additional directions for further research. I argue that American higher education fails students from low-income families and inequality is perpetuated by often well-meaning educators and public policy. I then end with notions to consider on the changing purpose of higher education in society asserting the public benefit and moral imperative of doing a better job in educating children from low-income families.

Findings

The following is a list of the important conclusions I've reached in this journey pursuing an understanding of the fate of college students from low-income families:

• Merit-based Admissions Doesn't Work for Low-Income Students

Meritocracy narrowly construed as test scores or grade point average without consideration of obstacles and the environmental context will not work for the poor. The meritocracy model argues that those who are the most innately intelligent will be most successful in life and should rise to the top in college admissions. However, the clear impact of economic class on college going can be seen in the fact that those youth who are similarly prepared in high school enroll at different rates depending on their parent's income and educational level. Differences in average parental education for those in the top and bottom have widened as well, leading to what some experts call a doubling of the benefit for the upper class through college attendance. The larger socio-political context and function of higher education in society prevent a meritocratic admissions system from working.

- Changes in Financial Aid Policy Alone Will Not Correct Inequality

It is a simple truth that students from poor families do not go to college because they cannot afford to do so. Financial aid alone does not solve the problem for two reasons. First, even full scholarships do not replace foregone wages while attending college. In many cases, those families in extreme poverty depend on the wages of older children for survival. Second, for both practical and cultural reasons, college loans are not a practical option for low-income students. With good reason, poor families are very hesitant to take on loans. With a lack of surety in the economic value of a college degree, taking on the risk of such a financial burden for a family already living on the economic edge is simply not sensible. Finally to complete the economic picture, students who do attend college report a need to both work and send money to their families. In sum, the weight of poverty suffocates even more generous efforts at financial aid than we have today.

- Low-income Students Lack Worldliness

Students from low-income backgrounds often suffer from a lack of general experience and knowledge of the world. This lack directly impacts the students in the classroom because of a limited frame of reference and context for learning new things. Additionally, low-income students then miss out later after graduation in finding a productive career path because of a more limited knowledge of the world, and network of opportunity. In this way, the social isolation, typical of many low-income families, further exacerbates the deficiency in these students.

- Student Stories Describe Difficult Adjustment Problems in College

The difficulty in adjustment for first-generation college students is first largely a cultural one. College has a culture with strong rules of behavior that is foreign to many students. The traditional university clearly values literacy norms in line with the elite eastern preparatory schools which are completely foreign to middle-class, let alone low-income, students. I found adjustment issues when attending college fell into three main categories or domains of experience: personal, family/cultural and structural. The individual or personal level was filled with stories of students going through identity formation issues characteristic of their developmental stage. In many ways this first domain is less controllable and is a place where social realities become apparent. The family sphere gets us into the cultural issues which are in many ways the most powerful influence on the experience of first-generation college students. Finally, the larger unequal socio-political environment provides a context for the family and personal experiences.

- Student Stories Describe Great Tension with Parents

I was frankly shocked by what I heard from students about their parents. While some students talked about appreciation for the sacrifices of their parents, they also spoke about suffering from alcoholic parents and various forms of abuse and manipulation. Those especially talented and lucky students who do make it to college often suffer under extraordinary pressure by their families to succeed. The fate of their families often rests on the young student's shoulders and this pressure contributes to their feelings of resentment.

- Elite Colleges are Controlled by and Primarily Serve the Upper Classes

Unfortunately, the fact that elite colleges are for the children of the wealthy is of no surprise to anyone. Economists and social theorists point out that the creation of an elite class has occurred in all societies and appears to be a natural tendency. Elite universities have gamed the admissions process to advantage the privileged through various means including admission on subjective "character," the use of biased standardized tests, and giving preference to special admission athletes who disproportionately come from upper-class families. Given the conservative rhetoric against affirmative action policies, it is ironic to find that admissions policies to this day often give advantage to upper-class families.

- The Dependence on Text-Based Education Hurts Low-Income Students

For those who are not native English speakers, the pedagogical dependence in college on textbooks is an especially clear disadvantage. Echoing what was presented in chapter one, the economist Thorstein Veblen makes the important point that the way one speaks is evidence in society of family lineage. Those from upper-classes speak in ways that gives a connotation of leisure: "Great purity of speech is presumptive evidence of several successive lives spent in other than vulgarly useful occupations" (Veblen, 2006, p. 102). This dependence of teaching in college on the oral and written language of leisure is a legacy of our education system which excludes low-income students in a practical manner.

- There May be Better Opportunity for Low-Income Students at Private Universities

As detailed in the second chapter, outside of the top elite schools, the privates actually serve a higher percentage of students from low-income families. This fact is an embarrassment for American public higher education.

- Students from Low-Income Families are Completing College Less Often

While there has been some increase in the number of students from poor families going to college, there has also been an increase in the failure of those same students to complete their degrees.

- Beliefs About the Undeserving Poor Are Behind College Public Policies

Increasingly conservative views placing blame on the poor for their condition in America have become prominent at the end of the twentieth century and are behind public funding, financial aid and admission policy changes that do not favor low-income students. Reduced public funding for higher education over the past three decades, financial aid redirected to the middle-class since the Reagan administration, and the turning back of affirmative action policies all reflect the change in public attitudes towards the poor.

- Americans No Longer Believe the Education Myth

Americans no longer hold a singularly idealistic vision of college. While students do talk of college as a route to better living and working conditions, many also speak about it as a place that is not appropriate for everyone and as four years spent with limited personal benefit. Furthermore, there is an understanding that students have very different college experiences, especially those from poor families.

Recommendations for Further Research and Analysis

It is a common perception among the middle class that low-income students have less ability and drive and these are the reasons for poor academic performance. Ell Brantlinger (2003) in her analysis of the liberal attitude to public education, *Dividing Classes: How the Middle Class Negotiates and Rationalizes School Advantage*, argues that Americans waiver between believing students of varying backgrounds are the same in school on the one hand, or very different on another. This schizophrenic attitude towards education has led to different approaches to education policy, with a general insistence that the poor become more like the middle class in order to succeed. As we've seen by the example of adjustment problems for poor students in college, it is counter-productive to insist the low-income become middle-class by simply attending school; they lack material wealth and the associated advantages. With this understanding of the need to take a fresh look at public policy to correct educational inequality, I offer the following suggestions for further research and examination.

- Examine How Public Higher Education Can be Redesigned Specifically for Low-Income Students

The findings of this book should have special meaning for public universities because land grant universities established by the Morrill Act of 1862 are charged with providing wide access to advanced education. Students from two public universities, one in the West and the other in the South, are profiled in this book and reveal many of the specific challenges encountered. For various reasons, including most importantly a decrease in funding, land grant universities do not serve low-income students as well as they should. As we saw, except for the most selective colleges such as Harvard, Yale and Princeton, private universities have a larger percentage of lower-income applicants (Economic Diversity of Colleges, 2007). Private or independent universities are filling gaps left by the public, land-grant universities in providing access to lower-income students. This fact serves as both an example of the failure of public higher education and perhaps a partial remedy going forward.

For instance, one reality is that low-income students cannot afford to stop working in college. Although colleges have adapted somewhat to students who work, they are still extremely resistant to meeting the demands of this group. We must face the reality that this resistance is class-based and stands in the way of confronting basic inequality in our society. The dreaded for-profit universities are successful because traditional higher education has failed low-income students (Berg, 2005). Requirements at public research universities, such as the University of California that necessitate students to attend full-time, are simply unfair to those that out of necessity must work while attending school. In addition to changing the format of education to accommodate working students, universities need to pay attention to the practical and emotional barriers to college attendance low-income students face.

- Analyze How to Make Tax Rates More Equitable

The United States gave the wealthy tax cuts at the end of the twentieth century. According to the United States Congressional Budget Office, between 1977 and 1999, the top 1 percent in annual income received a federal tax cut of 13 percent, worth an average of more than $40,000. The Center on Budget and Policy Priorities notes about these data that "changes in federal tax policy over the period have exacerbated, rather than lessened, the large growth in income disparities that has occurred in the private economy" (Shapiro and Greenstein, 2007). On the international level, the United States' lower comparative tax rate means that public education is less supported. In this way, there is a lessened effect of redistribution of wealth through public college opportunities for the poor.

At the end of the twentieth century when funding for public higher education began to flatten, scholars started noting a change in attitude towards education and mobility. One can argue for increased funding of higher education, but resources tend to benefit those most that are prepared and positioned to take advantage of the opportunities presented. On the other hand, reduced funding tends to first cut out those who are least prepared. Voters seem to want to try to give preference to those who show merit, that the best educational system is one that is completely competitive—a meritocracy. Rather than an affirmation of the belief in mobility through education in America, I view this development as resignation to the fact that not all are created equal and that a certain amount of unfairness in society is inevitable.

- Consider the Goal of Serving Low-Income Students as a Priority Over Seeking Prestige

The insane competition by universities to climb over each other in the *US News and Report* rankings has had a directly negative impact on poor students because the quality measures work against them. A concentration on such data as financial status, student academic test scores, research dollars, endowments, and reputations make it less attractive for selective institutions to accept lower-income students. Universities need to reject the pursuit of higher ranking and instead formally work towards using measures of serving low-income students, such as percentage of Pell Grant recipients, to assess their own success. The mad scramble to outrank each other is damaging the budgets and soul of pubic universities in particular. According to a special report by the *Chronicle of Higher Education*, the *US News and World Report* ranking methodology especially hurts public institutions (Van Der Werf, 2007, p. A13). Measures such as alumni giving rate, student-faculty ratio, acceptance rate, and financial resources handicap institutions that are focused on serving the broad public. In their book *In Pursuit of Prestige: Strategy and Competition in US Higher Education*, Anthony Brewer and Susan Gates (2002) argue that the pursuit of prestige often linked to sports, research, and faculty reputation by colleges is risky and expensive. In terms of a pure business analysis, some institutions, especial for-profits, opt out of the competition and instead focus on meeting student needs directly. The authors claim that because most universities seek prestige, it leaves the opportunity for those that don't, and this is more likely to occur at privates. Again, the success of the privates in serving low-income students over pursuing a higher national rating is an embarrassment to public universities.

- Analyze How to Reduce Inefficiencies

Here is a simple and important truth: *The low productivity of American universities hurts poor students most*. Students from wealthy families are not bothered by continual fee increases. While such hikes are inconvenient for middle-class students, only low-income students are prevented from attending college as a result. Inefficiencies are numerous, but let me point to one obvious inefficiency: university scheduling. It is time for universities to operate year round. There is no excuse for the schedule at most universities in which the facilities are used at full capacity only seven to eight months. If enrollment were better managed at public universities, more low-income students could be served in greater numbers. At any public university, hundreds, if not thousands, of additional poor students could be accommodated at little additional cost simply by enacting an enrollment on space-available basis policy.

- Evaluate the Impact on Grades and Standardized Tests on Student Self Confidence

Our current grading and measurement system in higher education disadvantages those who have the most ground to make up—the lower classes. The EOP counselor specifically made this point articulating the need to use different measures of success for low-income students. While their academic records may be mediocre, the actual change in students can be "incredible." Instead, our grading system now ends up being a constant attack on low-income students who often end in a cycle of reduced effort and poor grades. The echo of the accomplishment of a single low-income college graduate can reverberate through subsequent generations and have a very large impact, greater than that of one more high-achieving child from an advantaged family. Peter Drucker challenged the perceived value of a Harvard education in a seminar that I attended in graduate school claiming that this premiere institution admits well-prepared students from advantaged families, and after four years, produces graduates who are well prepared and advantaged. Exactly what has the university done? Looked at in terms of productivity, Harvard University is much less productive in teaching/learning than an average community college. The lesson: in education we measure the wrong thing.

Final Thoughts

What if all this "tinkering" with higher education were done, would there still be considerable inequality in higher education? One of the clear findings coming from the large picture that emerges out of this book is that the larger social and political context for low-income students is very weighty and complex. Vast inequality and poverty in America is the environment within which universities operate. One would be naïve to think that any effort by higher education alone could overcome poverty and injustice, and thus more directly impact the lives of low-income students. However, I believe that the recommendations for further study made here and by others based on a more full understanding of the plight of low-income students in college can make a significant difference.

The myth that college moves the poor as a group up in society is false. While it is inspiring to tell stories of individual struggles and success through education, as we often like to do in higher education, it deludes us into thinking we are more successful than we plainly are. Most importantly, it prevents us from confronting our clear failings in serving the needs of low-income students. The hard fact of the matter is that college is a primary way that wealthy families transfer privilege to their children, while at the same time functioning to certify the inadequacy of the disadvantaged.

I would never want to dissuade a child from a low-income family from attending college. However, it is important that we as a society separate out individual stories of successful mobility through education and a general pattern of the disadvantaged moving up in American society. This book has shown in detail how the intended and stated mobility function of college in a general way is not working and why. What's more, I illustrated how Americans no longer hold a purely idealistic vision of college. While the rhetoric of college as a place for unbounded opportunity remains to some degree, American attitude towards higher education is more realistic and grounded than ever before. Students do talk of college as a route to better living and working conditions, but many also speak about college, and especially some elite colleges, as a place that is not appropriate for everyone. Overall there is an increased understanding of how many college-going experiences differ based on class and the college attended. The Horatio Alger success through education stories of the early twentieth century clearly no longer suit the twenty-first century public mind set.

Part of the reason for this altered attitude towards college is an understanding that there is not to begin with a level playing field for students. The education myth disillusionment represents an acceptance of inequality in American society that is reflected more broadly in our social policies. As shown in the fact that 94 percent of applicants are admitted to their first or second choice universities, low-income students intuitively understand the nature of the college class system and are not even trying for admission to many of the elite universities (Soares, 2007, p. 11). It is not the case that low-income students are being turned away from the best universities—they are not even trying to get in. Americans have come to know into which universities they are most likely to get accepted—in a real and deeply unsettling sense they have come to know "their place."

America is far too comfortably unequal. Although we like to think of ourselves as being a generous and philanthropic people, the fact is that the United States does the least among advanced countries to prevent childhood poverty. The following figure (8.1) reveals the small amount of resources our government puts into combating poverty.

Unfortunately, the reality in America today is the poor are increasingly comprised of children. Official national poverty rates reveal that today's children are poorer than they have been in the past and that the distressing circumstances are worse in America than in many other Western developed countries. In fact, more than 20 percent of children live in poor families; 40 percent of ethnic minority families fall into this category. Even in those families where parents are working full-time there is an incidence of 12 percent poverty.

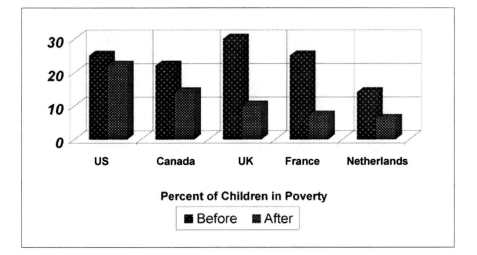

Figure 8.1 International comparison of government intervention in childhood poverty
Source: Fischer, Hout, Jankowski, Lucas, Swidler and Voss, 1996 (based on data from Rainwater and Smeeding, 1995).

How has such an advanced nation arrived at this dismal position? The following figure is a visual representation of the causes of social inequality in general.

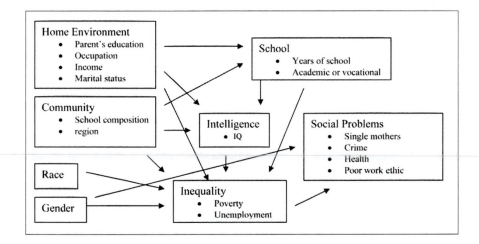

Figure 8.2 Model of social inequality
Source: Based on data from Fischer, Hout, Jankowski, Lucas, Swidler and Voss, 1996.

In this graphic representation one can see that education, and college in particular, is just one factor in the creation and perpetuation of poverty. Furthermore, school as a feature in an individual's chances in life is heavily influenced by home environment and the community. The evaluation of subsequent "intelligence" by society through various filters such as standardized tests and school academic records then also stands between college and resulting social position.

Peter Sacks in his book on economic class and education describes the myth of higher education mobility: "America's education system is driven by class distinctions to a degree most Americans don't acknowledge and perhaps don't even comprehend" (Sacks, 2007, p. 5). He points out, using interviews and data from various sources, that too often politicians and university presidents completely ignore the social class issue and instead focus on race and gender enrollment data.

> The cruel joke on lower-income students is that no amount of academic preparation, taking tests, or filling out college applications can overcome the lack of financial support, unless the students happen to be academic all-stars, whom universities heavily recruit for the sake of their own financial self-interest. (Sacks 2007, p. 184)

He argues for not only the need to better address and understand the way class is operating in universities, but to change what is valued in colleges by the public by emphasizing economic diversity. Sacks directs attention to surveys such as the one done by the *Washington Monthly* which rather than focusing on endowments and test scores uses criteria designed to score the ways universities serve the public good including the number of Pell Grant recipients. Using these criteria, MIT is number one, followed by UCLA.

We are increasingly unequal and self-satisfied in America. The public expectations of college are cynically self-interested and almost completely divorced from an understanding of how the education of individuals benefits us all. Furthermore, as a civilization, we have shirked our human obligation to support each other, especially the weakest. The great social mobility ideal of college has become, except for those exceptional few who beat the odds, merely a device to perpetuate advantage. We are becoming a society in which everyone knows their place, where the wealthy go to the best colleges and the poor face bleak futures. To make matters worse, in this brave new world we use education not only to deprive low-income children of a future, but as a way of claiming to scientifically put them in their rightful spots. They are poor because they are uneducated; they are uneducated because they are poor and dull-witted, we are told. America demonstrates in the failure of its educational system astounding callousness.

This book includes a case study relating the moving stories of children of recent immigrants to America. Their struggles tell of the bitter hardness of building a decent life for their families, and the challenges they encounter in trying to enter and complete college. However, the dirty little secret, that the racist blogs demonstrated in their attacks on these children of migrant farm workers, is that not all in the United States today are sympathetic to the plight of the disadvantaged, let alone concerned about what might happen to them in college. The dismal statistics on poverty in America, which effect women and children disproportionately, combined with increasingly reactionary welfare, financial aid, and public education policies reveal the disturbing comfort that society seems to now have with extreme inequity. The passionate efforts of many in the education community alone cannot change the basic unfairness of our society. We must do better. The fate of those students presented in this book, and those like them to come, as well as that of our society as a whole, rest upon our actions.

Appendix A: Institutional Demographics

CSUCI Demographics 2007 (CSUCI Fact Sheet):

- Enrollment: 3,599 students
- Gender: Female: 61 percent, Male: 39 percent
- Undergraduate Median Age: 23
- Race and Ethnic Composition: White/Non-Latino: 53.9 percent, Hispanic: 26.3 percent, Asian American: 6.5 percent, African American: 2.7 percent, Native American: 9 percent, Unknown: 9.7 percent
- Average high school GPA: 3.1
- Average ACT Score: 21
- Average SAT Score: 979

ASU Demographics 2007 (ASU Common Data Set):

- Enrollment: 6,588
- Gender: Female: 65 percent, Male: 35 percent
- Undergraduate Median Age: 25
- Race and Ethnic Composition: White/Non-Latino: 59 percent, Hispanic: 3 percent, Asian American: 3 percent, African American: 27 percent, Native American: .3 percent, Unknown: 7.7 percent
- Average high school GPA: 2.96

Appendix B: Social Mobility and Higher Education/Informal Learning Interview Instrument

General Demographic Information

1. Interview Subject:
2. Occupation:
3. Age:
4. Gender:
5. Race:
6. Current Social/economic class (self-described): upper, middle, lower
7. Parent's class (self-described):
8. Subject educational level:
9. Parental college/educational background:

College Experience

10. When growing up, what was your family's attitude towards college?

   a. Did you have many books, magazines, newspapers?
   b. Did you typically have discussions about politics, religion or things you read about?

11. Before attending, what did you think college would be like?

   a. Did your parents/family members tell you about college?
   b. How was the reality different?

12. Describe any work experience you had while attending college?

   a. How was your college experience different as a result of working?
   b. How was working while attending college viewed by other students?

13. How did family obligations affect your college experience?

14. Gender (if woman): How did your gender influence your options in college?

15. Race (if racial minority): How did your race influence your options in college?

16. What was it like when you returned home on holidays and vacation?

    a. Did your parents and friends have trouble understanding your new experience?
    b. Did you feel you had to give up some of your own cultural background?

17. In what ways was it necessary in college to adopt a common form of behavior in order to succeed?

    a. How is the behavior linked to social class?

18. What challenges did you have in college?

19. How did your sense of self or identity change as a result of attending college?

20. *(if faculty member) In your teaching experience, what differences have you observed in first-generation college students?*

    a. In what ways do they struggle?
    b. How do they succeed?

Career

21. What role did college play in sorting out career paths for you?

22. Describe your transition from college to work.

    a. How important were family and friends in identifying career opportunities for you?
    b. Did family and friends play any role in subsequent career transitions?

23. How does your career path compare to that of your classmates in college?

    a. Do they tend to have different occupations?
    b. How has your network from college played a role in your career?

24. Describe your attitudes towards your career.

a. In what way is your work personally fulfilling?
b. How has your career path given you social status?
c. Any regrets?

Mobility/Impact

25. *How would (or will be) your life be different now if you had not attended college?*

26. Have you benefited more or less than others from your college experience? Why?

27. *Should society support all equally including those who demonstrate less "talent" for a specific field? Why?*

28. Does education lead to greater equity in society?

a. Who benefits most from public higher education?
b. Who should pay?
c. Does public higher education lead to a redistribution of wealth?

Appendix C: Additional Data Tables

Table A.1 Percentage distribution of full-time, full-year dependent undergraduates according to type of institution, by family income: 1989-90 and 1999-2000

Family income	Public: 2-year	Public: 4-year	Private: Not-for-profit 4-year	Private: For-profit less than 4-year
1989-90				
Total	15.5	52.4	28.0	4.1
Lowest quarter	16.4	47.0	28.0	8.7
Lower middle quarter	19.7	53.5	22.8	4.0
Upper middle quarter	15.5	56.4	25.2	2.9
Highest quarter	10.6	52.4	35.7	1.3
1999-2000				
Total	19.4*	51.3	27.0	2.4*
Lowest quarter	24.7*	47.4	22.9*	5.0*
Lower middle quarter	22.3	51.9	23.8	2.0*
Upper middle quarter	18.6	51.7	28.0	1.7*
Highest quarter	12.6	53.9	32.6	0.9

Note: Detail may not sum to totals because of rounding; * Represents statistically significant change from 1989-90.
Source: US Department of Education, NCES, 1989-90 and 1999-2000 National Postsecondary Student Aid Studies (NPSAS: 90 and NPSAS: 2000).

Table A.2 Percentage of full-time, full-year dependent undergraduates who received grants, and among those with grants, average amount received (in 1999 constant dollars), by family income and type of institution: 1989-90 and 1999-2000

Family income and type of institution	Percentage with grants		Average amount	
	1989-90	**1999-2000**	**1989-90**	**1999-2000**
Total	44.8	56.9*	$4,200	$5,400*
Family income				
Lowest quarter	77.0	83.8*	4,600	5,500*
Lower middle quarter	48.8	60.1*	3,900	5,300*
Upper middle quarter	36.6	47.5*	3,900	5,700*
Highest quarter	20.3	38.5*	4,200	5,300*
Type of institution				
Public 2-year	33.0	43.6*	1,900	2,400*
Public 4-year	36.5	51.7*	3,200	3,800*
Private not-for-profit 4-year	65.2	75.7*	6,200	9,000*
Private for-profit less than 4-year	57.1	63.4	2,900	2,900

Note:* Represents statistically significant change from 1989-90.
Source: Wei, Li and Berkner (2004). A Decade of Undergraduate Student Aid: 1989-90 to 1999-2000 (NCES 2004-158), tables 5, A-1.10, A-2.10.

Table A.3 Percentage of full-time, full-year dependent undergraduates who took out loans, and among those who borrowed, average amount, by family income and type of institution: 1989-90 and 1999-2000

Family income and type of institution	Percentage with loans		Average amount	
	1989-90	1999-2000	1989-90	1999-2000
Total	30.1	45.4*	$3,900	$6,100*
Family income				
Lowest quarter	46.0	48.9	3,500	5,200*
Lower middle quarter	35.8	50.0*	3,800	5,700*
Upper middle quarter	27.5	49.3*	4,200	6,400*
Highest quarter	13.1	34.5*	4,800	7,400*
Type of institution				
Public 2-year	8.2	14.2*	2,200	3,200*
Public 4-year	26.0	46.6*	3,300	5,300*
Private not-for-profit 4-year	44.7	63.1*	4,500	7,600*
Private for-profit less than 4-year	66.1	74.4	4,700	7,200*

Note: Includes all student borrowing through federal, state, institutional, and private loan programs, and parental borrowing through the Parent Loan for Undergraduate Students (PLUS) program; * Represents statistically significant change from 1989-90.

Source: Wei, Li and Berkner (2004). A Decade of Undergraduate Student Aid: 1989-90 to 1999-2000 (NCES 2004-158), tables 7, A-1.6, A-2.6, A-3.6, and A-4.6. Data from US Department of Education, NCES, 1989-90 and 1999-2000 National Postsecondary Student Aid Studies (NPSAS: 90 and NPSAS: 2000).

Table A.4 Percentage distribution of 1989-90 and 1995-96 beginning post-secondary students by their status at the end of 5 years, by student characteristics and year first enrolled

Student characteristic and year first enrolled	Completed (highest level)			No degree or certificate		
	Bachelor's degree	Associate's degree	Vocational certificate	Still enrolled at 4-year institution	Still enrolled at 2-year institution or less	Not enrolled
Sex						
Male						
1989-90	24.5	10.2	11.3	10.0	5.6	38.4
1995-96	23.5	10.7	9.6	14.1	6.6	35.6
Female						
1989-90	26.9	12.1	14.4	6.3	4.8	35.4
1995-96	26.3	9.3	13.4	9.6	6.6	34.8
*Race/ethnicity**						
Asian/Pacific Islander						
1989-90	34.4	8.5	11.5!	13.5	6.4	25.7
1995-96	35.7	10.6!	6.9	16.0	7.6	23.2
Black						
1989-90	16.9	8.8	16.1	8.2	5.3	44.7
1995-96	14.5	5.2	16.9	11.2	7.2	45.1
White						
1989-90	27.3	11.6	12.3	7.9	4.3	36.6
1995-96	27.8	10.3	10.6	11.4	6.3	33.6
Hispanic						
1989-90	17.8	11.5	15.7	6.8	11.8	36.4
1995-96	15.2	11.8	14.4	11.4!	7.4	39.8
Family income						
Lowest quarter						
1989-90	16.7	11.5	17.2	7.3	4.9	42.3
1995-96	15.0	14.0	14.9	10.7	6.1	39.4
Middle two quarters						
1989-90	24.6	11.6	13.2	7.8	5.2	37.5
1995-96	23.7	9.5	12.5	11.4	7.4	35.5
Highest quarter						
1989-90	38.4	9.8	7.7	9.5	5.5	29.1
1995-96	41.0	5.9	5.7	12.8	5.4	29.2

Note: ! Interpret data with caution (estimates are unstable due to small sample sizes); * Black includes African American, Pacific Islander includes Native Hawaiian, and Hispanic includes Latino. Racial categories exclude Hispanic origin. Estimates for American Indians are excluded due to extremely small sample sizes.

Source: Wei, Li and Berkner (2004). A Decade of Undergraduate Student Aid: 1989-90 to 1999-2000 (NCES 2004-158), tables 7, A-1.6, A-2.6, A-3.6, and A-4.6. Data from US Department of Education, NCES, 1989-90 and 1999-2000 National Post-secondary Student Aid Studies (NPSAS: 90 and NPSAS: 2000).

Table A.5 Percentage distribution of 1989-90 and 1995-96 beginning post-secondary students by their status at the end of 5 years, by student characteristics and year first enrolled

Student characteristic and year first enrolled	Completed (highest level)			No degree or certificate		
	Bachelor's degree	Associate's degree	Vocational certificate	Still enrolled at 4-year institution	Still enrolled at 2-year institution or less	Not enrolled
Sex						
Male						
1989-90	24.5	10.2	11.3	10.0	5.6	38.4
1995-96	23.5	10.7	9.6	14.1	6.6	35.6
Female						
1989-90	26.9	12.1	14.4	6.3	4.8	35.4
1995-96	26.3	9.3	13.4	9.6	6.6	34.8
*Race/ethnicity**						
Asian/Pacific Islander						
1989-90	34.4	8.5	11.5!	13.5	6.4	25.7
1995-96	35.7	10.6!	6.9	16.0	7.6	23.2
Black						
1989-90	16.9	8.8	16.1	8.2	5.3	44.7
1995-96	14.5	5.2	16.9	11.2	7.2	45.1
White						
1989-90	27.3	11.6	12.3	7.9	4.3	36.6
1995-96	27.8	10.3	10.6	11.4	6.3	33.6
Hispanic						
1989-90	17.8	11.5	15.7	6.8	11.8	36.4
1995-96	15.2	11.8	14.4	11.4!	7.4	39.8
Family income						
Lowest quarter						
1989-90	16.7	11.5	17.2	7.3	4.9	42.3
1995-96	15.0	14.0	14.9	10.7	6.1	39.4
Middle two quarters						
1989-90	24.6	11.6	13.2	7.8	5.2	37.5
1995-96	23.7	9.5	12.5	11.4	7.4	35.5
Highest quarter						
1989-90	38.4	9.8	7.7	9.5	5.5	29.1
1995-96	41.0	5.9	5.7	12.8	5.4	29.2

Note: ! Interpret data with caution (estimates are unstable due to small sample sizes); * Black includes African American, Pacific Islander includes Native Hawaiian, and Hispanic includes Latino. Racial categories exclude Hispanic origin. Estimates for American Indians are excluded due to extremely small sample sizes; See supplemental note 3 for information on income quartiles. Detail may not sum to totals because of rounding.

Source: Horn and Berger (forthcoming). College Persistence on the Rise? Changes in 5-Year Degree Completion and Postsecondary Persistence Between 1994 and 2000 (NCES 2004-156), table 5-B. Data from US Department of Education, NCES, 1989/90 and 1995/96 Beginning Postsecondary Students Longitudinal Studies (BPS: 90/94 and BPS: 96/01).

Table A.6 Percentage of high school completers who were enrolled in college the October immediately after completing high school, by family income and race/ethnicity: 1972-2004

Year	Total	Family income[1]		Middle	High	Race/ethnicity[2]					
		Low		Middle	High	White	Black		Hispanic	
		Annual	3-year average[3]	Annual		Annual		3-year average[3]	Annual	3-year average[3]
1972	49.2	26.1	†	45.2	63.8	49.7	44.6	†	45.0	†
1973	46.6	20.3	†	40.9	64.4	47.8	32.5	41.4	54.1	48.8
1974	47.6	—	†	—	—	47.2	47.2	40.5	46.9	53.1
1975	50.7	31.2	†	46.2	64.5	51.1	41.7	44.5	58.0	52.7
1976	48.8	39.1	32.3	40.5	63.0	48.8	44.4	45.3	52.7	53.6
1977	50.6	27.7	32.4	44.2	66.3	50.8	49.5	46.8	50.8	48.8
1978	50.1	31.4	29.8	44.3	64.0	50.5	46.4	47.5	42.0	46.1
1979	49.3	30.5	31.6	43.2	63.2	49.9	46.7	45.2	45.0	46.3
1980	49.3	32.5	32.2	42.5	65.2	49.8	42.7	44.0	52.3	49.6
1981	53.9	33.6	32.9	49.2	67.6	54.9	42.7	40.3	52.1	48.7
1982	50.6	32.8	33.6	41.7	70.9	52.7	35.8	38.8	43.2	49.4
1983	52.7	34.6	34.0	45.2	70.3	55.0	38.2	38.0	54.2	46.7
1984	55.2	34.5	36.3	48.4	74.0	59.0	39.8	39.9	44.3	49.3
1985	57.7	40.2	35.9	50.6	74.6	60.1	42.2	39.5	51.0	46.1
1986	53.8	33.9	36.8	48.5	71.0	56.8	36.9	43.5	44.0	42.3
1987	56.8	36.9	37.6	50.0	73.8	58.6	52.2	44.2	33.5	45.0
1988	58.9	42.5	42.4	54.7	72.8	61.1	44.4	49.7	57.1	48.5
1989	59.6	48.1	45.6	55.4	70.7	60.7	53.4	48.0	55.1	52.7
1990	60.1	46.7	44.8	54.4	76.6	63.0	46.8	48.9	42.7	52.5
1991	62.5	39.5	42.2	58.4	78.2	65.4	46.4	47.2	57.2	52.6
1992	61.9	40.9	43.6	57.0	79.0	64.3	48.2	50.0	55.0	58.2
1993	62.6	50.4	44.7	56.9	79.3	62.9	55.6	51.3	62.2	55.7
1994	61.9	43.3	42.0	57.8	77.9	64.5	50.8	52.4	49.1	55.0
1995	61.9	34.2	42.1	56.0	83.5	64.3	51.2	52.9	53.7	51.6
1996	65.0	48.6	47.1	62.7	78.0	67.4	56.0	55.4	50.8	57.6
1997	67.0	57.0	50.6	60.7	82.2	68.2	58.5	58.8	65.6	55.3
1998	65.6	46.4	50.9	64.7	77.5	68.5	61.9	59.8	47.4	51.9
1999	62.9	49.4	48.5	59.4	76.1	66.3	58.9	58.6	42.3	47.4
2000	63.3	49.7	47.8	59.5	76.9	65.7	54.9	56.3	52.9	48.6
2001	61.7	43.8	50.0	56.3	79.9	64.2	54.6	56.3	51.7	52.7
2002	65.2	56.4	51.0	60.7	78.2	68.9	59.4	57.2	53.3	54.7
2003	63.9	52.8	53.1	57.6	80.1	66.2	57.5	60.0	58.6	57.7
2004	66.7	49.6	†	63.5	79.3	68.8	62.5	†	61.8	†

Note: — Not available. Data on family income were not available in 1974; † Not applicable because data for one of the three consecutive years are missing or one of the years is not applicable; [1] Low income is the bottom 20 percent of all family incomes, high income is the top 20 percent of all family incomes, and middle income is the 60 percent in between. See supplemental note 2 for further discussion; [2] Included in the total but not shown separately are high school completers from other racial/ethnic groups. Black includes African American and Hispanic includes Latino. Race categories exclude Hispanic origin unless specified; [3] Due to small sample sizes for the low-income, Black, and Hispanic categories, 3-year averages also were calculated for each category. For example, the 3-year average for Blacks in 1977 is the average percentage of Black high school completers ages 16-24 who were enrolled in college the October after completing high school in 1976, 1977, and 1978; Includes those ages 16-24 completing high school in a given year. The Current Population Survey (CPS) questions about educational attainment were reworded in 1992. Before then, "high school completers" meant those who completed 12 years of schooling; beginning in 1992, it meant those who received a high school diploma or equivalency certificate. In 1994, the survey methodology for the CPS was changed and weights were adjusted.

Source: US Department of Commerce, Census Bureau, Current Population Survey (CPS), October Supplement, 1972-2004, previously unpublished tabulation for 2004 (November 2005).

Table A.7 Average net access price for full-time, full-year dependent students after grants and loans, by type of institution and family income: 1989-90, 1999-2000, and 2003-04 (in constant 2003-04 dollars)

Type of institution and family income	1989-90	1999-2000	2003-04
Public 2-year			
Total	$7,100	$7,700	$7,700
Low income	5,900	6,100	6,000
Lower middle income	7,500	7,900	7,800
Upper middle income	7,700	8,600	8,700
High income	7,300	8,900	8,800
Public 4-year			
Total	8,700	8,800	9,300
Low income	6,200	5,700	6,000
Lower middle income	8,200	8,200	8,700
Upper middle income	9,300	9,400	10,000
High income	10,500	11,200	11,600
Private not-for-profit 4-year			
Total	14,700	14,000	15,300
Low income	9,100	8,100	10,200
Lower middle income	11,800	11,900	12,400
Upper middle income	14,100	13,400	14,600
High income	20,700	19,700	21,000
Private for-profit less-than-4-year			
Total	10,900	9,600	9,300
Low income	9,500	8,100	8,000
Lower middle income	11,200	10,300	9,700
Upper middle income	12,500	10,700	10,000
High income	14,700	14,000	12,600

Note: The cutoff points for low, lower middle, upper middle, and high income were obtained by identifying the incomes at the 25th, 50th, and 75th percentiles. Adjusted to 2003-04 constant dollars, in 1989-90, the values were $32,900, $55,400, and $85,800. In 1999-2000, they were $34,200, $59,600, and $91,600. In 2003-04, they were $32,400, $59,400, and $91,800.

Source: US Department of Education, National Center for Education Statistics, 1989-90, 1999-2000, and 2003-04 National Postsecondary Student Aid Studies (NPSAS: 90, NPSAS: 2000, and NPSAS: 04), previously unpublished tabulation (September 2005).

Table A.8 Earnings of the civilian population 18 to 64 years by educational attainment, age, and work status: 2000

Age and work status	Associate degree	Bachelors degree	Masters degree	Professional degree	Doctoral degree
18-64 years:					
Worked in 1999:					
Number with earnings	1,261,760	2,999,343	1,020,571	378,005	191,226
Mean annual earnings	36,480	52,832	67,601	93,767	80,000
Worked full-time, year-round:					
Number with earnings	770,175	1,897,931	643,378	252,344	134,095
Mean annual earnings	45,625	64,802	82,109	109,567	91,799
18-24 years:					
Worked in 1999:					
Number with earnings	114,812	176,793	9,893	3,513	637
Mean annual earnings	14,278	20,503	24,299	18,546	21,484
Worked full-time, year-round:					
Number with earnings	33,061	56,336	3,089	1,071	D
Mean annual earnings	24,109	33,861	37,879	27,988	D
25-34 years:					
Worked in 1999:					
Number with earnings	297,477	896,533	223,113	81,299	30,173
Mean annual earnings	30,531	43,292	50,966	54,585	52,159
Worked full-time, year-round:					
Number with earnings	173,704	561,824	133,542	48,914	19,957
Mean annual earnings	37,746	52,288	63,659	67,331	60,571
35-44 years:					
Worked in 1999:					
Number with earnings	386,646	890,538	299,865	118,229	56,296
Mean annual earnings	40,444	60,964	75,005	95,190	76,461
Worked full-time, year-round:					
Number with earnings	254,549	605,726	203,493	81,148	41,910
Mean annual earnings	48,094	72,152	88,567	109,914	86,088
45-54 years:					
Worked in 1999:					
Number with earnings	329,992	724,149	321,022	116,607	61,487
Mean annual earnings	43,079	60,435	73,385	114,649	92,173
Worked full-time, year-round:					
Number with earnings	226,954	488,781	209,857	83,246	44,221
Mean annual earnings	50,207	70,892	86,964	128,108	104,028
55-64 years:					
Worked in 1999:					
Number with earnings	132,833	311,330	166,678	58,357	42,633
Mean annual earnings	41,057	57,718	67,977	108,273	87,695
Worked full-time, year-round:					
Number with earnings	81,907	185,264	93,397	37,965	27,779
Mean annual earnings	50,654	72,056	84,974	124,891	103,812

Note: Geographic area: California; All race and ethnic groups, both sexes; - Represents zero or rounds to zero; "D" indicates data suppressed due to fewer than 50 unweighted cases; Internet release date: October 2006; Data based on a sample. For information on

confidentiality protection, sampling error, nonsampling error and definitions, see www.
census.gov/prod/cen2000/doc/sf3.pdf.
Source: US Census Bureau, Census 2000.

References

A "perversion of democracy". (1959, January 25), *Los Angeles Times*, p. B4. Retrieved May 25, 2007, from ProQuest Historical Newspapers *Los Angeles Times* (1881-1985).

A vocationally deprived generation. (1964, June 8), *Los Angeles Times*, p. A4. Retrieved May 25, 2007, from ProQuest Historical Newspapers *Los Angeles Times* (1881-1985).

Adelman, C. (2004), *Principal indicators of student academic histories in postsecondary education, 1972-2000.* Washington, DC: United States Department of Education, Institute of Education Sciences.

Anderson, C. (1994), *Black labor, white wealth: The search for power and economic justice.* Edgewood, MD: Duncan and Duncan.

Aristocracy and democracy in education. (1926, October 31), *New York Times*, p. E8. Retrieved May 25, 2007, from ProQuest Historical Newspapers *New York Times* (1851-2003).

Ashworth, J. (1998, April), A waste of resources? Social rates of return to higher education in the 1990s. *Education Economics.* Vol. 6, Issue 1, p. 27-45.

Astin, A. (2002), *The American freshman: Thirty-five year trends, 1966-2001.* Cooperative Institutional Research Program, American Council on Education, UCLA.

Avery, C., Fairbanks, A. and Zeckhauser, R. (2003), *The early admissions game: Joining the elite.* Cambridge, MA: Harvard University Press.

Barnes, J. (1896), *A Princetonian: A story of undergraduate life at the college of New Jersey.* New York, NY: G.P. Putnam's Sons.

Baum S. and Lapovsky, L. (2006), *Tuition discounting: Not just a private college practice.* New York, NY: The College Board.

Baum S. and Lapovsky, L. (2008), *Trends in college pricing.* New York, NY: The College Board.

Beller, E. and Hout, M. (2006), Intergenerational Social Mobility: The United States in Comparative Perspective. *The Future of Children.* Vol. 16. No. 2, pp. 19-36. The Woodrow Wilson School of Public and International Affairs at Princeton University and The Brookings Institution.

Berg, G.A. (2005), *Lessons from the Edge: For-profit and non-traditional higher education in America.* Westport, CT: Praeger/American Council on Education, Higher Education Series.

Bernstein, B.B. (1971), *Class, codes and control. Volume 1 Theoretical studies towards a sociology of language.* London, UK: Routledge & Kegan Paul.

Bernstein, J., Boushey, H., McNichol, E. and Zahradnik, R. (2002), *Pulling apart: A state-by-state analysis of income trends*. Washington, DC: Center on Budget and Policy Priorities, Economic Policy Institute. Retrieved May 24, 2007 from http://www.cbpp.org/1-18-00sfp.htm.

Bird, C. (1975), *The case against college*. New York, NY: David McKay Company, Inc.

Bishaw, A. and Iceland, J. (2003), *Poverty 1999, Census 2000 Brief.* US Census Bureau. Retrieived May 24, 2007 from http://www.census.gov/prod/2003pubs/c2kbr-19.pdf.

Blau, P.M. (1967), *The American occupational structure*. New York, NY: The Free Press.

Board of Admissions and Relations with Schools (BOARS) (n.d.), *The use of admissions tests by the University of California*. Retrieved May 8, 2007, from http://www.ucop.edu/news/sat/summary.pdf.

Bodilly, S. and Beckett, M.K. (2005), *Making out-of-school time matter: Evidence for an action agenda*. Santa Monica, CA: Rand Corporation.

Bombardieri, M. (2007, January 19), Many Hub graduates struggle in college: Remedial classes often necessary, study finds. *The Boston Globe*. Section: Metro, Page: 1A.

Boudon, R. (1973), *Education, opportunity and social inequality: Changing prospects in western society*. New York, NY: John Wiley and Sons.

Bourdieu, P. (1993), *The field of cultural production*. New York, NY: Columbia University Press.

Bowen, W.G., Kurzweil, M.A. and Tobin, E.M. (2005), *Equity and excellence in American higher education*. Charlottesville, VA: University of Virginia Press.

Bowles, S. (1976), *Schooling in capitalist America: Educational reform and the contradictions of economic life*. New York, NY: Basic Books.

Bowles, S., Gintis, H. and Groves, M.O. (eds) (2005), *Unequal chances: Family background and economic success (Introduction)*. Princeton, NJ: Princeton University Press.

Brantlinger, E.A. (2003), *Dividing classes: How the middle class negotiates and rationalizes school advantage*. New York, NY: RoutledgeFalmer.

Brewer, D.J. and Gates, S. (2002), *In pursuit of prestige: Strategy and competition in US higher education*. New Brunswick, NJ: Transaction Publishers.

Brigham, C. (1923), *A study of American intelligence*. London, England: Oxford University Press.

Brint, S. and Karabel, J. (1989), *The diverted dream: Community colleges and the promise of education opportunity in America, 1900-1985*. New York, NY: Oxford University Press.

Brown, H.D. (1886), *Two college girls*. Boston, MA: Ticknor and Company.

Buyer's market in college graduates. (1949, January 30), *Los Angeles Times*, p. A4. Retrieved May 25, 2007, from ProQuest Historical Newspapers *Los Angeles Times* (1881-1985).

Cassill, R.V. (1961), *Night school*. New York, NY: New American Library.

Chow, E.N. (1996), Introduction: Transforming knowledgement: Race, class, and gender. In Chow, E.N., Wilkinson, D. and Zinn (eds), *Race, class, & gender: Common bonds, different voices*. Thousand Oaks, CA: Sage Publications.

Choy, S. (2001), *Students Whose Parents Did not Go to College: Postsecondary Access, Persistence, and Attainment*, NCES 2001-126. Washington, DC: US Department of Education, National Center for Education Statistics. Retrieved May 24, 2007 from http://nces.ed.gov/pubsearch/pubsinfo. asp?pubid=2001126.

Cole, B. (2007, January 28), The future is now for minorities preparing for college. *Yakima Herald-Republic (WA)*, Section: Main/Home Front.

Coleman, J.S. (1968), *The evaluation of equality of educational opportunity*. Santa Monica, CA: The Rand Corporation.

College Board. (2006), *Advanced Placement Report to the Nation. College Board special report*. Retrieved May 24, 2007 from http://www.collegeboard.com/ about/news_info/ap/2006/index.html.

College Board. (2007), *2006 trends in higher education: Net price*. Retrieved May 8, 2007 from http://www.collegeboard.com/prod_downloads/press/cost06/ net_price_06.pdf.

College girls work. (1923, September 23), *Los Angeles Times*, p. 114. Retrieved May 24, 2007 from ProQuest Historical Newspapers *Los Angeles Times* (1881-1985).

Collins, R. (1979), *The credential society: An historical sociology of education and stratification*. New York, NY: Academic Press.

Conant, J.B. (1940, May), Education for a classless society. *The Atlantic Monthly*. Vol. 165, No. 5.

Conant, J.B. (1943, May), Wanted: American radicals. *The Atlantic Monthly*. Vol. 171, No. 5.

Conklin, E.G. (1921), *The direction of human evolution*. New York, NY: Charles Scribner's Sons.

Conley, D. (1999), *Being black, living in the red: Race, wealth, and social policy in America*. Berkeley, CA: University of California Press.

Correspondents of the New York Times (Keller, B. introduction) (2005), *Class matters*. New York, NY: Henry Holt and Company.

Corwin, M. (2001), *And still we rise: The trials and triumphs of twelve gifted inner-city students*. New York, NY: Harper Perennial.

Crane, C. (1985), *The western shore*. Salt Lake City, UT: Peregrine Smith Books.

Cross, K.P. (1976), *Beyond the open door: New students to higher education*. San Francisco, CA: Jossey-Bass Inc.

Dalrymple, T. (2001), *Life at the bottom: The worldview that makes the underclass*. Chicago, IL: Ivan R. Dee.

Danziger, S. and Waldfogel, J. (eds) (2000), *Securing the future: Investing in children from birth to college*. New York, NY: Russell Sage Foundation.

Davis, J. (2003), *Unintended consequences of tuition discounting*. Indianapolis, IN: Limina Foundation for Education. ERIC #: ED476666.

Day, J.C. and Newburger, E.C. (July, 2002), *The big payoff: Educational attainment and synthetic estimates of work-life earnings.* Washington, DC: US Census Bureau.

Durkheim, E. (1977), *The evolution of educational thought: Lectures on the formation and development of secondary education in France.* London, UK: Routledge & Kegan Paul.

Dye, T. (2002), *Who's running America? The Bush restoration.* Upper Saddle River, NJ: Pearson Education.

Economic Diversity of Colleges, Derived from FISAP & IPEDS. Retrieved May 24, 2007, from http://www.economicdiversity.org/variables.php.

Education and Labor. (1900, September 3), *Los Angeles Times*, p. 16. Retrieved May 25, 2007, from ProQuest Historical Newspapers *Los Angeles Times* (1881-1985).

Education and the rich life. (1954, December 7), *Los Angeles Times*, p. A4. Retrieved May 25, 2007, from ProQuest Historical Newspapers *Los Angeles Times* (1881-1985), p. A4.

Educational ideals. (1941, January 20), *New York Times*, p. 16. Retrieved May 24, 2007, from ProQuest Historical Newspapers *New York Times* (1851-2003).

Ellwood, D.T. and Kane, T. J. (2000), Who is getting a college education? Family background and the growing gaps in enrollment. In Danziger, S. and Waldfogel, J. (eds), *Securing the Future: Investing in children from birth to college.* New York, NY: Russell Sage Foundation.

Equality and equal education. (1953, March 29), *Los Angeles Times*, p. B4. Retrieved May 25, 2007, from ProQuest Historical Newspapers *Los Angeles Times* (1881-1985).

Erikson, R. and Goldthorpe, J.H. (1992), *The constant flux: A study of class mobility in industrial societies.* Oxford, UK: Clarendon Press.

Ewen, E. and Ewen, S. (2006), *Typecasting: On the arts and sciences of human inequality.* New York, NY: Seven Stories Press.

Farrell, J.T. (1943), *My days of anger.* New York, NY: Vanguard Press.

Farrell, J.T. (1963), *The silence of history.* Garden City, NY: Doubleday and Co.

Feagin, J.R., Vera, H. and Imani, N. (1996), *The agony of education.* New York, NY: Routledge.

Fischer, C.S., Hout, M., Jankowski, M.S., Lucas, S.R., Swidler, A. and Voss, K. (1996), *Inequality by design: Cracking the bell curve myth.* Princeton, NJ: Princeton University Press.

Fitzgerald, R.A. (2000), *College quality and the earnings of recent college graduates*, NCES 2000-043. United States Department of Education. Project Officer: Shelley Burns. Washington, DC: National Center for Education Statistics.

Freeman, R.B. (1976), *The overeducated American.* New York, NY: Academic Press.

Galton, F. (1998), *Hereditary genius.* London, England: Macmillian and Company.

Golden, D. (2006), *The price of admission: How America's ruling class buys its way into elite colleges and who gets left outside the gates*. New York, NY: Crown.

Gould, S.J. (1981), *The mismeasure of man*. New York, NY: W.W. Norton & Company.

Gould, S.J. (1995), Curveball. In Fraser, S. (ed.), *The bell curve wars: Race, intelligence, and the future of America*. New York, NY: Basic Books.

Groves, M.O. (2005), Personality and earnings transmission. In Bowles, S., Gintis, H. and Groves, M.O. (eds), *Unequal chances: Family background and economic success*. Princeton, NJ: Princeton University Press.

Grubb, W.N. (1996), *Working in the middle: Strengthening education and training for the mid-skilled labor force*. San Francisco, CA: Jossey-Bass Publications.

Grubb, W.N. (2001), The varied economic returns to postsecondary education: New evidence from the class of 1972. *The Journal of Human Resources*. 28, pp. 365-382.

Grubb, W.N. (2004), *The education gospel: The economic power of schooling*. Cambridge, MA: Harvard University Press.

Grubb, W.N. and Lazerson, M. (1982), *Broken promises: How Americans fail their children*. New York, NY: Basic Books.

Hacker, A. (1995), Caste, Crime, and Precocity. In Fraser, S. (ed.), *The bell curve wars: Race, intelligence, and the future of America*. New York, NY: Basic Books.

Hacker, A. (1995), *Two Nations: Black and white, separate, hostile, and unequal*. New York, NY: Charles Scribner's Sons.

Hall, O. (1953), *The corpus of Joe Bailey*. New York, NY: Viking Press.

Halsey, A. H. (1980), *Origins and destinations: Family, class, and education in modern Britain*. Oxford, Great Britain: Clarendon Press.

Halsey, A. H. Lauder, H. Brown, P. and Wells, A.M. (eds) (1997), *Education, Culture, Economy, Society (introduction to part six)*. Oxford, Great Britain: Oxford University Press.

Hansen, W.L. and Weisbrod, B.A. (1969), *Benefits, costs, and finance of public higher education*. Chicago, IL: Markham Publishing Company.

Hawthorne, N. (1828), *Fanshawe*. Boston, MA: Marsh and Capen.

Heckman, J.J. and Lochner, L. (2000), Rethinking education and training policy: Understanding the sources of skill formation in a modern economy. In Danziger, S. and Waldfogel, J. (eds), *Securing the future: Investing in children from birth to college*. New York, NY: Russell Sage Foundation.

Herrnstein, R.J. and Murray, C. (1996), *The Bell Curve: Intelligence and class structure in American life*. New York, NY: Free Press Paperbacks.

Heyns, B. (1978), *Summer learning and the effects of learning*. New York, NY: Academic Press.

Higher education of women. (1873, November 3), *New York Times*, p. 4. Retrieved May 24, 2007, from ProQuest Historical Newspapers *New York Times* (1851-2003).

Hill, C.B. and Winston, G.C. (2006), How scarce are high-ability, low-income students? In McPherson, M.S. and Schapiro, M.O. (eds), *College access: Opportunity or privilege?* New York, NY: College Board.

Hinton, D.B. (1994), *Celluloid ivy: Higher education in the movies 1960-1990*. Metuchen, NJ: The Scarecrow Press.

Holbrook, R. (1900), *Boys and men: A story of life at Yale by Richard Holbrook*. New York, NY: Charles Scribner's Sons.

Horn, L. and Berger, R. (forthcoming), *College Persistence on the Rise? Changes in 5-Year Degree Completion and Postsecondary Persistence Between 1994 and 2000* (NCES 2004-156). Retrieved May 24, 2007 from http://nces.ed.gov/pubs2005/2005156.pdf.

Hout, M. (2005), *Berkeley's comprehensive review method for making freshman admissions decisions: An assessment*. A report to the Committee on Admissions, Enrollment, and Preparatory Education (AEPE) and the Associate Vice Chancellor – Admissions & Enrollment. Berkeley, CA: University of California, Berkeley. Retrieved May 8, 2007 from http://academic-senate. berkeley.edu/committees/pdf_docs_consolidate/Hout_Report.pdf.

Hout, M. Raftery, A.E. and Bell, E.O. (1993), Making the grade: Education stratification in the United States, 1925-1989. In Shavit, Y. and Blossfeld, H.P., *Persistent inequality: Changing educational attainment in thirteen countries*. Boulder, CO: Westview Press.

How good are colleges? (1939, January 2), *New York Times*, p. 22. Retrieved May 24, 2007, from ProQuest Historical Newspapers *New York Times* (1851-2003).

Hoxby, C.M. (ed.) (2004), *College choices: The economics of where to go, when to go, and how to pay for it*. Chicago, IL: The University of Chicago Press.

Husband, J.B. (1923), *High hurdles*. Boston: Houghton Mifflin Co.

Iceland, J. (2006), *Poverty in America: A handbook*. Berkeley. CA: University of California Press.

Illich, I. (1983), *Deschooling society*. New York, NY: Harper Colophon Books.

Immerwahr, J. (2004), *Public attitudes on higher education: A trend analysis, 1993 to 2003*. San Jose, CA: The National Center for Public Policy and Higher Education. Retrieved May 24, 2007 from http://www.highereducation.org/reports/pubatt/.

Jencks, C. and Phillips, M. (eds) (1998), *The black-white test score gap*. Washington, DC: Brookings Institute Press.

Jencks, C., Smith, M., Acland, H., Bane, M.J., Cohen, D., Gintis, H., Heyns, B. and Michelson, S. (1972), *Inequality: A reassessment of the effect of family and schooling in America*. New York, NY: Basic Books.

Jensen, A.R. (1972), *Genetics & education*. London, England: Methuen & Co.

Johnson, O. (1968), *Stover at Yale*. New York, NY: Macmillan Company.

Jonsson, J.O. (1993), Persisting inequalities in Sweden. In Shavit, Y. and Blossfeld, H.P. *Persistent inequality: Changing educational attainment in thirteen countries*. Boulder, CO: Westview Press.

Kahlenberg, R. (1997), *The remedy: Class, race and affirmative action*. New York, NY: Basic Books.

Kahlenberg, R.D. (ed.) (2004), *America's untapped resource: Low-income students in higher education*. New York, NY: The Century Foundation Press. Introduction, pp. 1-16.

Karabel, J. (1986), Community colleges and social stratification in the 1980s. In Zwerling, S.L. (ed.), *The community college and its critics*. San Francisco, CA: Jossey-Bass.

Karabel, J. (1989, May 19), Report by the committee on admissions and enrollment Berkeley division, Academic senate, University of California.

Karabel, J. (2005), *The chosen: The hidden history of admission and exclusion at Harvard, Yale, and Princeton*. New York, NY: Houghton Mifflin.

Karabell, J. and Halsey, A.H. (1977), *Power and ideology in education*. New York, NY: Oxford University Press.

Kerckhoff, A.C. (1974, December), Stratification processes and outcomes in England and the US. *American Sociological Review*. Vol. 39, No. 6, pp. 789-801.

Kohn, M.L. (1989), *Class and conformity: A study in values, with a reassessment*. Chicago, IL: The University of Chicago Press.

Kramer, J.E. (1981), *The American college novel: An annotated bibliography*. New York, NY: Garland Publishing, Inc.

Krueger, A.B., Rothstein, J. and Turner, S. (2006), Was Justice O'Connor right? Race and highly selective college admissions in 25 years. In McPherson, M.S. and Schapiro, M.O. (eds), *College access: Opportunity or privilege?* New York, NY: College Board.

Lareau, A. (2003), *Unequal childhoods: Class, race, and family life*. Berkeley, CA: University of California Press.

Lemann, N. (2000), *The big test: The secret history of the American meritocracy*. New York, NY: Farrar, Straus and Giroux.

Leonhardt, D. (2005, May 24), The college dropout boom. *New York Times*. National Desk, p. 1-7.

Lichtenstein, J. (1901), *For the blue and gold: A tale of life at the University of California*. San Francisco: A.M. Robertson.

Lieberson, S. (1985), *Making it count: The improvement of social research and theory*. Berkeley, CA: University of California Press.

Lucas, S.R. (1999), *Tracking inequality: Stratification and mobility in American high schools*. New York, NY: Teachers College Press.

Lyons, J.D. (1962), *The college novel in America*. Carbondale, IL: Southern Illinois University Press.

Machin, S. and Gregg, P. (2003), A lesson for education: University expansion and falling income mobility. *New Economy*, pp. 194-198.

Massey, D.S. and Mooney, M. (2007, February), The effects of America's three affirmative action programs on academic performance. *Social Problems*. Vol. 54, No. 1, pp. 99-117.

Mayer, S.E. (1997), *What money can't buy: Family income and children's life chances*. Cambridge, MA: Harvard University Press.

Mazumder, B. (2005), The Apple falls even closer to the tree than we thought. In Bowles, S., Gintis, H. and Groves, M.O. (eds), *Unequal chances: Family background and economic success*. Princeton, NJ: Princeton University Press.

McDonough, P.M. (1997), *How social class and schools structure opportunity*. Albany, NY: State University of New York Press.

McPherson, M.S. and Schapiro, M.O. (1998), *The student aid game: Meeting need and rewarding talent in American higher education*. Princeton, NJ: Princeton University Press.

McPherson, M.S. and Schapiro, M.O. (eds) (2006), *College access: Opportunity or privilege?* New York, NY: College Board.

Middelbury College: Middlebury Ad Hoc Committee. (2002), Cited in Bowen, W.G. and Levin, S.A., *Reclaiming the Game: College Sports and Education Values*. Princeton: Princeton University Press.

Morrah, D.W., Jr. (1962), *Me and the liberal arts*. Garden City, NY: Doubleday and Co.

Mortenson, T.G. (1991, January), *Equity of higher education opportunity for women, black, Hispanic, and low income students*. Iowa City, IO: American College Testing.

Murray, C.A. (1984), *Losing ground: American social policy, 1950-1980*. New York, NY: Basic Books.

Nairn, A. (1980), *The reign of ETS: The corporation that makes up minds*. The Ralph Nader Report on the Educational Testing Service. Unpublished.

New York Times Poll Class Project. March 3-14, 2005. Retrieved June 10, 2005 from http://www.nytimes.com/packages/pdf/national/20050515_CLASS_GRA PHIC/classpoll_results.pdf.

Newman, B. (2007, January 28), College worth every cent – Students grapple with rising costs. *Amarillo Globe-News (TX)*, Section: Local News.

Oren, D.A. (1985), *Joining the club: A history of Jews and Yale*. New Haven, CT: Yale University Press.

Perkinson, H.J. (1995), *The imperfect panacea: American faith in education*. Boston, MA: McGraw Hill.

Phelps, R. (2007, January 14), *Hitting the books ... and a job – College students find time to work*. Longview News-Journal (TX).

Rainwater, L. and Smeeding, T. (1995), *Doing poorly: The real income of American children in comparative perspective*. Working paper no. 127, Luxembourg Income Study. Syracuse, NY: Maxwell School of Citizenship and Public Affairs, August.

Rosen, J. and Lane, C. (1995), The sources of *The Bell Curve*. In Fraser, S. (ed.), *The bell curve wars: Race, intelligence, and the future of America*. New York, NY: Basic Books.

Rothstein, S.W. (ed.) (1995), *Class, culture, and race in American schools: A handbook*. Westport, CT: Greenwood Press.

Sacks, P. (2007), *Tearing down the gates: Confronting the class divide in American education*. Berkeley, CA: University of California Press.

Schools and their Influence. (1909, May 19), *Los Angeles Times*, p. 114. Retrieved May 25, 2007, from ProQuest Historical Newspapers *Los Angeles Times* (1881-1985).

Shapiro, I. and Greenstein, R. (2007), *The widening income gulf*. Washington, DC: The Center on Budget and Policy Priorities, p. 2. Retrieved May 8, 2007, from http://www.cbpp.org/9-4-99tax-rep.htm

Shavit, Y. and Blossfeld, H.P. (1993), *Persistent inequality: Changing educational attainment in thirteen countries*. Boulder, CO: Westview Press.

Shockley, W.B. (1992), *Shockley on Eugenics and Race: The application of science to the solution of human problems*. Washington, DC: Scott-Townsend Publishers.

Smeeding, T.M. (2002), *Globalisation, inequality and the rich countries of the G-20: Evidence form the Luxembourg income study (LIS)*, Reserve Bank of Australia 2002 Conference Proceedings. Globalisation, Living Standards and Inequality: Recent Progress and Continuing Challenges 27-28 May 2002. Retrieved May 8, 2007 from http://www.rba.gov.au/PublicationsAndResearch/Conferences/2002/smeeding.pdf.

Smetanka, M.J. (2007, January 19), A match not a prize: College: What's in a big name? *Star Tribune: Newspaper of the Twin Cities (Minneapolis, MN)*, Edition: METRO, Section: NEWS, Page: 1A.

Smiley, J. (1995), *Moo: A novel*. New York, NY: Fawcett.

Soares, J.A. (2007), *The power of privilege: Yale and America's elite colleges*. Stanford, CA: Stanford University Press.

Sorokin, P.A. (1959), *Social and cultural mobility*. Glencoe, IL: The Free Press.

Sowell, T. (2004), *Affirmative action around the world: An empirical study*. New Haven, CT: Yale University Press.

St. John, E.P. (2003), *Refinancing the college dream: Access, equal opportunity, and justice for taxpayers*. Baltimore, MD: The Johns Hopkins University Press.

Staff. (2005, January), Ever higher society, ever harder to ascend. *Economist*. Vol. 374, Issue 8407, pp. 22-25.

Staff. (2007, January 15), Poll shows awareness of king. *The Post-Standard* (Syracuse, NY), Edition: Final, Section: Local, Page: B3.

Stanton-Salarzar, R.D. (2001), *Manufacturing hope and despair: The school and kin support networks of US Mexican youth*. New York, NY: Teachers College Press.

Steele, C.M. and Aronson, J. (1995), Stereotype threat and the intellectual test performance of African Americans. *Journal of Personality and Social Psychology*. Vol. 69, No. 5, 797-811.

The 'right' to go to college. (1979, February 27), *Los Angeles Times*, p. C4. Retrieved May 25, 2007, from ProQuest Historical Newspapers *Los Angeles Times* (1881-1985).

The "new departure" in colleges. (1871, July 2), *New York Times*, p. 4. Retrieved May 25, 2007, from ProQuest Historical Newspapers *New York Times* (1851-2003).

The college diploma. (1922, April 14), *Los Angeles Times*, p. 114. Retrieved May 24, 2007, from ProQuest Historical Newspapers *Los Angeles Times* (1881-1985).

The deadly college bookworm. (1927, December 9), *New York Times*, p. 24. Retrieved May 24, 2007, from ProQuest Historical Newspapers *New York Times* (1851-2003).

The education of the free. (1942, June 18), *New York Times*, p. A4. Retrieved May 25, 2007, from ProQuest Historical Newspapers *New York Times* (1851-2003).

The education of women. (1873, August 30), *New York Times*, p. 4. Retrieved May 24, 2007, from ProQuest Historical Newspapers *New York Times* (1851-2003).

The immigration problem. (1916, January 15), *Los Angeles Times*, p. 114. Retrieved May 25, 2007, from ProQuest Historical Newspapers Los Angles Times (1881-1985).

The quantity of education. (1952, January 12), *Los Angeles Times*, p. A4. Retrieved May 25, 2007, from ProQuest Historical Newspapers *Los Angeles Times* (1881-1985).

The Status of Education. (1922, January 31), The *Los Angeles Times*, p. 114. Retrieved May 25, 2007, from ProQuest Historical Newspapers *Los Angeles Times* (1881-1985).

Too much higher education. (1883, June 27), *New York Times*, p. 4. Retrieved May 25, 2007, from ProQuest Historical Newspapers *New York Times* (1851-2003).

Train, A.C. (1917), The world and Thomas Kelly. New York, NY: Charles Scribner's Sons.

Turner, S.E. (2004), Going to college and finishing college: Explaining different educational outcomes. In Hoxby, C.M. (ed.), *College choices: The economics of where to go, when to go, and how to pay for it*. Chicago, IL: The University of Chicago Press, pp. 13-62.

Umphlett, W.L. (1984), *The movies go to college: Hollywood and the world of the college-life film*. London, UK: Fairleigh Dickinson University Press.

United States Census Bureau. *Census 2000*. Retrieved May 24, 2007 from http://www.census.gov/main/www/cen2000.html.

United States Congress. (2002, June), *Empty promises: The myth of college access in America*. Report of the Advisory Committee on Student Financial Assistance. Washington, DC: Retrieved May 8, 2007 from http://www.ed.gov/about/bdscomm/list/acsfa/emptypromises.pdf.

United States Department of Commerce, Census Bureau. (2005, November) *Current Population Survey (CPS)*, October Supplement, 1972-2004, previously unpublished tabulation for 2004. Retrieved May 24, 2007 from http://nces. ed.gov/programs/coe/2006/supnotes/n02.asp.

United States Department of Education. (2002), *National Education Longitudinal Study of 1988 (NES:88/2000)*, Fourth Follow-up, Student Survey, 2000. National Center for Education Statistics. Retrieved May 24, 2007 from http:// nces.ed.gov/surveys/nels88/.

United States Department of Education. (2004), *National Center for Educational Statistics, US Department of Education. Where are they now?* A description of 1992-93 bachelor's degree recipients 10 years later. Statistical analysis report. Retrieved May 24, 2007 from http://nces.ed.gov/pubsearch/pubsinfo. asp?pubid=2007159.

United States Department of Education. (2004), *National Center for Education Statistics, 1993-2003 Baccalaureate and Beyond Longitudinal Study*. Retrieved May 24, 2007 from http://nces.ed.gov/surveys/b&b/.

Van Der Werf, M. (2007, May 25), Rankings methodology hurts public institutions. *The Chronicle of Higher Education*. Vol. LIII, No. 38, p. A13.

Veblen, T. (2006), *Conspicuous consumption: Unproductive consumption of goods is honourable*. New York, NY: Penguin.

Weber, M. (1930), *The protestant ethic and the spirit of capitalism*. London, Great Britain: Routledge.

Wei, C.C. and Horn, L. (2002), *Persistence and attainment of beginning students with Pell grants (NCES 2002-169)*, US Department of Education. Washington, DC: National Center for Education Statistics. Retrieved May 24, 2007, from http://nces.ed.gov/programs/quarterly/vol_6/6_3/4_1.asp.

Weil, D. (1979), *Continuing Education*. New York, NY: Ransom, Wade Publishers.

Weller, G.A. (1993), *Not to eat, not for love*. New York, NY: Harrison Smith and Robert Haas.

West, C. (2001), *Race matters*. New York, NY: Vintage.

Whippoorwill, T. (pseudo.) (1845), *Nelly Brown: Or, the trials, temptations and pleasures of college life*. Boston: "The Yankee Office."

Wilson, W.J. (1978), *The declining significance of race: Blacks and changing American institutions*. Chicago, IL: The University of Chicago Press.

Wilson, W.J. (1987), *The truly disadvantaged: The inner city, the underclass, and public policy*. Chicago, IL: University of Chicago Press.

Winston, G.C. and Zimmerman, D.J. (2004), Peer effects in higher education. In Hoxby, C.M. (ed.), *College choices: The economics of where to go, when to go, and how to pay for it*. Chicago, IL: The University of Chicago Press, pp. 395-424.

Wolfe, A. (2002), *Does education matter? Myths about education and economic growth*. New York, NY: Penguin Books.

Wolfe, T. (2004), *I am Charlotte Simmons*. New York, NY: Farrar, Straus & Giroux.

Young, M.D. (1994), *The rise of the meritocracy*. New Brunswick, NJ: Transaction Publishers.

Index

CPSIA information can be obtained
at www.ICGtesting.com
Printed in the USA
LVOW10*0852070318
568946LV00007BA/120/P